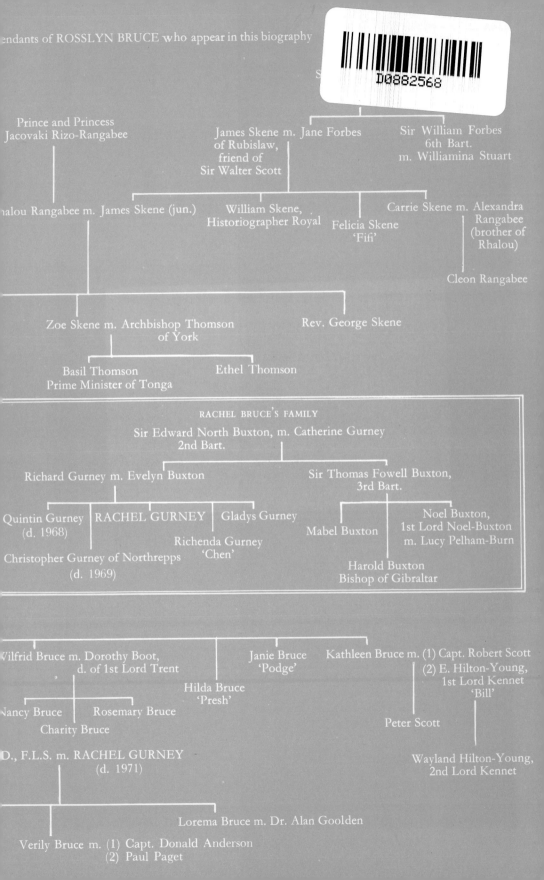

Prince and Princess
Jacovaki Rizo-Rangabee

James Skene m. Jane Forbes
of Rubislaw,
friend of
Sir Walter Scott

Sir William Forbes
6th Bart.
m. Williamina Stuart

halou Rangabee m. James Skene (jun.)

William Skene,
Historiographer Royal

Felicia Skene
'Fifi'

Carrie Skene m. Alexandra
Rangabee
(brother of
Rhalou)

Cleon Rangabee

Zoe Skene m. Archbishop Thomson
of York

Rev. George Skene

Basil Thomson
Prime Minister of Tonga

Ethel Thomson

RACHEL BRUCE'S FAMILY

Sir Edward North Buxton, m. Catherine Gurney
2nd Bart.

Richard Gurney m. Evelyn Buxton

Sir Thomas Fowell Buxton,
3rd Bart.

Quintin Gurney
(d. 1968)

RACHEL GURNEY

Gladys Gurney

Richenda Gurney
'Chen'

Christopher Gurney of Northrepps
(d. 1969)

Mabel Buxton

Noel Buxton,
1st Lord Noel-Buxton
m. Lucy Pelham-Burn

Harold Buxton
Bishop of Gibraltar

Wilfrid Bruce m. Dorothy Boot,
d. of 1st Lord Trent

Janie Bruce
'Podge'

Kathleen Bruce m. (1) Capt. Robert Scott
(2) E. Hilton-Young,
1st Lord Kennet
'Bill'

Hilda Bruce
'Presh'

Nancy Bruce

Rosemary Bruce

Charity Bruce

Peter Scott

D., F.L.S. m. RACHEL GURNEY
(d. 1971)

Wayland Hilton-Young,
2nd Lord Kennet

Lorema Bruce m. Dr. Alan Goolden

Verily Bruce m. (1) Capt. Donald Anderson
(2) Paul Paget

THE LAST OF
THE ECCENTRICS

A Life of Rosslyn Bruce

by

VERILY ANDERSON

HODDER AND STOUGHTON
LONDON SYDNEY AUCKLAND TORONTO

BX
5199
.B77A8
1972

To
RACHEL BRUCE

Author's Acknowledgments

I am grateful to Lord Hailsham and Hodder and Stoughton for permission to reproduce the poem that appears on p. 284, to Mr. Nikita Bruce and Constable & Co. for extracts from *Silken Dalliance* by H. J. Bruce, and to Mr. Cecil Roberts and Hodder and Stoughton for extracts from *The Growing Boy*.

I should also like to express my grateful thanks for all the assistance given by Dr. David Bradby; Sir Harry Brittain, Pilgrim Emeritus; Commander Merlin Bruce; Colonel Peter Clifton; Sir Noël Coward; Mrs. Patricia Dykes; Mr. John Hersey; Mr. H. R. F. Keating; Miss Gwen Newham; Mrs. Kirkby Peace; Mr. Giles Playfair; Mr. Peter Scott. And above all my thanks go to Mr. Paul Paget for his patient help with the book and index, during which process he became my husband.

Contents

Chapter   *page*

1   Line and Family   11
2   Seventh Child of a Seventh Child   23
3   Darling Carlton   35
4   Beastly Boy   46
5   Edinburgh and Oxford Freshman   58
6   Honourable Member for Dogs   70
7   Bruce *v.* Belloc   82
8   The Curate's Egg   97
9   St. Anne's, Soho   110
10   Young Londoner   125
11   Thatch and Feudalism   138
12   Macedonian Sorrow   150
13   Fall upon Fall   162
14   Bruces in Love   175
15   Married Bliss   189
16   The New Church   203
17   Very Brave and English Gentlemen   215
18   Rosslyn in America   227
19   Aftermath   240
20   The Goodly Heritage   252
21   Our Father which art in Herstmonceux   266
22   Seventh Heaven   281
23   Green Mouse, Rose Tinted   297
   Index   309

Illustrations

	facing page
Jane and James Skene of Rubislaw	32
Rhalou Rizo-Rangabee	32
Sir Walter Scott's letter to James Skene and Rosslyn's transcription	33
Rosslyn, aged two	64
Wilfrid, Rosslyn and Lloydie	64
The family at Scarborough	64
Worcester College Commemoration Ball, 1893	65
The Strafford Club in costume	65
Queen Victoria with her Skye terrier, bred by Rosslyn	96
Rosslyn in 1894	96
Bicycling in County Derry	96
Oxford Union Society Committee, 1895	97
Frederick, 4th Earl of Bristol and Bishop of Derry	128
Rosslyn as senior curate at St. Anne's, Soho	128
Gervase Bruce at Clifton, 1905	129
Noel Buxton's election poster, 1905	129
Rosslyn on Aerial	160
Clifton Hall, 1906	161
The Glebe, Clifton	161
Clifton cottages	192
May Day procession	192
Purity, Rosslyn's dove	193
Rachel Gurney of Northrepps	193
Lady Bruce, Rosslyn and Kathleen Scott at Clifton	193
Merlin, Rhalou and Erroll	256

Illustrations

Rosslyn with Rhalou at Herstmonceux   256
Wedding reception for Rosa Bane at Herstmonceux Rectory   257
Merlin and Joan's wedding reception   257
Colonel Claude Lowther's weeping cupid   288
Herstmonceux, 1934   288
Rosslyn with two of his dogs   289

CHAPTER ONE

Line and Family

'The secret of breeding a champion,' Rosslyn Bruce pointed out in his classic of the dog world, *Fox Terrier Breeding, The Line and Family Method*, 'is that the dam's dam's dam is the chief factor in a pedigree, over and above the sire's sire's sire.' Thus he maintained that traits handed down from his own forebears through his beautiful young mother— she never had time to grow old—were of more importance than those from his father in producing the kind of person he became.

Possibly this was because his own dam's dam's dam was a romantic Byzantine princess who, in the year 1832, sent her comely sixteen-year-old daughter out shopping in Athens with her nurse. As they passed down a quiet street within sight of Mount Olympus, an English mastiff appeared and frightened the girl — or so she said— into running into the nearest house and leaping on the table. The dog chased her, barking playfully. Its handsome young master, over from Malta to shoot wild duck, followed, fell in love at first sight, lifted her off the table, sold his commission in the 73rd Regiment —later the 2nd Black Watch—and married her.

The bride was Rhalou, daughter of Prince Jacovaki Rizo-Rangabee, head of an old and influential Phanariot family, and his lovely wife Princess Zoe Lapidi.

The bridegroom, then aged twenty-one, was James Skene, junior, son of James Skene of Rubislaw, whose close friendship with Sir Walter Scott was described in the introduction to the first canto of *Marmion*: Their summer walks, 'As thou with pencil, I with pen the features traced of hill and glen', their talks, 'whose topics ranged from grave to gay', and their 'blythesome nights when fires were bright and lamps beamed gay'.

In his dedication to *Ivanhoe*, Sir Walter said that the Secretary to the Antiquaries of Scotland, was the best amateur draughtsman in the kingdom. 'Mr. Skene is here intimated, to whose taste and skill the author is indebted for a series of sketchings exhibiting the various localities alluded to in these novels.' Mrs. James Skene had also known Sir Walter well since her brother, Sir William Forbes, had married Scott's first love, Williamina Stuart. After the total wreck of Sir Walter's fortunes, he frequently sought refuge from visitors with the Skenes. He said he drew inspiration from the Jacobite leanings of both their ancestors. Jane Skene's father was Sir William Forbes, 5th Bart., nephew and heir of the indomitable Jacobite, Lord Pitsligo of Monymusk, who took part in the first attempt to recover the throne from the Stuarts in 1715 and, in his seventieth year, had some hair-raising escapes disguised as a beggar in the army of the Young Pretender.

Sir Walter let the younger Skene children climb on his knee to exchange stories with him. Once Fifi, the youngest—who was to have so strong an influence on her—great-nephew, Rosslyn Bruce—pretended to read one of Scott's books—*The Abbot*—but Sir Walter snatched it away as being unsuitable. After Sir Walter's death the Skenes took their four younger daughters to France to be educated in Paris. Fifi was taught the piano by Liszt, 'a wild-looking, long-haired, excitable man'. The Skenes then moved on to Greece and bought a house, eight miles from Athens, large enough to share with their son, James, and his wife, Rhalou and their children. Fifi's three sisters married but she never seemed to have time for marriage. She was tall, red-haired and full of talent and an enjoyment for the funny side of life. Thanks to the Rizo-Rangabees, she was invited everywhere and was 'much at Court'. She had a fine contralto voice and sang before Queen Amelia. She was also a daring rider and when out with the Queen's favourite maid of honour, was passed by the Queen who, watching her antics, forbade her to ride with her Court ladies again. But Fifi's greatest delight were her half-Greek nephews and nieces, of whom there were eventually seven. She would play with her three favourites, George, Zoe and Janie—who was to become Rosslyn's mother—among the pillars of the Temple of Jupiter and would go for nursery walks with them up to the Acropolis and to the Temple of the Caryatides who, they told her, wept each night for the sisters the wicked Lord Elgin had carried off to the British Museum.

The family travelled a great deal and once, on the Danube, Fifi took the children to see a pasha's wife who received them in curl papers and was much excited about the beauty of Janie's auburn hair, asking whether it was dyed with henna as were the palms of her own hands. Fifi believed in broadening the children's sense of social service by pointing out such horrors as a drowned sailor being picked up in a boatman's hook, or slaves being sold in the market, or the head of a wounded brigand, cut off by a grinning peasant 'to cure him'. In fact it only developed, at any rate in Janie, a fear of horrors that lasted into the next generation as unnatural squeamishness.

'My little sister and I,' wrote Zoe later, 'saw a funeral of an old general, his body exposed and clad in his uniform, from our nursery window; and later, when we were digging in our gardens in the country, Janie exclaimed, with a look of horror on her face, "Oh Zoe, stop, befear'd we dig up old Cantacuzene".'

But most frightening of all were the tales the children's nurses told them of the cruelty and horrors of the Turkish rule. For Janie and Zoe, for the rest of their lives, there were no good Turks.

Fifi tempered her lessons in the starkness of life with English, drawing and music. She had a book of her own poems published which she illustrated herself. Her brother—Janie's father—James Skene, was also a writer and fine amateur singer. He had now joined the British Diplomatic Service. He was described at the time as 'a brilliant scholar, remarkable linguist and a charming man'. He lived for a while among the Arabs as a sheik which he recorded in *Rambles in the Syrian Desert*.

When Janie and Zoe were seven and eight years old their Skene grandparents decided to return to Scotland. Fifi persuaded James and Rhalou to let the little girls go too to be educated in Edinburgh. Here Fifi's brother, William Skene, lawyer and archaeologist lived and received them.

Five years later the Skenes moved to Oxford where they bought a house in the newly-built Beaumont Street. Fifi was accepted by

Oxford society on the strength of her work in the prisons and the regular articles she contributed to magazines about it. Zoe and Janie were able to study music and attend lectures.

Both had inherited their mother's and her mother's outstanding good looks. Heads turned when Zoe walked down the street and, like her mother at the same age, she fell irrevocably in love at sixteen.

Dr. William Thomson was a young cleric with a reputation. He had been rusticated from Queen's College for assault after a debate. He was the anonymous author of a controversial religious treatise, *Outlines of the Laws of Thought*. He was already a Fellow of Queen's College. The Skene grandparents liked him more and more. Zoe's mother, Rhalou, however, sent a curt message from Constantinople: 'Don't let Zoe marry that priest.'

The Crimean War had already broken out, but Janie went straight off to the Bosporus to plead with her mother on her sister Zoe's and William's behalf. But Rhalou was adamant. After the Greek custom, she had arranged a marriage for Zoe with an English peer who had admired her photographs.

Granny Skene, whose twinkling blue eyes, over a decisive chin, look out from under a cosy bonnet in her portrait, wrote advising Janie:

> to storm the position and carry it by assault as people want Lord Raglan to do with Sebastopol. I do not think your present plan of advancing your entrenchments by slow degrees, and proceeding by sap and mind will ever make any progress. Paint in vivid colours the attachment between the two lovers and the happiness they look forward to, *thanks* to your mother. I think she will probably give in at once and, though there might be a scene of weeping, Mama [she added mischievously] does not dislike a scene.

She was right and Rhalou gave in. Rhalou's husband, young James Skene, was now acting as Private Secretary to the British Ambassador at Constantinople, Lord Stratford de Redcliffe. Janie, who wrote to Zoe saying how hard it was 'to keep up the steam in this horridly stupid place, where everybody is on bad terms with their neighbours', attended an ambassadorial party at which Lord Stratford was 'particularly kind and attentive' to her. As a result she was able to go with her mother to visit her brother George who, as a midshipman, had been wounded and was recovering in a makeshift hospital at Scutari. The appalling sights, smells, and the suffering of the wounded, through lack of nurses and hospital appliances, incited Janie to write a long letter to her grandfather at Oxford. He sent it to *The Times* and it was immediately published, which helped to stir up the feelings of the public.

Fifi had already trained a corps of nurses during an outbreak of cholera in Oxford. Now she offered her nurses to Florence Nightingale who had started enlisting recruits to send to the Crimea. Florence Nightingale eventually sailed with thirty-four volunteers, three of whom were Fifi's nurses.

Janie was back in Oxford for her sister's wedding to Dr. Thomson, who had just been given the important living of All Souls, Langham Place in London. Janie stayed often with them and Zoe took pleasure in taking her travelled and entertaining sister 'about' with her. When Dr. Thomson was made Provost of Queen's College, Oxford, Zoe was known there as 'the Queen of Queens'. By now her children had begun to arrive and so her parents moved into Frewen Hall so that their grandchildren would have a larger garden to play in. This lovely old house had, for the past year, been lived in by the Prince of Wales under the supervision of 'a dour Scotsman', Colonel Bruce. When the Prince visited Oxford after his marriage, he brought his bride to the house to see where he had lived. The Skenes entertained him by showing him the exquisitely bound prayerbook that Charles I had given to one of their ancestors.

In 1862 the Thomsons shared a holiday house in Wales with the Gladstones. Mr. Gladstone was then Chancellor of the Exchequer. Janie stayed on with the children of both families after their parents had left. She wrote to Zoe: 'The children's joke is to call me Mama so sometimes I'm not quite sure if I am you or myself.'

With the birth of Zoe's fifth child came Dr. Thomson's appointment to the bishopric of Gloucester and Bristol. With the birth of the next, came an even more surprising appointment. The Bishop wrote to Janie, who was caring for the children at Frewen Hall:

My dear Janie,

I have had a sharp attack of toothache which ended, at least I hope so, in chloroform and a touch of the lancet.

Just as I was coming out of the chloroform trance, there arrived a letter from Palmerston to announce that the Queen had authorised him to offer me the vacant office of Archbishop of York. You may suppose that this news has caused an excitement in the family. So that when I come to you it will not be to fetch you to Gloucester after all.

Love to all the chickees. Yours affectionately,

W. Gloucester and Bristol

Zoe, who had already warned him of the dangers of chloroform in disturbing the mind, exclaimed, when she heard the news, 'There! what did I tell you? Those beastly narcotics again.'

The *Oxford Review* noted: 'Due to periodical increases in the family circle, it has been impossible for Mrs. Thomson to be present to receive congratulations on the rapid progress of her husband.'

Professor Max-Muller observed to Bishop Wilberforce: 'It is a curious thing that whenever Mrs. Thomson presents her husband with a baby, the Archbishop of York has always got preferment.'

The Bishop replied: 'Mrs. Thomson had better be very careful, because there are only Canterbury and heaven before him.'

When Janie's turn came to fall in love, she was twenty-seven and *her* 'young priest', a distant cousin of the royal tutor, was thirty-four. Alas, Granny Skene, who would have delighted in leading another granddaughter into battle, if only to tease her daughter-in-law in Greece, had died the year before. This time it was Zoe herself who singled out the Rev. Lloyd Bruce, rector of an obscure parish in Wiltshire, from Janie's plentiful admirers as being 'dull, shabbily dressed and too old'. Zoe's parties had deliberately included the potential great of the time, from whom she intended her sister to choose wisely. Janie wrote admitting that Mr. Bruce had declared himself and she had agreed to let him call at Frewen Hall.

A tiny tear-besmirched letter, deeply edged with black for their lately departed grandmother, exists, in a miniature envelope, equally black-edged.

Dearest Zoe,

I just write a line to tell you that I have nothing yet to say. Mr. Bruce did not come today and I find that I could not have heard from him by earlier post than tomorrow morning. I will let you know as soon as possible what he says. I hope, darling, that you are not still vexed with me. I can only say that nothing could ever make up to me for the loss of your love. I wish you believed that if I have done wrong in this matter it was from a mistaken sense of duty and never from cold-heartedness or ingratitude.

Yours in great haste, Janie.

In her next letter she said that Mr. Bruce had written to Fifi that he could come on Tuesday to talk over matters with her . . .

as he thinks he can so much better explain by word of mouth than in writing. I shall be thankful when this wretched suspense is over. Much more of it would very soon finish me. The children are well and happy. Will you thank the Absp very much for his letter which raised my spirits a good deal and made me hope that you and he were thinking less hardly of me than you have done, but altogether I rather wish myself in the backwoods. I have not been able to eat, sleep or settle down to anything since this day week.

Perhaps worst of all, was Janie's beloved brother George being so hurt by her not confiding in him that he vowed he would never have anything to do with her again.

Aunt Fifi, to whom Janie had told all, wrote to Zoe from Frewen Hall:

Dearest Zoe,

Please tell the Archbishop from me that Mr. Bruce wrote to me this morning and he possesses £5,000 of his own which he can settle on Janie. He says he will make these arrangements with her father. I am so grieved about George. I feel as if he were cut off from us from his not being able to write to Janie. I myself wished her to go and see him. I wish so much you could come, in haste, ever affectionately, your Felicia Skene.

Mr. Bruce, it seemed, had not till then thought of finding out how much money his father had left him. It was not till they were on the doorstep of his brother's London house, where he took Janie to stay, that he explained that his brother, Sir Hervey Bruce, 3rd Bart., being ten years older than himself, and having been a regular in the 1st Life Guards, Lieutenant and then High Sheriff of Londonderry, and now M.P. for Coleraine, was sometimes a little overweening in his ways. Though, Lloyd added dryly, it was said that the only time he was heard in the House of Commons was when a Liberal or an Irish member rose to speak, whereupon Hervey got up on his seat and crowed like a bantam cock. Janie might also find Lady Bruce somewhat unbending. She was sister of Sir Robert Clifton, M.P. whose Nottinghamshire estate of the same name had been in the family since the Norman Conquest. Both Sir Hervey and Lady Bruce were, Lloyd thought, unnaturally proud of the common origin of their families in the 'Competitor', grandfather of King Robert the Bruce.

The granddaughter of Prince Jacovaki Rizo-Rangabee, Grand Postelnic of Wallachia, stiffened.

In her first letter to Zoe from the Bruces' London house she wrote: 'Lady Bruce seems to think me proud and conceited and that is why she was cold about the marriage. I am not afraid to dispel the idea,' and she pressed on with plans for the wedding in September:

As quiet as it can possibly be made. Nobody but brothers and sisters. Happily, Lloyd and I quite agree on our views on that subject. Oh! dear Zoe, I wish you could see him a little more with my eyes. The more I see him, the more I find to like and respect in him. You really have got *quite* the wrong impression of him and what distresses me is I feel that I myself gave that impression. The day *will* come when you will find that you have done him an injustice. I'm sure I am going to be very happy and if you could see how considerate he is for me in every way you would be of the same mind.

At last George, at Filey, answered his favourite sister's letters.

Dearest duck,

I am so glad I do not know *him* yet and if I make his acquaintance and learn about him through you I shall probably feel more charitably disposed towards one who takes possession of *my property* (that's you) in so arbitrary a manner. I could not bear to have been on just acquaintance terms with one who is to be so much to you (who *is* for all I know). The photograph you sent me I hope to have replaced by a better one. I am sure it cannot do him justice. Oh Janie, we have been so far away from each other and I shall feel so lonely when my unmarried sister goes. We shall never more have those little confidential talks before going to bed in which we used to tell each other our secrets. You don't know how I have missed them and how I have been unreasonable enough to look forward to them. However when I know more of *your* darling I dare say I shall be more resigned to make haste and console.

P.S. I wrote you a horrid letter for last mail because I was vexed that you did not tell me more about it but on looking over your letter again I could not bring myself to post it.

Before Janie had time to reply she heard that her temperamental brother had collapsed and Zoe had rushed to Filey to nurse him. After two days Janie wrote to Zoe:

I can't rest longer without seeing George so I am going to start tomorrow morning. I hope you don't mind my coming. It would be such a relief to my mind and I can at least read aloud to him and spare you that. Do not mind preparing a bed for me, for any sofa will do quite well.

As Janie tiptoed into the sickroom, George announced that he now expected to live. Zoe returned to her children and moving into Bishopthorpe and Janie took over.

'Dearest Zoe,' she wrote, 'He is very much as you left him, the pleurisy is not worse but he is not much better and he still has poultices all over him. The turtle soup unfortunately is quite tainted.' Next day she wrote: 'His appetite is growing immense. He is always asking for food and has already come to puddings and jam on his bread. He has his chest rubbed which he greatly enjoys. Mama has told my old friends of my engagement but complains that I have not written to them myself.'

Janie continued to concern herself entirely with George's health, to his great satisfaction, till just before the wedding.

She wrote from Filey:

Fifi is leaving everything at Frewen Hall till I go and it will all be a horrid mess I know. I have got into a state of worry that is misery. Such is life. Nothing ever will go smoothly for me I fear. Will you answer Aunt Georgie at once that she too may not take offence? George is to sit in another room today for change of air. Lloyd writes that Lady Barnard is to be in Ireland when we go. We must try to get Grandpa to sit in Fifi's room, else I do not know how we shall cram all the people in. If it should happen to be a wet day it will be all over with us.

Then came a frantic note from Frewen Hall:

If you are going to shop before you come down and are at Marshall and Snelgrove's will you please get me *two knitted petticoats* to wear under my crinoline. Ten shillings is the price. White and mauve are the prettiest. Tell Miss Knoakes too please, that she *must* send my wedding dress on Saturday. I am in such a fright that it will be too late if only sent on Monday. Yours in haste.

However, all was well and Rosslyn's parents were safely married on October 6th, 1863, at St. Michael's, Oxford, to which church Fifi devoted herself throughout her fifty years in Oxford.

The honeymoon was to be spent in Ireland at Downhill, the vast marble and granite palace on the edge of the cliff where Lloyd and his brothers had been brought up. This 'monster bathing box' had been left in 1803 to their grandfather, the Rev. Sir H. Hervey Bruce by the rumbustious 4th Earl of Bristol and Bishop of Derry, from whose grandfather, the 1st Earl, Rosslyn was twice descended, once through the eccentric Bishop's daughter.

A contemporary memoir describes the Bishop as 'splendid but fantastical; engaging, often licentious in conversation. His progress from his diocese to the metropolis, and his entrance into it, were perfectly correspondent to the rest of his conduct. To every town on the road he seemed to call, and was received with honours as he passed by, full of spirits and talk.' He became a well-known figure as he bowled along the roads of Germany and Italy in his great coach, and Hotels Bristol all over the continent were named after him.

'Lord Bristol has been particularly civil to me,' young Hudson Gurney wrote to his mother from Rome. 'His table is surrounded by prelates and artists, and his Lordship's wit keeps one in continual laughter the whole time, even in debating serious subjects and saying seriously good things.'

The Earl–Bishop built Downhill in about 1775 on the cliffs of Antrim, using local granite with all the marble for the interior, as well as the pictures and statues, brought from Italy. He then started to build another vast mansion in the form of a rotunda at Ickworth in Suffolk. Both are now National Trust properties.

'Downhill is a great rambling place as large as a college,' Janie wrote to Zoe from her honeymoon. 'Three parts of it is in ruin, having been burnt down twelve years ago.'

Life at Downhill was a mixture of Irish make-do and high formality. Sir Hervey dressed like one of his own keepers by day but always came down to dinner in full evening dress, even if he dined alone. The Bishop's old Irish silver was exquisite, though sometimes mixed on the sideboard with dog bowls. Sir Hervey detested dogs but his son placed them, and the tame grouse running about the house with them, high above human importance and was heard to say, when offering to peel a peach for a stately dowager sitting on his right: 'May I peel this peach for you? It's too ripe for the monkey.'

How comforting dull Lloyd's behaviour must have been to Janie on their honeymoon!

We have not quarrelled yet, dear and I rather think we are each day less likely to do so, [she wrote to Zoe] I see it would take a great deal to ruffle Lloyd's temper and mine will improve under his guidance. I am very happy, old Zoe, and I do not find now that I have any coldness from his part to complain of, and all the other fears that I had before I was married must have been rather fancy, for I cannot see a trace of them now. I am not afraid of having a hard life before me either, for he seems to underrate my strength and will hardly let me do anything.

A fortnight later she was writing:

Lady Bruce and I get on famously. I like her immensely now and feel quite at home with them all. The only thing that mars my happiness at all is that they sit up so late at night that I am always quite worn out before I can go to bed.

CHAPTER TWO

Seventh Child of a Seventh Child

'Here I am in my new home!' Janie wrote to Zoe in her first letter from Hale Rectory, Wiltshire. 'The house is undoubtedly small but I neither fainted nor went into hysterics when I saw it last night. It is a very nice little snuggery and is all fresh and clean and I do not see what we should do with a larger house.' A month later she was thanking for books that 'will be the greatest value. I was becoming almost useless from constant sickness so shall be most grateful if the remedies your book suggests are effectual,' and she went on to inquire about Mrs. Afflick, the family midwife. Zoe's inevitable reply was that of course Janie must go to Bishopthorpe palace for her first confinement and Zoe would care for her and her baby with her own hands.

It is clear from the constant letters beginning 'You are an old darling again' and 'so many substantial benefits to thank you for I hardly know where to begin', that Zoe showered her sister with baby linen, clothes for herself, hampers of food and every imaginable comfort. 'Lloyd came up and found me sitting on the floor beaming and admiring everything like a child with a new doll, and calling you a duck and an angel and all sorts of feathered fowls.'

As her time drew near Janie wrote: 'I quite expect "Nellie" to make her appearance soon after our arrival.' But Bishopthorpe was kept waiting for nearly a month. The only engagement that could not be put off was the Judges' Dinner. Zoe wrote of it afterwards:

A few hours before the dinner the doctor had to be sent for and Lady Wightman, widow of a judge, volunteered to stay with my sister during the dinner hour. Janie said afterwards she had a vision of me coming in to kiss her in a dress of blue satin and white lace on my way down to dinner. The doctor assured me that I should be back in time. The Archbishop begged me to say nothing to the judges as it would make them uncomfortable. All went well until a little note was brought me during the fish course written by Lloyd Bruce "A little girl born. Both doing well." I gave a sigh and was able to carry on the conversation much better. At the pudding course another little note was brought me from Lloyd saying "Another little girl born. All three doing well." This second note was too much for Lord Blackburn's curiosity and he could not help asking what the notes were about. I was wondering what to say and had sent the notes on to the Archbishop. As soon as he looked at them he confided the contents to the High Sheriff's wife who promptly made a sign for the ladies to leave the table and I was thus released and able to go up to my sister where I saw the little twins in the same basinette, facing each other.

For the rest of the evening names were discussed for the twins. Judge Blackburn remarked that had they been boys he would have asked to have them called Themis and Justitian. Other suggestions relating to the moment of their birth were Soup and Fish, to be known collectively as the Superficial Twins. Both little girls were fair and exceedingly pretty, but Elma, the elder, was only about half the size of the other. Her delicacy and the distance from doctors, family and friends, incited Zoe to suggest a move. The Archbishop offered Lloyd the parish of Barton-in-Fablis, a mile down the river Trent from Lady Bruce's family home of Clifton, and a mile downstream to Thrumpton, home of the 8th Lord Byron, cousin of the poet and old friend of the Nottinghamshire Bruces.

The Archbishop was very much averse to what he called 'the monstrous Simony now prevailing' by which he meant 'the procuring for a person any spiritual charge from consideration of interest rather than fitness.' Evidently, therefore, he felt Lloyd was fit for this tiny parish with its picturesque but damp rectory. The Archbishop may not even have been aware then that in its grounds lay valuable gypsum which the rector was free to exploit.

Janie gave birth to her third daughter at Barton, with Zoe in attendance, as she was for all her sister's confinements. In return, Janie despatched the most promising material from her husband's confirmation classes as nursery maids to Bishopthorpe, where a new baby arrived shortly after a royal visit to the palace.

By the time Janie's first son, Douglas, was born, Barton was becoming less attractive and she longed to leave. She was soon pregnant again and passing through one of these eras well known to young mothers of one epidemic after another, trouble with helps and too little money. Lloyd felt the only hope of procuring more money was to remain rector of Barton till the gypsum could be mined. But he was no businessman and whenever he was advised to go ahead with investing money in the mine, someone would warn him to pull out at the last minute. For a while they had to be content with long exchanges with curates of healthier parishes, in one of which Janie gave birth to a second set of twins.

It was not so much the bearing of six children in just over three and a half years, Janie said, that caused her complete collapse in 1868 but the rearing of them. Formerly bright, energetic and easily moved to make others about her laugh, she was now pale, listless and so weak that she had to be fed at half-hourly intervals to be kept alive at all. Her diet sheet remains, this being the first day:

9 a.m.	Beef tea
9½	Champagne
10	Chicken broth
10½	Arrowroot with milk
11	Turtle soup or beef tea
11½	Medicine
11¾	Champagne
12	Custard pudding
12½	Beef tea
1 p.m.	A sandwich of chicken or mutton with a little brandy and water
2	Medicine
2½	Chicken broth
3	Champagne

3½	A cup of milk
4	Brandy and water
5	A cup of cocoa
5½	Turtle soup
6	A cup of tea, with two teaspoonsful of brandy with a little heated butter
7	Medicine
7½	Beef tea
8	Cocoa with a rusk
9	Chicken broth, followed by champagne
10	Arrowroot with milk
11	Cup of tea with brandy
12	Chicken broth and champagne
1	Cocoa
2 o'clock	Cup of tea. Brandy
3	Beef tea and a glass of champagne
4	Arrowroot and medicine
5	Cocoa
6	Beef tea and champagne
7	Tea and toast
8	Arrowroot with brandy and medicine

No wonder a London specialist diagnosed Janie's trouble, including a recurring pain in the back, as hysteria.

Zoe came for the collapse and even *she* agreed with the rest of the family that for Janie to have another baby would be unnecessary, foolish and probably lethal.

Not many months passed before Janie wrote to her, in a letter commenting on their old friend Mr. Gladstone becoming Prime Minister, that 'a false alarm caused a useless commotion about myself.'

She had now completely recovered and was helping to augment their income by illuminating photograph albums which Zoe helped to sell to rich friends for three guineas each. The work was delicate and the result exquisite. On each page a different motif decorated slip-in frames for family photographs. Wild flowers, corn ears, her own jewellery all suggested motifs for the illuminations, into which she worked gold leaf.

The family had just returned from a Yorkshire curacy in 1870 when news came from Greece of Janie's mother's death. Rhalou Skene, still remarkable for her beauty, and until then in rude health, had died suddenly of a fever. She was fifty-three.

A bishop and fifteen priests of the Greek Church officiated at her funeral, while sixteen priests of other denominations and hundreds of children headed the procession. A military guard of honour, formed with sergeants with arms reversed, surrounded the bier of which the consuls of France, Russia, Austria and Italy were the pall bearers. The streets were lined with soldiers, all shops were closed, flags were hung at half mast and funeral services were performed in every church.

Lloyd wrote the next letter to Zoe, as he often did in a crisis.

We were, as you may suppose, very much shocked by the sad news contained in your letter, having had no idea of Mrs. Skene's illness. Our post frequently does not arrive until nearly 11 o'clock and as I was attending a choral festival, Janie opened yours. Last night, putting some tokens of mourning on the children's frocks diverted her attention in a measure.

Janie wept for the letters she loved to receive from her exuberant mother—always in French, using large all-embracing words—and for the visits even though they left her slightly sapped. She had so longed for her to see her new grandchild, but in a few days she had recovered enough to write:

All our children have got the whooping cough in case you dislike coming to us now. You would not be the least in the way, quite the contrary, only I fear it will not be pleasant to hear the eternal coughing that goes on. Gwennie's is at the height, Douglas is also bad and began with croup and, following your advice I am rubbing them with linament, and giving them no meat. Night is the worst and when one begins they all follow suit. I have the baby at night to release the nurse, and Allie takes alternate nights with her. Uncle William has a horror of whooping cough, never having had it. He most generously insists on our accepting £50 for the expenses of a trip to Cleethorpes.

Uncle William Skene, Fifi's eldest brother, had never married but his generosity to his nephews and nieces and their children never ceased. Whooping cough apart, he was always ready to have them in his house in Edinburgh or take them for holidays with their parents. Within half a day's drive of 20, Inverleith Row, he had a private beach where many of them learnt to swim, near Dunbar, and a Hebridean island where the boys learnt to row and fish.

Three weeks after Rhalou Skene died, the Franco–Prussian War broke out. Carrie, William and Fifi's sister, who had married Rhalou's diplomat brother, fled from Paris with her younger children, leaving two of her sons fighting on opposite sides. Her husband was on a mission to Constantinople and it was only thanks to money sent by the Archbishop that the Rangabees were able to cross the channel.

In England, family doors were immediately opened to them. Beds were made up at Bishopthorpe, and at Fifi's in Oxford and at Barton Rectory. Carrie chose to go to Barton first, ignored the whooping cough, and amazed Janie by her cheerful attitude as she joked and 'lionised' her children in the village, in face of such terrible adversity in fares.

Carrie was back at Barton in the late autumn when Janie realised that another 'commotion about herself,' after a lapse of three years, turned out to be justified. Zoe had arranged to take her to a royal function in the spring and Carrie assured her she could still go. 'You'll have to wear a label saying "this side up",' she suggested, and went on to deplore the fact that Janie's mother would no longer be there to claim, according to the Greek peasant belief, second sight for her grandchild who would be the seventh child of a seventh child.

On Christmas Day Janie wrote to Zoe: 'I am very glad I shall see Uncle William and I hope you will break to him the awkward news that No. 7 is expected in August, as I dare not face him with such an impediment to all his kind plans for me to go abroad with him.'

On January 3rd, 1871, she complained:

It is just a month now since I had to write to Mrs. Afflick to tell her the unwelcome news that I should want her in the beginning of August. Now today I get the enclosed letters which I think are very wrong and unfair. I really do not want her to martyr herself to me. Don't worry about me, dear, for I am in perfect health and can walk about bravely. It may be that I shall be better than ever after it, if I have a good time and am well nursed. Dr. Graham thought it could be so.

By the time the baby was due the elder twins, Elma and Zoe would have reached their seventh birthday, Irene would be five, Douglas four, and the 'second version of Bruce twins', Lloydie and Gwennie, would be three and a half. All were good-mannered, obedient, house-trained and, at any rate during the summer, in bounding good health. Janie could see their pink cheeks and golden curls bobbing about the garden at Barton Rectory, an incentive rather than a deterrent to adding to their numbers.

Janie went on with the photograph albums.

Lady Byron took the first book to London. I hope it will give satisfaction. The second will be more carefully done and has a prettier binding. It is rather difficult to keep one's hand always steady when posterity gives a violent kick but happily that impediment can't last for ever.

Zoe was determined that Janie should have her baby in London where she could have the best attention, even though she was in better health than for years.

To emphasise parental delight over the seventh child, the god-parents discussed were all titled and immensely grand.

Of Lady Georgiana Milner, who was also expecting, Janie wrote to Zoe:

Georgie writes most ecstatically on being delighted to be the second godmother. She's young and perhaps a little quick but I trust that as she grows older she will grow wiser and become a sober matron.

But Georgie had no time to grow older. Only five weeks before Janie's baby was due came the news that Georgie had gone to

Edinburgh to have her baby. 'Georgie had all the good doctors money could buy and yet she died. There is really a very nice doctor here who with Mrs. Afflick will give me all the aid I ought to expect from human skill.' Janie was so well now it seemed a pity to take a long journey. Nottingham was supposed to have exceptionally good medical men. So Zoe packed her bag, and proceeded with Mrs. Afflick to Barton where she despatched the six Bruce children to Bishopthorpe to be with her own nine.

The seventh child of a seventh child was born on August 14th, 1871. All went better than ever before. Lloyd heard the lusty sound of his son's voice as he crossed the lane separating the rectory from the church.

Lord Rosslyn wrote from 40, Upper Brook Street, London on August 21st:

My dear Bruce,

I was delighted to think Mrs Bruce got so well over her troubles and can sympathise the more truly as Lady Rosslyn was happily confined of a daughter after protracted waiting yesterday morning at 6 a.m. and thank God is going on now as well as possible. It will give me very much pleasure to lend my name to your boy and I trust that the influence and example of his father may render any interference on my part unnecessary. With best regards to Mrs. Bruce. Give my love to Mrs. Afflick.

Sincerely, Rosslyn.

After Zoe had left, Lloyd wrote to her at Bishopthorpe:

I am very proud of Master Rosslyn. I think he is quite the best baby of the seven, whatever he may turn out thereafter, and he seems to bear with much complacency the separation from his mother from 10 o'clock at night till 7 o'clock in the morning, so that Janie will I hope continue to have good nights. She has been out in the garden and thinks all the children look well after their month away.

Janie's handwriting verges almost imperceptibly into Lloyd's:

I have sent you the green ribbons packed by mistake. I tried the lessons this morning and got on capitally. Lloyd suggests our sending them to the village school for an hour in the morning but I'm not sure that would be the answer. Feeling much better. You have made me and the children so very comfortable for the winter. Lloyd says he never saw me in anything so nice and useful as my shepherd's plaid.

The baby was christened at Barton before he was four weeks old, Francis Rosslyn Courtenay. His three godfathers were his cousin, the 21st Lord Forbes, Premier Baron of Scotland; the 20th Earl of Erroll; and the 4th Earl of Rosslyn, High Commander to the General Assembly of the Church of Scotland and Captain of the Corps of Gentlemen at Arms. Lady Georgiana was replaced by Amy Monkton-Milner, who afterwards completed the imposing list by becoming Lady Fitzgerald.

At last Janie had time to enjoy a baby. 'Baby has engrossed me a good deal this week.' When he had a cold she was uneasy. However, it passed 'and I am thankful to have my jolly little boy crowing and laughing at me again,' she wrote when he was ten months old. 'I have weaned him or rather he has weaned himself while he was ill and now he prefers pudding to me.'

He was born into a gap in the otherwise crowded family pattern. This allowed him to reign supreme for a while, untrammelled by the demands of a twin or another baby less than a year old or younger than himself.

The damp at Barton drove the Bruces out again, this time to Scalby near Scarborough. Again there were moments when they hardly knew where to turn for money, but Janie's natural resilience buffered the children from their cares.

'Lloyd thinks things go on better in a money point of view and comfort now I am cook,' she wrote to Zoe. 'Lord Forbes and another clergyman came to lunch in blissful ignorance that I had cooked it all.' She really enjoyed cooking and only occasionally wrote of her disasters. Mostly she was surprised how untired it left her, considerably less so than her other creative work of illuminating the photograph albums.

The Byrons tutor taught the older children and, to save money, 'for

music, I have put them into the church choir,' Janie admitted cheerfully.

Zoe and the Archbishop's generosity in both money and time
continued. Throughout Janie's letters are frequent practical references to the way, again and again, these important, immensely busy
people took trouble on behalf of their less successful dear ones, sending them food, clothing, toys, books and very often money. The
Archbishop had no private income but his higher pay made this help
possible, though his expenses were enormously greater.

'Lloyd's tenants have all paid up bravely this time,' Janie wrote,
after a crisis, 'and we are quite flush again for the present so no need
to help at all. I would really much rather try to pay our own way.'

At Christmas she was writing again:

> You really are a witch to find out all our wants as you do. Every
> one of the children's frocks and knickers fit like a glove and the
> boys are in great glee with their soldier's clothes. They think they
> are quite at liberty to fight now and go stumping about the house
> in single file shouldering arms, Rosslyn included.

Rosslyn at two years old was undoubtedly a charmer. With his
mischievous blue eyes, pink cheeks and fluffy fair hair, he waddled
about the lawn back at Barton, to his mother's delight, trying to
persuade a hen to an egg-laying point of view. His lifelong fascination with birds and beasts was already evident. Janie was distraught
one day when she learnt that he had disappeared from the garden.
She was sure he had been kidnapped. Eventually he was found in the
pigsty, asleep, with fifteen piglets, against the sow.

Rosslyn was such a success and Janie felt so well now that prudence
was thrown to the four winds and once again babies came crowding
into the nursery. Still the gypsum went unmined and still the garden
was too often under water.

On Christmas Day 1874 came a letter from Zoe giving Lloyd the
tip that the excellent living of Stokesley in the North Riding of
Yorkshire was vacant and to apply for it. Lloyd did so.

> We had almost given up thinking of Stokesley when your letter
> came this morning addressed by the Archbishop, [Janie wrote]

Jane (née Forbes) and James Skene of Rubislaw, friends of Sir Walter Scott. Their son married Rhalou (*below*), daughter of Prince Jacovaki Rizo-Rangabee, of Athens.

Sir Walter Scott's handwriting (*left*) and Rosslyn Bruce's transcription of Scott's letter to his great-grandfather.

My dear Shene

I have been suffering great trouble from the toothache and Naysmith the dentist who has been with me has just extracted the offending piece of ivory. He imposes as an additional penance, the injunction that I should remain at home today, which I comply with very reluctantly as it prevents my having the pleasure of waiting on you but in view of the Clerks table I must not risk rheumatism in the jaw. Yours ever

Walter Scott

Castle Street
Wednesday

This Shene, to whom Scott dedicated marmion (Cant 4) was my great grandfather. R.B.

when I must confess my heart beat quickly for a few minutes. One is but human you see, but I shall be glad when I hear that it is settled as, in spite of all one's philosophy, you can't help feeling unsettled at times. You will remember how it used to be when a bishophric was vacant in the old Queen's College days?

But the Archbishop must have had second thoughts about Lloyd's being able to manage the upkeep of so large a rectory as Stokesley and he wrote offering him instead a prebendaryship of York with duties that included acting as private chaplain to himself. To this the Archbishop added the personal gift of the price of a curate for Barton to tide things over in Lloyd's absence.

The following year he offered him the parish of Carlton-in-Lind-rick near Worksop. It was not much nearer to York but there was an excellent stipend, a lovely garden with the church forming one side of it and an attractive Jacobean house with Georgian facings. A banked-up terrace kept the walls dry and the whole of the attic floor was paved with stone composition, as in Italy, so that if the pantile roof leaked, at least the two floors beneath the attic were well protected. From the many nursery windows were magical views of the lake at Carlton Hall and of a rushy mill pool.

Particularly delightful to Janie was the architectural beauty of the early English church with its fine Norman doorway, priest's door and font, a Saxon window, rare stained glass and a bossed roof carved with the arms of the ancient family of Dacre.

'This will be like beginning life again,' Janie wrote to the Arch-bishop. 'I hope you may be persuaded to come and give the house a warming and gladden your eyes by the sight of the comfort that you have bestowed on us,' for he and Zoe had showered them with beds and carpets.

In fact the new life began with Janie having to nurse a carpenter, sent to make good urgent repairs, who had collapsed with a stroke.

The house looked in a most deplorable state yesterday [she wrote to Fifi]. The rain never ceased for two days and the men carried the mud on their boots into every corner of it. I found the three maids standing in a mournful group after they arrived; they seemed to think it was quite a hopeless undertaking and looked ready to run away, but I soothed them down as best I could and assured them we should soon get things comfortable again. The vans did not arrive till twelve o'clock having stuck on the road from the rain and darkness.

Eventually Janie found herself helping to paper the bedrooms with her own hands.

Before they were finished came a letter from her father, James Skene, proposing a visit. Since Rhalou's death he had been more frequently to England, usually bringing two or three of the Arab horses with which he did more to improve the racing stock of Great Britain than was appreciated by his family. It was said afterwards that he virtually introduced the Arab blood to this country that has helped to produce some of the greatest winners.

Janie's concern for him, however, was with getting a room safely dried out in time for him to sleep in on this, his first visit to the new home.

CHAPTER THREE

Darling Carlton

Rosslyn was three and a half when the family moved to Carlton. All his earliest and dearest memories dated from then. Janie painted him in water colours in his sailor suit, with his blond hair almost to his waist. When it was cut he boasted: 'My muvver cried when my curls were cut off.'

As to his second sight, he saw mysterious other worldly beings everywhere. 'Look! An old man hammering up in the tree!' He pointed up to the bushy foliage of an ilex. His mother would peer up and see no one till he explained how the leaves formed the old man's nose and chin and arm and how the wind made him raise his arm to wield the hammer. In the clouds he saw faces, too, and animals and birds and egg-shells. The world was full of miracles that his perceptive mind and keen eyesight never missed. Carlton rectory garden was full of birds' nests and Rosslyn was fascinated by what always remained the greatest miracle of all, a chick pecking its way out of an egg. He was so anxious to try it out himself that he went to the kitchen and asked for eggs to sit on. When they were refused, he took a clutch of tennis balls up to the hay loft and was found sitting intently on them.

He loved the village passionately. It was like a toy village, so charming were the blacksmith's shop, post office, inn, mill, farm and a few cottages.

The Hall was very grand and the Ramsdens, who lived in it, were Plymouth Brethren. At first the Bruces found them hard to get on with, till the children befriended Robbie Ramsden, who was the same age as Rosslyn. His father had died soon after he was born, leaving him overridden by women who considered him delicate.

The two little boys were pushed out together and while their nursery maids stood gossiping Rosslyn showed Robbie how to rock his pram so that both wicker prams went bowling downhill in a race that made Rosslyn shout with joy and left Allie, his nursery maid, screaming.

The older children were shocked and often embarrassed by their little brother's obstreperous behaviour, which their mother only laughed at. Gwennie, the youngest of all the twins and nearest in age to him, however, secretly thought him funny. In a train a stranger asked how old he was and he answered with seraphic smile: 'I's not old at all. I's young.'

Janie took her brood with her when she went by train to Bishop-thorpe. Rosslyn's godmother, Amy Milner, describes a visit when he was there:

When the Archbishop entered the room with a long-clothed baby in his arms and little toddling things beside him for games and romps with the children, he put off the part of Archbishop and descended on all fours to take that of a roaring lion. He was much delighted when a small nephew approached him with double fists, and said 'Archbishop, shall I knock you down?' but at the same time begged him not to be frightened.

The palace, rather like the Archbishop, was very imposing and ecclesiastical-looking on one side, but homelike and delightfully holidayish on the other.

The river Ouse ran beneath the window of my mother's room, [wrote the Archbishop's son, Basil]. And we had only to float past with some craft of our own building, a raft with a packing-case to sit on, and speak ever so gently and she would be at the window with alarm in her eyes and unconcern—or what she thought was unconcern—in the tone of her voice.

There was much exchange of children between Bishopthorpe and Carlton Rectory. If the Archbishop's children were backward in their lessons they were packed off to their Uncle Lloyd to give them special coaching. The homemade craft was introduced on to the

Carlton Hall lake, where Rosslyn aided and abetted in some of Robbie Ramsden's first duckings and later taught him how to fish and look for birds' nests.

The Archbishop's daughter, Ethel, often came to Carlton where she and her Aunt Janie were liable to become hysterical with laughter over their efforts to smarten each other up for visits to London or parties. When the Archbishop went to Paris for a convention in June 1876 they asked him to bring Ethel back a bonnet. 'I have got Ethel a bonnet—not splendid, but passable. Black straw, wreath of white flowers over cream gauze, cream coloured frill inside. It passes muster quite well. The old woman who sold it passed through all the worst of the commune and assured me that horse was not at all bad to eat, and ass was delicious.'

After a gay time taking Ethel to art galleries and concerts, Janie wrote to Zoe: 'Rosslyn says I have come back a much merrier mama than before I went to London. I feel so well just now I cannot moan about anything.'

On the next visit to Bishopthorpe, Rosslyn heard the Archbishop speak, not in church, but at a meeting. The subject was a favourite one of his mother and aunt's, the wickedness of the Turks who would cut off arms and legs for no more serious reason than he would tweak his sister's hair.

At six Rosslyn was expelled from a day school for hiding behind a door as two mistresses went by and flicking up their petticoats. 'I only wanted to see,' he said sorrowfully, 'if they had legs.'

At his next school, when his father went to fetch him, he found him in the punishment room writing out a hundred times 'I must not say damn, I must not say damn'. However here he learnt to read and from then on would be found either in floods of tears over some harrowing deathbed scene in a nursery melodrama, or efficiently making notes from a bird fancier's handbook or from the current edition of *Fur and Feather*. In the holidays he wrote a biography 'Primrose, the lonely life of a yellow hen, written from experience by R. Bruce.'

He made friends with the miners' sons in the next village and exchanged mice and cage birds with them. One boy brought back a canary sold to him by Rosslyn for fourpence, complaining that it only had one leg. 'You said you wanted it to sing,' Rosslyn said, reluctantly returning the fourpence, 'you never said you wanted it to dance as well.'

Rosslyn's sisters gave him a birthday present of a splendid album bound in red. Into this he copied records from scraps of paper made of all the birds he had kept and their fates. The first was a robin called Ruby, 'killed by a cupboard door'. The next was 'exchanged for 3d.' Another died from staggers, one escaped, and the rest were exchanged for other birds.

Meanwhile he had acquired his first dog, a pug called Una. At a meet of hounds Rosslyn wriggled his way into the presence of the veteran sportsman, Parson Jack Russell, who was not so much a breeder of fox terriers as an owner and worker. He bought in any lively white or partly white terrier irrespective of coat. From Mr. Judd he bought a bitch whom he called Juddy who founded the main female line of smooth fox terriers up to this time. Rosslyn went home and recorded in bold juvenile letters in his notebook: 'Mr. Russell told Sir Thomas that an ideal fox terrier should be over 17 lbs and under 20 lbs and a rough haired terrier is best the same size.'

In spite of his precocity over dog- and bird-breeding, Rosslyn remained affectionately babyish at home, particularly with his mother who continued to lavish extravagant exoneration on him, which was often resented by the others.

When his mother called him her precious boy, Hilda his younger sister, objected: 'Aren't I precious too?' for which she was rewarded with the nickname of 'Presh' which lasted throughout her life.

'Why does Mama kiss and hug Rossie so much when he was just so very naughty?' his rotund younger sister, known as Podge, asked.

There were now eleven children, the last of whom, Kathleen, was the prettiest and strongest of them all. Rosslyn adored his mother's final baby and nursed her as tenderly as though she were a newly-hatched chick, calling her his 'Kiddy', which name he used privately for her until after she married.

With each of the four babies born after Rosslyn, Janie's earlier illness and pain in her back had returned. Now her sight was failing too and she had to give up her painting. Zoe insisted on her seeing a London specialist, and Lloyd too, who complained of stomach pains and sleeplessness.

I am using my spectacles for the first time, [Janie wrote to Zoe.] I hope to get much more used to them in time but they do not help me yet as much as I had hoped. The doctor here said he feared from my symptoms that the failure of sight was only from disease of the kidneys and he asked me to let him examine the water. When he had done so he said he found albumen in it and that I had better go to Parry. Parry did the same and found none. He said this might be accidental or the first doctor's examination might be, but more testing is needed to prove whether the disease really exists. He said my heart, etc., was weak. An oculist thoroughly examined my eyes and said that the left eye had paralysis of the optic nerve and the right was weak but healthy. He thought I might possibly recover the sight of the left eye and that there was no reason for fear that the sight would go entirely. He thought I might have burst a little vessel in the brain which pressed on the eye. I have given you a horrible history of my London proceedings but I am thankful to say that Parry gave a very good report of Lloyd. He has not to go again for four months and keep strictly on with the treatment. I asked him if he expected any substantial improvement in his case or if he merely meant to keep the disease in check as long as possible. He said it was by keeping it in check that the gradual recovery was attained and that he could not at all say this was a case that would yield or not but so far he had progressed favourably. We are all more cheerful. Rosslyn bears his cough most manfully.

Rosslyn, now too much of a handful for anyone but his mother for whom rest was essential, was sent off to board at Bussage Rectory with a bunch of other small boys who were taught by the rector. At eight years old he moved on to a prep school at Bournemouth—the fifth he claimed, more with pride than regret, that was unable to contain him.

At home Janie seemed to be recovering. Lloyd wrote cheerfully to Zoe: 'The latest on Janie is very good. She was out for a few minutes walk both yesterday and today.' Janie added that she felt quite herself again 'and my eyes are getting better every day. I send a letter found at Inverleith Row written by you when your handwriting was ladylike.'

She was well enough to go to the seaside for a few days, but here disaster overtook her. She wrote to Zoe in pencil:

I have been very badly since Thursday, two days in bed and two days creeping about wrapped up in a shawl but this time the nursing had nothing to do with it. It was the carelessness of that wretched housemaid who put damp sheets on my bed. Please say nothing about it for fear it should come round. Baby caught cold too and is much pulled down by it. I was too sleepy to think of pulling the sheets off though I might have been saved all this. Such a lot of people have called to inquire after me and I have never even returned their first visits. One sent me an inhaler so I suppose my illness has been exaggerated too.

Lloyd continued the letter:

Janie is now resting. She is very husky and also has a cold in the head.

This undated letter was probably the last she wrote.

Janie died of pneumonia, aggravated by Bright's Disease, on October 1st, 1880. She was forty-two.

The Archbishop was in Paris and telegraphed sympathy, saying he would return at once.

Fifi broke the news to Douglas and Lloydie at St. Edward's School, Oxford. Douglas remembered 'with tender recollection how she afterwards left us alone that we might talk to God about it'.

A much blotted letter with a small unintentional thumb print, crossing out and much inserting, came from Overton Hall School, Bournemouth.

My dear Papa,
    I am sorry I was not there to say goodbye to dear mother but it is an end to her pain at last I am glad to say, we shall all miss her so much. We shall never see her again in this world. Will you wright (sic) and tell me all about it. Mrs. Proctor let me come out of

school at 11 o'clock to write to you. It now 12 o'clock and I am thinking about you all at home going to church. It is so cold here and pouring rain. I wish it was fine for you. Please write to me soon your loving son Rossie.'

He was just nine.

Janie was buried in Carlton churchyard near a young copper beech standing almost in the rectory garden. The Archbishop of York took the funeral and afterwards put up a simple brass plate in the church in her beloved memory.

After officiating at York Minster a few days later, Lloyd wrote to Zoe:

I got home last night to find everything as comfortable as poor Sarah could make it but very very dreary. The children I find well and I am happy to say that they do sometimes ask about 'poor mama' though I find it impossible to respond as I should wish. I have written to the nurse as I was unable to speak to her at all before she left. The flowers have been kept fresh on the grave. Mrs. Ramsden is going to Bournemouth to look up Rosslyn.

In the spring he wrote more cheerfully to Fifi before going off to a convention with the Archbishop. 'The weather is beautiful so they all live in the garden, the girls picking flowers and the boys playing tennis, Rosslyn preferring his fowls, pigeons, etc. I believe you remain on after our departure to be entertained by Douglas and the younger members of my family and to civilise them more or less.'

Fifi found Rosslyn alone with his birds, still mourning his mother. It was not only civilising he needed but the loving attention of someone who understood the original spirit that caused so much of his naughtiness. Fifi persuaded Lloyd to send him to join his brothers at St. Edward's School, Oxford, the following term, where she could keep an eye on him. She had had a great deal to do with the founding of the school, which had begun in a small house opposite hers in New Road. Her first contact with the warden was when she asked if she might have one of the school cat's kittens. Young Mr. Simeon carried across the prettiest in the litter. 'She invited me to come and see her every evening, which I never failed to do,' he wrote afterwards 'and that close and deep intimacy lasted for thirty years. Her advice was invaluable.' It was Fifi who negotiated the school's being turned into a company and moved out into larger buildings at Summertown. It was Fifi who advised offering the school to the Woodard Foundation, and Fifi who walked two miles to Summertown every day to nurse the school coachman when he was ill. When Mr. Simeon had diptheria, she had him carried back to her house to nurse him there.

On the first day of the summer term, 1881, Fifi was waiting on the station platform, for the school train to come in, with three terriers at her skirt. 'She looked smooth and still as a marble statue,' wrote a contemporary. 'But at the sight of her great-nephews she sprang forth to meet them with a characteristic burst of animation.' Rosslyn, subdued in his new pea jacket and Eton collar, with his straw boater set squarely on his blond hair, was still small enough to be kissed. Fifi walked with them to the school, leaving their boxes for the luggage cart, for only in extreme cases of necessity would she ever ride in a cab or carriage.

Of the seven new boys that term all were parsons' sons except for one vice-admiral's. Also new was the music master, who started an enthusiastic orchestra, F. G. G. Jellicoe, brother of Admiral Jellicoe.

Douglas, now fourteen, gave his little brother the school rules to study, from which Rosslyn extracted those which he felt most deserved ridicule and copied them out for his sister's entertainment.

Matron *may* take away from hampers wines, spirits, etc. (*or she may not?*).

No boy may have gunpowder or strong acid, poison or other dangerous things. (*Catapaults have just been added as dangerous things. Hole in the window?*)

Moustaches are only allowed in the upper form.

One glass of beer per boy for breakfast and jugs of water for those who prefer it (*i.e. half the school.*)

(*And beer for supper*)

N.B. 'Spouts' are boys who have learnt their Greek and go through it for the ones who haven't.

Apart from cheeking his elder brother, Rosslyn seemed to settle down. He was bright and well ahead of the other boys in class, who nevertheless accepted him because he made them laugh. His delight in poetry endeared him to the English master, a great friend of Fifi's, Francis Paget, whom she tried to persuade to become headmaster. He later became Bishop of Oxford.

There seems to have been an easy atmosphere compared with most schools of the time, due, it was said, to the 'wonderful attractiveness of the warden'. Among Simeon's earlier pupils, was Kenneth Grahame and from this may have stemmed some of the freshness and charm of his book *The Golden Age*. Rat's happy boating days in *The Wind in the Willows* must surely have been founded on the river delights and study teas of the older boys at St. Edward's.

Rosslyn also had rat associations with the school. His nickname was the 'White Rat'. Another boy recollected:

Bruce and another new boy saw two men trying to drown a large white rat and they went up to them and asked to have it. One man said 'Let the little nipper have it for a bob'. Bruce explained he hadn't a shilling but he would give him all he had—threepence. They agreed. Half an hour later Topsy, a box of cotton wool and a raspberry bun were secretly stowed in the top locker in the second form. For a few days the secret was kept but people soon began to notice the boys taking bread away from meals in their pockets. Then everyone started doing it. We fitted her out with a gymnasium. Great was our surprise, but not apparently Bruce's, to find she had become the mother of a nest of ratlets.

It was only when they appeared in class that objections were raised. Rats, it was explained, were not allowed to be kept as pets. However much Rosslyn tried to insist that they were science—he was studying mixed breeding—the warden was adamant. 'Sorry,' he said. 'No rats.'

Rosslyn had promised the babies, when weaned, to various customers. To appease their disappointment, on his next half-holiday he bought a supply of other small mixed pets—tortoises and lizards to which he added a grass snake and other wild life found by himself.

He opened up his animal emporium in the boot room and his stock went like hot cakes. But the strange smells and alien scuffles were tracked down to him again. He wrote to his sisters that he had discovered that school rules after all seemed to be:

No boy may keep tadpoles in his spare ink pot.
Play boxes may not be used as hutches.
Broody finches may not sit in boot lockers.
Snakes are forbidden in boys' hat boxes and, I suppose, studies are intended for prefects and not monkeys.

A kidney-shaped hole had been dug out near the school and lined with wood. Here the smaller boys learnt to swim, scraping their knees on its shallow bottom, ready to give their parents an aquatic demonstration following choral eucharist at the summer Gaudy. It was a great day, with lunch and speeches, choral and orchestral excerpts and 'exhibitions of assault'.

When Douglas told his younger brothers that their father was bringing someone to the Gaudy as a surprise, Rosslyn hoped it would be Una, his pug dog. Lloydie thought it would more likely be the Archbishop. To Rosslyn's disappointment it was only Mrs. Parker, the rich widow of a Sheffield surgeon, who used to come to church fêtes and other occasions when his mother was alive. Usually he hugged to himself anything that belonged to his mother's life, but he could hardly hug Mrs. Parker, nor did he want to. She was, as always, smartly dressed, with a bustle as big as a camel's hump under a kind of wide-sleeved ruched riding jacket. Her bonnet was trimmed with feathers as *well* as roses, which seemed as extravagant as having butter *and* jam on your bread, which his mother used only to allow after a bad cold. The real surprise came from father.

Mrs. Parker was now his wife. They had been married on June 1st, exactly nine months, Rosslyn was quick to calculate, after his mother's death.

At first it seemed like bigamy. What would mother think of the plan? Lloydie, always the soul of sweetness and understanding, tried to mould the awful situation into something shapely and good. Mrs. Parker had been a friend of their mother and very kind, presenting all kinds of luxurious appointments to the church, especially an expensive monument to her first husband. Someone had to replace their mother to look after the children. They had only to think how lonely and lost their father was. And he needed help in the parish too.

Douglas, never renowned at school for tact, suggested they should call her mother in gratitude for her unselfishness in coming to look after them. Angrily Rosslyn said he would never call her anything but Mrs. Parker.

The only cheerful aspect of the whole dreadful calamity that Rosslyn could see was that Mrs. Parker's sister was married to Sir Luke Mappin who built the Mappin terraces at the London Zoo to exhibit goats and bears.

The marriage even seemed to have received the Archbishop's blessing. A cheerful letter from him described the recent painting by Frith of the Private View of the Royal Academy.

The scene is the large room; and the time, last May. Several principal figures are introduced and mine is to be one of the most prominent. There is some fun in the picture, for it introduces some of the aesthetic ladies of the day. Also one Oscar Wilde, who is a sort of lady killer poet of these times. I gave Mr. F. a long sitting and he has made a good head of me.

The handsome Archbishop, taller than ever in his stovepipe hat, is outstanding in his gaiters with the famous beauty Mrs. Langtry at his side and Oscar Wilde basking in the adoration of a set of unamed ladies representative of aestheticism and hero-worship. Gladstone, Teniel, Du Maurier and Robert Browning are on his left and Ellen Terry and Henry Irving to his right. The nearest and largest of all is bearded Anthony Trollope, taking notes.

CHAPTER FOUR

Beastly Boy

With Mrs. Parker in his mother's place at Carlton, it was hardly surprising that Rosslyn's behaviour at school deteriorated again. Nor was he any better at home. The elder children made a great effort to back up their stepmother at first. Elma, the eldest twin, even held family prayer meetings for the cause and must have seemed a whole generation away from the younger children, for even her uncle, Sir Hervey, referred to her by mistake in a letter to them as 'your Aunt Elma' instead of 'your sister'.

The five youngest must have been a handful. Rosslyn was either irrepressible, or in tears over changes made in his beloved mother's household arrangements. Douglas made an effort to control him and only just missed getting a brick dropped through a trap-door on his head with intent to kill, for his trouble. Lloydie drifted about pale, saint-like and either lazy or slightly ill, his father was not sure which.

Little Wilfrid, roly-poly, jolly and playful, was always ready to join in any of Rosslyn's more inventive pranks. But the increasing independence of the three youngest girls must have been even more exasperating for their stepmother than their rowdiness.

Hilda, with a mind like Aristotle, used it, aged eight, discussing Tractarianism with a knowledge entirely above the understanding of poor Mrs. Parker. Podge had a motherliness Mrs. Parker could never acquire, and Kathleen, the baby of three, had already dispensed with any of the uses of a mother.

Poor Mrs. Parker's efforts to handle this large and in many ways self-sufficient family were a failure from the beginning. Even Elma afterwards remembered feeling less sorry for her than for her father.

Whereas her mother 'was all gentleness and humility, this one was all pomposity and boss.' Once when Lloyd asked whether the fish at lunch was fresh or dried, she rose, walked round the table, and, to the astonishment of the children, said: 'Did you expect I'd give you stinking fish?' slapped his face and swept out of the room.

Gwennie, Lloydie's twin, next in age above Rosslyn, continued to keep a motherly eye on him. He wrote to her from school:

Dear Gwennie

I would rather you keep my little store of money and I will slowly though very surely send my money to you when I get any. I bought one nice cage at home and the rest I took to school. It went, as most school money goes, but the next store I hope won't go so carelessly. I bought five white rats but the warden would not let me keep them so I had to sell them but I have to buy them again at the end of the term.

Gwennie wrote back begging him to behave and stop buying rats, and he replied:

Dear Gwendoline from Rosslyn, News! change! fun! I have become sensible, no doubt you say 'doesn't seem so' but for all that I have. I have *bought* I mean purchased (sounds grander), a cock and hen green finch. Eoy porchoised thoise birrids for the un-surmountable surmount of ten—well not exactly pounds—but pence. I have given one of these lasting treasures to the cook, with-out no bribery too. Do you remember those twelve candles I brought to school. Every one except about a **dozen** have been stolen with the wicks too. It's *wicked*! It's scandalous! Thanks aw-fully for the threepence.

Rosslyn's passion for words and playing with them remained with him always. Once, when he came before the warden for calling a master a 'beastly man', he explained it was the highest praise he could think of, showing how much he loved and understood God's creatures. He himself was proud to be called a 'beastly boy'.

Next came his flea. He spent his whole life savings of five shillings on a performing flea circus. The flea, when harnessed by a fine wire loop to a carriage several times bigger than itself, drew it smoothly along the showman's miniature ring. Only when Rosslyn got flea and carriage home did he realise he had been swindled. This was not a trained flea at all. An ordinary flea could leap forty-five times its own height and this one did, with the carriage attached. He took it back and the showman explained how the jump could be taken out of a flea by putting it on a warm plate.

Rosslyn's performing flea hardly helped to smooth the path of his new stepmother. Her sister, Lady Mappin, was staying at Carlton. Rosslyn was sent for to remove his flea which her lady's maid had captured in an upturned medicine glass on her ladyship's pillow.

'Sorry,' he said. 'That's not my flea. Mine's a cock flea. That's her own.'

When Mr. Simeon, the warden, was married from the school, the happy couple returned under triumphal arches, stepping out of their carriage on to flowers strewn by little girls. Rosslyn watched the little girls and decided they were prettier and even more charming than fleas. He followed three of them to an oak tree and sat down under it with them.

'Have you got a sister?' one asked.

'Seven,' he replied, realising for the first time how valuable these hitherto mostly tiresome adjuncts could become as swaps with other boys' sisters.

'You mean she's seven years old?'

'No, I *own* seven sisters,' he said with a proprietory toss of his head.

When Rosslyn was twelve he and a form-mate, F. A. Churchill, whose father was a surgeon-major serving in Egypt, were fooling on the cricket ground while it was being rolled. Next time the horses came round, Churchill jumped on the roller, overbalanced and his right leg was jammed so tight that the machine had to be taken apart to get him out. Rosslyn, who was squeamish about the smallest cut, had to be taken to the sick bay too, with shock. Churchill contracted lockjaw and three days later died.

If Churchill's death revived Rosslyn's sorrow over his mother's, news from Bishopthorpe of the death of a favourite family dog, plunged him even more deeply into gloom. Rosslyn never forgot the details, written by the Archbishop to his son, of the death of 'poor old Cheviot'.

He was only a dog but we all loved him. He was called to dispose of a rat, failed to find it, and returned much excited and tired. Next day his ways were quite altered. He went about with his nose in the air, as if he was astonished at the world and went snapping not at persons but at the air. For four days he touched not a morsel of food and if he tried, it seemed to produce a kind of sickness. When he met me he bounded up against me and turning his head sideways made a loud snap as much as to say 'I must bite but I would not bite you.' I offered my stick to tempt him to a low jump. He went straight at it and tried to make his teeth meet but without anger or excitement. On Sunday he tried to bite Ethel when she was putting his chain on, then they thought he was mad and re-treated by the loft, in case they went out of the stable he got out But except for the snapping he was quiet and showed no anger. It was sad to see him thin and weak and looking so sad. After four days of complete fasting he had to be shot.

Rosslyn helped to choose Cheviot's successor, Scamp. 'Scamp killed three rats yesterday and one the night before,' wrote the Archbishop. 'The rat was very large and it had bit him but he finished it in good workmanlike style.'

Rosslyn owned three dogs as a schoolboy, Una, Dick (a fox terrier), and Zeeta (a collie). But it was still with his birds that he won prizes and kudos at Crystal Palace.

He was thirteen when his first letter to the press was published. It appeared in *Poultry*, on fattening and killing fowls. It was followed by several others in *Sporting Life,* including one on breeding tame birds with wild, which created considerable correspondence. 'In my experi-ence,' one letter ended, 'mule birds can only be bred in confinement.'

An excited bird fancier, who disagreed with him, arranged to meet him and was amazed to find the 'experienced expert' was a small tow-headed schoolboy with a cheerful grin.

There was trouble at school when Rosslyn led a schoolboys'

movement for the suppression of the bearing rein. The boys bought knives and went about the suburbs of Oxford cutting bearing reins, to the great annoyance of horse-owners and even more to the boys' fathers who had to pay for the damage.

But Lloyd was even more concerned when he heard that Rosslyn had been writing a school essay condoning the behaviour of a Church of England priest who 'elevated the patten and cup during communion, prostrated himself before them, used incense and lighted candles not needed for giving light and mixed water with wine for communion.'

Because of its High Church outlook, the school had already been accused of practising popery and had been nicknamed 'Edward's Monastery'. The warden wrote to Lloyd, evidently fearful that Rosslyn's letters to the press might take an ecclesiastical turn. 'I know Rome very well and I know what would be the result,' wrote Mr. Simeon. 'I want to protect him against himself.'

In April 1884, Lloyd was offered the excellent living of Stokesley that Janie had set her heart on when she was alive. Presumably Mrs. Parker, between her increasingly frequent trips abroad, must have made some official appearances in this much grander rectory, though her patience with the family itself continued to wane.

From Stokesley Rectory the first of the family was married. Zoe, just twenty-one, the second of the elder twins, had accepted the Rev. C. S. Newham, vicar of Christ Church, Paddington. There was a joint wedding for her and Miss Dagg, the family governess, whose train was carried by Kathleen. The rest of the sisters shared the duties of bridesmaids between the two brides. Mrs. Parker does not appear to have been at the wedding, though nearly two hundred others were. Lloyd commemorated the occasion with a present of a large tenor bell and the new peal of bells rang out for the first time.

Some of the younger Bruces went off afterwards to Bishopthorpe where a brother of Rosslyn's godmother, a keen racing enthusiast, was staying. Rosslyn listened attentively as he expounded on form and thoroughbreds to the Archbishop, who showed so much interest that his guest observed that he considered the Archbishop an immense loss to the turf. Robert Browning, an old friend of Aunt Zoe's was also at Bishopthorpe. When the Archbishop told him he had an early copy of *Bells and Pomegranates* which he valued very much, Browning replied, 'Ah, if you sell the book you would get much more money for it than I ever did for writing it.'

The meeting Rosslyn attended on this visit with his uncle was directed towards the abolition of drunkenness. There were loud cheers after almost every statement the Archbishop made but none so loud as when he was enlarging upon the virtues of moderation and said that his doctor had told him that some drink was good. 'Having been a teetotaller, I have a little lapse under that learned person's prescription.' (Loud cheers and shouts.)

At Stokesley Lloyd was now far from well. His continual pains and lack of appetite was said by Mrs. Parker to be imaginary and more kindly by his relations 'a state of mind brought on by his troubles'. By his second Christmas at Stokesley, he had been told he had an incurable 'gout of the stomach'. Uncle William had once again lent money and invited as many of the children as he could spare to stay in Edinburgh, provided one of the older girls went to help him.

On Christmas Eve 1885 Lloyd wrote to him from Stokesley.

Dear Mr. Skene,

I hope you have spent a pleasant Christmas, we have, considering the circumstances. All boys at home and well. Zoe and Cecil Newham visited us and seemed to be very happy and well. I don't think, considering my state, it would have done for Gwen (aged 17) to have been left here instead of Elma (aged 21 unmarried,) though I quite understand your feelings in the matter. Elma understands *something* about my affairs in general and is of course at present of more use to me than Gwen could possibly be. I well remember our arrangement was only tentative but then we did not know my state. Of course doctors can say nothing we can trust but my doctor said about a month ago that I *might* live on for three months more. Some days I feel there is a possibility of doing so, on other days I imagine a few hours will suffice, however I am glad I came home, I have put all my papers, etc., in the hands of a solicitor here, who with Douglas and Elma must make the best of them. I get confused at once if I attempt anything of the kind.

On washable panels in his leather writing case—a luxuriously fitted wedding present—are pencilled notes that are still legible today showing his efforts to overcome the confusion. He leaves the names and addresses of his trustees, William Skene, Janie's uncle; George Skene, her brother, now a country parson; the Archbishop of York, her brother-in-law; and his own brother, Sir Hervey Bruce and his cousin Bagot Delabere.

'L. S. B. hopes the funeral expenses will be exceptionally small on the grounds both of convenience and economy, not exceeding £10 or £12,' he scribbled. 'No hat bands, gloves or other useless paraphernalia.'

'All my documents of any value to be found in safe, the left-hand drawer beside the writing table in the library of Stokesley Rectory and a few Railway Stock in letter box in press under shelves in same room.' A list of his shares shows no signs of the gypsum having been mined in his day.

Rosslyn, only 14, and as tall as his brother Douglas, nearly 19! [his letter to William Skene went on] Poor Lloydie, nearly as *weak* as ever, though his present tutor speaks better of him than any preceding. I enclose a cheque for the amount advanced, with renewed thanks. I have no notion what my young ones are to do by and by, unless the Mrs. (who's in Sheffield and very poorly) takes them under her protection more or less. She may though. Before she went abroad she very positively declared she would have nothing to say to any of them. I hope and believe she is in a better frame of mind now.

Lloyd lived for exactly three months more and died in March 1886. Mrs. Parker seems to have retained her positive frame of mind.

Rosslyn must have felt less abandoned at this parental departure than before and more as though he were left in a position of trust. A passage, suggestive of his early reading, in an essay he wrote on 'The Joy of Living' could explain the protective devotion he showed to his younger brothers and sisters throughout their lives:

The hardly perceptible movement of the hand of a dying father, as we take our leave after what seems to be our last prayer together, which asks a last favour which is not to be misunderstood, and the look of infinite relief and assurance which rests upon those fading eyes as we assure him softly, slowly, deliberately, that we will be personally responsible for the welfare of his wondering little ones, God knows there is a wealth of joy in it.

Lloyd was buried beside his first wife at Carlton. His brother, Sir Hervey, came to the funeral and looking round at the eleven children his eye alighted on the ferret peeping from Rosslyn's pocket. He was the only one with whom he felt he had anything in common and he invited him to spend the next holidays at Downhill with his twin grandsons of the same age, Ronnie and Percy, and their younger brother Benjie. The Archbishop and Zoe added the rest of the Lloyd Bruces to their own nine at Bishopthorpe.

Downhill was a great success. The twins were delightful, with a kind of cynical wit they had acquired from Eton, unknown at the less sophisticated St. Edward's. Though Rosslyn had heard about Downhill from his mother, he was still amazed by its size and bleakness, with the formality of meals on the one hand and lack of comforts on the other.

Benjie described the bare, windswept grass round the house:

that led to sheltered glens of almost tropical exuberance, with a burn that flowed down into the sea, arched over by stunted trees and walled in by rocks till it left the glen to spread out over the sands of the seashore. That shore was a bather's dream and a child's paradise. On the shorter stretch between the burn and the cliffs, were rocks of all sizes and shapes dotted here and there. Rocks for undressing on and for headers into the sea; pools round the rocks ideal for shrimping . . . With such a shore; with trout fishing in the lake, with unlimited scope in the glens for the woodmanship we boys were experts in, especially the bonfire part, with good shooting of all kinds . . . life should have been perfect; out-of-doors it was. Indoors we were saved by our sense of humour from foundering under the grand-parental rule.

Rosslyn learnt from a Downhill gamekeeper how to train a cormorant to fish for him with a collar round its neck to prevent it swallowing the fish. Within a week of attending his first race meeting he was contributing to *Sporting Life* on form. He got on well with his eccentric uncle, who was less stern with him perhaps through having lost his parents, than with his grandsons.

He was shown a portrait of the Bishop of Derry, 4th Earl of Bristol, which is now at Ickworth, Suffolk. It was painted by the gay and beautiful artist, Madame Vigée Le Brun, whose own self-portrait is also at Ickworth. Later Benjie pointed out in the picture the same charm and sweetness of expression that Rosslyn wore, particularly, like the bishop, after making some outrageously border-line remark.

Back at school Rosslyn began to work more earnestly. He joined the Debating and Dramatic society, swam, rode and played rugger for the school. Though he was tall for his age, he still had 'the face of an angel, with a bright pink and white complexion. No wonder Rossetti asked his mother to sit for him,' observed Mrs Humphry Ward at Fifi's house.

Fifi kept open house to the senior boys at St. Edward's and many others who had passed on into Oxford life. Here Rosslyn joined in with discussions to which Fifi would toss a word of wisdom or anecdotes about her prison work. She was very funny about tramps and 'other oddities' that passed through her hands.

As to the truth, [she said] you might as well try to get that out of a crocodile as out of a tramp. The marriage rite is of course in their eyes entirely superfluous. It is convenient to have a woman to tramp along with them, to help them, cook, carry or invent fictions by which they can draw pence from the pockets of the simple. If they quarrel they can just fight it out or part company. Sometimes they will change partners with another couple as easily as at a dance. 'I say old chap I likes y'woman better'n mine here, let's swap. I'll throw you in a bit of baccy with my wench, as yours is a bit younger.'

'All right I'm willing. I'm sick of my 'oman's tantrums. I'll try it out with yours.' And the transfer is made with the utmost ease.

Fifi was delighted when her nephew Cleon Rizo-Rangabee in Athens won the dramatic prize in the first Olympic Games. 'It's in the blood,' she said and encouraged Rosslyn to keep on with his writing.

In July 1887, just before his sixteenth birthday, Rosslyn left St. Edward's. Though his father had not been able to leave enough money for another two year's fees, a prefect who had reached his standard in work and games in his last year could surely have been paid for by one of the better off relations or even by the school itself? Possibly stipulations were made, contrary to the conscience of a wilful adolescence. Maybe his prefect's study had become too crowded with lame dogs, foxes and birds. Perhaps he decided that he must earn his own living. Whatever the reason there is no record that this was one of the schools that found Rosslyn too much for it. He went off to Ireland again where he met, at Downhill, the son of the Irish Lord Chancellor, a young neighbour of his own age, Hugh (Hugo) Law, who later became a close friend. Through Hugo he met lively red-headed Noel Buxton, already, at seventeen, filled with enthusiasm for politics and philanthropy. They took to each other at once, both sharing a bizarre, eccentric sense of fun and adventure. Noel was the son of Sir T. Fowell Buxton, 3rd Bart., M.P., later Governor of South Australia.

Rosslyn returned from Ireland bursting with excited ideas about politics and women's suffrage. When he next saw Fifi he presented her with a booklet, bound by himself with a needle and cotton 'Thirty-three reasons why I am an Irish home-ruler after hearing Sir T. F. B.'

Rosslyn wrote to his godfather, Lord Forbes.

Dear Rosslyn, [came the reply from the House of Lords]
   I send you a book today which will tell you all about the progressive programme and I send you also a pamphlet on London County Council work which may interest you. I am always sorry when hot-headed enthusiasts and fadists whether they call themselves Radicals or Progressives, have too much of their own way because in the pursuit of our favourite object they generally do not see how much they dislocate the social system but in the case

of London I think landlords have it rather too much their own way.

And he went on to expound on the business side of house owning.

Rosslyn's head was buzzing with plans for his future in politics, on the stage or in a circus. Uncle William settled the matter for him by finding him a place as a clerk in the banking part of his own office in Edinburgh. He was to live with him at 20 Inverleith Row.

William Skene, W.S., L.L.D., D.C.L., D.L., was a gentleman of the old school, courtly and somewhat stately in manner. Strangers often thought him haughty and austere. People who knew him better found him genial and humorous with a great love for children and young people. There was hardly a time during his last fifty years when there were not some of his nephews and nieces or greats being educated at or from his house. When Rosslyn arrived at Inverleith Row, Wilfrid was already there attending the Edinburgh Academy and their younger sisters were doing lessons there with a governess. The house was accustomed to having children at their books clustered round the heavily fringed plush-clothed table or playing hide-and-seek under the monster pieces of elaborately carved furniture, some of which still survive in the family. Another child would be practising on the carved-footed piano. Uncle William was a good amateur musician and encouraged them to play and sing. A piper came regularly to the house for dancing classes in the long library, to which other Edinburgh children came, including Compton Mackenzie, R. Bruce Lockhart and a charming family of girls, the Misses Francis. Most holidays a dance was held in the library with pipers walking up and down. Uncle William still, at seventy-eight, took parties of children to swim at his private beach near Dunbar. The boys swam in the nude while the girls turned their backs at a discreet distance. Decorum was observed in all things.

Meal times could be heavy going. No child might speak till the meat course was finished, and then on certain days, only in French, German or Greek. When Podge kept the icing off her Sunday cake on the side of her plate as a treat to eat at the end, Uncle William whipped it away to prove the folly of storing up on earth where moth and rust doth corrupt. He was a staunch Episcopalian with an impressive knowledge of the Bible and its literary development in English and German. He not only conducted Bible classes and a Sunday School but actually owned the fabric of his church, which he later presented to the congregation. On Sundays the blinds were kept down at 20 Inverleith Row until after church and no books were allowed to be read but the Bible.

Uncle William had now been appointed Her Majesty's Historiographer for Scotland, one of the last remaining relics of the Royal Household of Scotland. Inspired as a boy by his father's old friend, Sir Walter Scott, William Skene had made a special study of the Scottish Highlanders and had written several books on their origin and history. He had a rare literary faculty for arranging, analysing and classifying his facts and presenting them in a striking form. The stories he told the children of the whims and oddities of former generations held their attention provided he slipped in a little frivolity. Sometimes he wrote them fairy stories.

As a family lawyer, specialising in landed and trusted estates he was the foremost consultant in Scotland in cases of disputed succession and peerage claims. It was his success as a pedigree lawyer in tracing missing family links and recovering lost documents that fired Rosslyn's more serious preoccupation with the pedigrees of animals.

Under Uncle William's directorship, Rosslyn was able to take time off to attend lectures at Edinburgh University. Even with political meetings in the evenings, a dramatic society to act for and games to be played, Rosslyn still found time to encourage Wilfrid at school football matches and little girls from his great-uncle's dancing class to write to him. Evelyn La Coeur writes in a childish hand from 17, Inverneath Place: 'Dear Rossling, I would be very glad to come to your bank to borrow a stamp. I am going to ask Wilfrid to take this round so I hope he will give it to you safely without looking at it. Goodbye.'

CHAPTER FIVE

Edinburgh and Oxford Freshman

The garden at Uncle William's was just large enough for Rosslyn's animals' and birds' pens and aviaries. He supplied the house with eggs and frequented the bazaars and market places buying and selling bargain pets and poultry. From the proceeds of these and from writing about them he was able to travel to many of the leading shows at which he usually cleared the rest of his expenses with prize money. For thirty-five shillings he bought Rona, a five-week-old Skye terrier puppy by the acknowledged supreme champion, Old Burgundy. Skyes were the Edinburgh dogs of the day.

Compton Mackenzie wrote that 'there was hardly a doorstep in Edinburgh at that time without a Skye stretched out on it.' One of Rosslyn's happiest negotiations was in finding and despatching to his Great-Aunt Fifi the Skye terrier that was to be her dearest companion for the last ten years of her life. Fifi wrote from 13, New Hall Street, Oxford, on August 5th, 1888:

Dearest Rossie,

Thank you a thousand times for the immense service you have done me in getting the much desired doggy for me. I most willingly agree to your wishes. I do not for a moment believe I shall ever part with him while I am alive for I am certain to adore him and make him my special friend. But if ever anything so unlikely happened, you alone should have him and when I die he most certainly shall be my legacy to you. I shall be only too glad to have you to take care of him when I'm gone. I like his name 'Tatters' and I am looking forward with the most intense delight to having him on Tuesday. I conclude that you are sending him by L.M.W.

railway first train in the morning which arrives at 9.30 and I shall meet that and all subsequent trains till he comes. If not, would you mind sending me a telegram. I will return you stamps for the telegram if you have to send it but if I do not hear from you I shall meet that first train. I am very glad it is a dog and not a wife you have written about. Marriage is such a lottery and it is a terrible thing for a young man to be hampered with a disagreeable woman.

Your loving Fifi.

That year Uncle William was being painted by Sir George Read. The portrait was commissioned by friends and admirers and willed to the National Portrait Gallery. It was one of Rosslyn's duties to read to Uncle William during the sittings. Another was to relieve his great-uncle of one of his Sunday School classes, which led to all kinds of other good works. Rosslyn wrote and put on plays for the Boys' Brigade and organised displays of gym and combat in the winter and athletic sports and cricket in the summer. There were few playing fields available in Edinburgh so the company often trekked out to the edge of the country. The fifth Edinburgh Company, of which he became captain, was said to be the least military of any in the Boys' Brigade, but always the most imaginative. Undernourished illiterate east-enders saw rainbows and sunsets in their lives that they would otherwise never have dreamt existed. To be taken birds-nesting by their captain was something boys were prepared to go hungry for all day, to save the fourpenny train fare to the country.

Rosslyn usually had, besides a few dogs, two or three boys if not the whole gang at his heels. They helped him to clean out his animals and accompanied him to shows within walking distance, where they were admitted free as 'Kennelmen' or 'cage men'.

With his uncle the Archbishop of York's strong leanings against drunkenness still affecting him, Rosslyn became an enthusiastic member of the Junior Temperance Lodge in Earl Grey Street, experimenting on its behalf with white rats and finding them belligerent when drunk and lethargic and miserable in their hangovers. He signed the Pledge and the only alcoholic drink he tasted for years was communion wine; not that he had any need for extra stimulants. Just to turn up at a political meeting or a parish gathering or even to talk to strangers in the train were to him what a couple of double Scotches would be to other men. His short holidays were now mostly spent at Scarborough, in a house bought for his sisters from their father's estate and presided over in the kitchen by Allie, who had started at Barton as Rosslyn's nursery maid. She still found Rosslyn shocking but irresistible, so his sick finches continued to be revived beside the kitchen range and his nursing bitches to drink the best milk.

Mr. Blunt, vicar of Scarborough, later Bishop of Hull, became a great friend and would go for long walks with the Bruces at low tide. With him, Rosslyn thrashed out many of his theories, and he, probably more than anyone, curbed Rosslyn's desire to take the world by storm via the political polling booths or theatre box office. This kindly and humorous clergyman drew Rosslyn's attention to the need for young men of his calibre in the Church, where his academic mind, his originality, his enthusiasm, his ability to hold an audience, his love of people and particularly little children, and above all his simple but intense faith could take not the world, but heaven by storm. 'Conviction can build cathedrals; opinions cannot,' he quoted, when suggesting that Rosslyn could bring the greatest happiness to others by returning to full time education, if this were possible, with a view to going on later into the Church.

A few months later came a letter from Rosslyn's lieutenant in the Boys' Brigade: 'Dear Sir, I have just heard that you have passed with flying honours to Oxford. I really hope it is the case. May I add my respectful congratulations. Yours respectfully, James Greenaway.'

The brigade gave him a parting present and had a certificate ornamented and inscribed with their 'appreciation of the services rendered by you not only to the boys of our own Company but to the Brigade in general by your example and zeal. We regret that the post of Captain will soon be vacant and also the loss of the Captain who is beloved and respected by us all and we are certain that the Company was never so prosperous before as it has been under your care for which we beg to tender you our best thanks and sincerest esteem.'

Rosslyn framed it, attached his B.B. badge to the frame and hung it in the bathroom of every house of which he afterwards became master.

Meanwhile the warden of St. Edward's School, Oxford, wrote:

My dear Rosslyn,

I was not altogether surprised at the news contained in your letter for I thought your mind was set in the direction of taking Holy Orders. It is very good of your uncle to give his permission and encouragement to such a scheme and I have not a word to say against it. I think a clergyman's life is the happiest in the world for a man who has a real vocation. But you are giving up the prospect of a comparatively easy life for one of hardship and poverty and you have no doubt faced this and prefer the House of the Lord to the tents of the world! The first question is that of cost. There is no difficulty about finding a good tutor in Oxford or elsewhere but they are expensive people and a tutor in Edinburgh could probably cost much less. Write to me after consulting with your uncle. There are many distractions in Oxford too and I should personally prefer a country place if I was going to read hard for an examination. We have good accounts of Aunt Fifi. She talks of *walking* up here on Sunday week. My kindest regards to your uncle and believe me, always affectionately yours,

Algernon Barrington Simeon.

The money to pay for Oxford came, surprisingly, from Mrs. Parker. She must have had a great change of mind, for Rosslyn had led her more of a dance than perhaps any of them. He passed the necessary exam, was interviewed and offered a place at Worcester College, Oxford, for Michaelmas 1890.

Schooled in Oxford with his eldest brother lately down from Worcester, Rosslyn already knew something of the traditions of the university. He knew for instance that the gold tassels still dangling from some caps were the distinguishing marks of the nobility and not, as believed by poor Verdant Green, whose fabulous adventures as a freshman were still popular reading, badges of drunkenness. He knew that Worcester was known as Botany Bay through being the most distant college. Verdant was told: 'It's a delicate way of referring to the temporary sojourn that any undergrad has been forced to make there.'

Clearly this was a period in Rosslyn's life when he could indulge in his delight in a certain amount of frivolity, to lighten the serious study before him of Plato and Aristotle. He was to read classics, with additional lectures in theology, logic and philosophy, and on behalf of the animals and birds he brought with him, biology.

At nineteen he was tall, still fair-haired and athletic. Worcester, being a small college, expected those who were any good at games to pull their weight, wet and dry. Rosslyn appeared on the river on his first morning for weight, strength and form to be estimated and immediately found himself pulling in a college 'Challenge Four' under the severe eye of a senior cox. From then on he went out in a skiff or pair or four most days, sometimes rowing in an eight down to Iffley with its beautiful old mill and Norman church.

Wearing his St. Edward's rugger colours, he next presented himself on the playing fields to be tried out for the college fifteen. The ground was then some way from the college though later swampy fields beyond the lake were drained for the purpose. When Oxford was under water he ran through the hedges in a country steeplechase, or followed hounds on foot. Better still, if he could borrow a horse, he went out with Johnnie Delabere with the Heythrop hunt.

Worcester had a country air about its attractive gardens and enviable lake. Rosslyn's first three years were spent in college in rooms looking out on to what was then called the old cottages, their gables befrilled with carving like the lace under the poke bonnets of a row of old ladies. The walls were thickly clothed in green creepers with trees and bushes almost joining them. Geraniums tumbled from stone urns and flowerbeds ornamented the lawns beside the broad walk, a delight to stroll along on Sunday afternoons. Beyond it were the half-hidden seats and garden arbours and the charming old house where Dr. Daniel, the Dean (later the Provost,) lived with his family. Rosslyn had already met the Daniels at Fifi's but was still rather in awe of them, especially Mrs. Daniel, an ardent church worker and amateur impresario and craft worker.

Considerably less awe-inspiring was the Junior Proctor, H. T.

Gerrans, M.A., who wore elastic-sided boots and a single flattened curl on each side of his forehead. Rosslyn called him 'The perfect paragon of unparalleled precocity,' after being reprimanded for bringing a terrier into college. He tried again, wrapping the dog ostentatiously in brown paper.

'The rule is no dogs,' Mr. Gerrans told him.

'Nor horses, nor pigs nor cows?'

'The rule is no dogs,' it was repeated, 'and the fine is a guinea a time.' To tease him Rosslyn went off and hired a cow for two and six and led it into the quad.

His written excuse for a puppy being found in his unused wine bin was that it seemed obvious to a tee-totaller that that was what a 'whine bin' was for. Quoting from Virgil's *Aeneid* 'Arma virum-que cano' he eventually softened the dons' hearts and was allowed to keep his dogs in the mediaeval pigsties of Worcester College. He exercised them with the help of a more or less equal-sized pack of bewitched girls, whose names Rosslyn had a confusing habit of bestowing also on the livestock of the moment. It was never quite clear when he said, 'I'm keeping Dorothy in my wardrobe till her foot gets better,' whether he referred to a girl or an iguana. A post-card to his brother with the news 'Poor Hilda died today. I shall have to get another,' turned out to refer to his brood bitch and not to his sister.

Fifi, who was never seen out walking without one of her dogs trot-ting beside her, usually Tatters, often joined him on dog walks.

Fifi had a strong belief in the immortality of animals and, half playfully, justified her vegetarian habits by asking: 'How could I meet the ducks and chickens in a future state whose bodies I have cut up in this?'

To Professor T. H. Huxley, author of *Zoological Evidences of Man's Place in Nature* and inventor of the word 'agnostic', she introduced Rosslyn as 'seldom having less than a small menagerie about him and generally two or three pets on his person.' Wearing a cassock and surplice, Rosslyn had been illustrating a talk to the children of her Sunday School, and in a lesson about Eden had, she said, won the complete attention of some ninety little people by illustrating his point with a grass snake. 'Imagine my horror,' said Aunt Fifi, 'when a bright five-year-old boy told me in an alarmed whisper, "Please, governess, that clergyman has got the devil in his pocket".'

So far Rosslyn's experience in public speaking had been confined to Sunday Schools and temperance meetings. Now he widened his scope by joining several debating societies and a dramatic club. He also joined one or two dining clubs involving serious speech-making, though when dining in hall he sat with the other men in training at the noisy athletes' table where bear-fighting was kept up fairly incessantly.

His uncle the Archbishop paid his entrance fee to the Union, which had begun in 1823 not long before his own Oxford days, as the United Debating Society, 'for the discussion of any subjects not immediately involving theological questions'. However it soon had to dissolve itself for the purpose of excluding turbulent members who persistently interrupted the debates 'with their boorish folly'. In 1825 it was reorganised as The Oxford Union Society.

Archbishop Thomson left no mark on the Union himself, having been rusticated in his last year after his assault on another undergraduate. In his day the Union met in its members' rooms and was not taken very seriously. Once, when a message was sent by the Proctors to dislodge a meeting, with 'much respect to the constitutional forms of procedure, the messenger was desired to withdraw while the message was taken into consideration.' Soon the Society became rich enough to buy its own house. On to this was built a large hall to use for debates and reading rooms, whose walls were decorated with scenes from *Morte d'Arthur*, painted by Rossetti, assisted by William Morris and Burne-Jones. Unfortunately they used water-colour distemper and the so-called frescoes soon faded.

By Rosslyn's time a new wing had been built with a smoking room and library of some forty thousand volumes, and a billiards room and a dining room, where breakfast, lunch and dinner were served. Any resident member of the University of Oxford could be proposed for election as a subscribing member, which cost him a pound entrance fee and twenty-five shillings a term. From this nursery of debate had already emerged many famous politicians, professors, headmasters of public schools, deans and diplomats, and a fair sprinkling of governor generals, lord chancellors and archbishops.

Rosslyn, aged two, his dress trimmed with
Greek key patterns.

Wilfrid, Rosslyn and Lloydie Bruce soon after
their mother's death.

At Scarborough, after their father's death. Gwen, Rosslyn, Kathleen, Janie, Lloydie and, in front,
Hilda, with Zoe and Elma (holding Zoe's babies) and Wilfrid.

Worcester College, Oxford, Commemoration Ball, 1893. Rosslyn is seated, nine from the left, holding a female trophy.

The Strafford Club, Oxford, dines in costume. Acworth, Bourne, Bruce (*centre*), Gibbons and G. C. Lamprieu.

During Rosslyn's first term as a member, the Queen, the Crown Prince of Denmark and the Prince of Wales, who was a life member, all subscribed to a two thousand pound decorations fund. The same term Gladstone accepted an invitation to address the House on Homer. As former M.P. for the University of Oxford, and already three times Prime Minister, he filled the House to its capacity of over eight hundred.

Sixty years before, as Secretary of the Union, young Gladstone had moved a resolution condemning the administration of the Duke of Wellington. The motion was carried, and in the heat of the moment, Gladstone had entered in the minutes 'concerted cheering from the majority of one'.

Afterwards Rosslyn had the honour of being congratulated by the Guest of Honour on being 'the son and nephew of two of the dearest and most beautiful young ladies of old Oxford'. Mr. Gladstone remembered the shared holidays in Wales in the early sixties with the young Provost of Queen's College and his wife and her then unmarried sister, Miss Janie Skene. Afterwards when letters came from them, his children covered them with kisses.

Without this kind of influence, a freshman had to distinguish himself in open debate, after the House had been thrown open and a note passed to the President permitting three minutes talk, before his name could be printed on the bills that circulated every college in Oxford. The Speakers 'on the paper' had to wear full evening dress—tail suit, white waistcoat and tie. In fact Rosslyn had soon been mentioned in *The Oxford Review* as having 'heckled the Librarian a good deal and rather unjustifiably twitted the President. The pertinacity with which that member maintained his position called for loud applause. He had taken great pains to present a small placard and when he could not get the President to concede his permission the Secretary was appealed to with the approval of the House.' The President was the amiable W. H. Cozens Hardy, who was well able to stand up to a bit of freshman's cheek.

The Union audience was strange and elusive. It would rock with laughter over a gimcrack epigram and yet was often cruelly critical.

After making his maiden speech 'on the paper', it was reported in

o

Isis that Rosslyn, having been accused of being surrounded by touts and tricksters had brought the House down with a modest 'When in truth, Sir, I was sitting in the midst of our guests and the standing committee.'

Rosslyn also joined the Worcester College Debating Society, a small in-college version of the Union, using the same procedure for its miniature elections for President, Treasurer and Secretary. He was first heard here when a young speaker was rebuked for referring to a Scottish forebear 'who was so strong that he could heave an ox over a wall'. 'People who boast of their ancestors,' Defoe was quoted, 'are like potatoes in that their best part is underground.' Rosslyn instantly leapt to his feet to misquote Pope with 'Those who on length of pedigree enlarge, produce the bull. We look for the discharge.' But the matter did not end there. After much twitting over Bruce and the bull, Rosslyn, typically, translated the literary into the three dimensional and appeared out hunting mounted on a bullock.

Another cause for raised eyebrows was the elephant he kept in a disused cart shed. When asked what biological data he had gathered from this experiment, he replied: 'Well, it is rather like keeping rabbits except it has one hundred rabbit power eating capacity.' He bought stale bread and buns cheap from a baker and then, having learnt the dodge from a professional showman, sold the buns in bags to the gullible public for the pleasure of feeding them to his baby elephant.

It was Max Beerbohm, then at Merton, who observed: 'Undergraduates owe their happiness chiefly to the consciousness that they are no longer at school. The nonsense that was knocked out of them at school is all put gently back at Oxford and Cambridge.'

Not that Max Beerbohm himself made much of his opportunities. Rosslyn saw very little of him at Oxford though afterwards in London they met frequently. There was a legend in Oxford that each term when Max Beerbohm arrived he drove straight to Merton in a ramshackle hansom ('all good hansoms go to Oxford when they die,') unbuttoned an immaculate pair of boots, put them away neatly in his cupboard, assumed a pair of pumps, decanted the first of a dozen bottles of good sherry for the entertainment of his intimate friends and then sat down and waited patiently and without any outward emotion for term to end, when he put on his boots again and drove back to the station.

Rosslyn's friends to start with were those he had already made in Ireland and Edinburgh, particularly Hugo Law and his own cousin Johnnie Bagot Delabere, son of the vicar of Prestbury who had been prosecuted under the Public Worship Regulation Act for illegal ceremonial.

Rosslyn's great-aunt continued to be his chief confidante. Fifi never tired of hearing about his latest young ladies.

She was a self-confessed matchmaker and once Rosslyn asked her why she herself seemed so content with her own single blessedness.

'Only think what a bore it would be always to have a snuffy old man sitting on the opposite side of the fire,' she said. In fact there were often two or three snuffy old men to be found not far from her fire. The former lights of Oxford, some now grown old and shuffly, others still gathering great audiences and congregations, continued to call. Most of the more ancient ones were bachelor parsons, for the necessity for Fellows to take Holy Orders and resign on marriage had only gradually been abolished since Fifi first settled in Oxford in 1850.

Hitherto Rosslyn had regarded them merely as no more than the plush curtains and other relics of Fifi's mid-Victorian arrival in Oxford. Now, the output of their prime being his required reading, his interest waxed. Not only were there the Oxford literati, the Arnolds and the Huxleys, but others from afar who called when visiting Oxford—Coventry Patmore and the other contributors to the pre-Raphaelite organ, *Germ*, Rossetti and George Meredith. Ruskin came and 'poor deaf Swinburne' and even the Poet Laureate, Alfred Lord Tennyson himself, of whom Rosslyn's Aunt Zoe had once asked innocently, 'Who is that brigand-like man with all that black hair?'

In the wake of the poets inevitably walked Augustus Hare, the popularity of whose literary 'Walks' in the great cities were at their height. He was now working on a history of the Quaker Gurneys of Earlham for which he sought information from Fifi on prison visiting.

Some of the older callers whom Rosslyn vaguely remembered when he was at school, had fallen by the way. Dr. Pusey's bowed and uncouth figure was no longer to be seen on the stairs, heading for

Fifi's drawing room. For years this leader of the Tractarian movement and supporter of the Church's union with the Church of Rome had bombarded Rosslyn's relations with his illegible rhapsodies against sin, advising them curtly against marriage and other earthly worthlessnesses.

Archbishop Thomson, who had heard him preach in his youth, admitted that 'Pusey carried his self-denying so far—even apparently to the extinction of all pleasures of sense and intellect, which have no direct theological bearing. I, who believe in the divine mission of poets and who exult in poetical studies, could not go along with his doctrines.'

Rosslyn's uncle, Sir Hervey Bruce, warned him: The Pusey letters suggest a man lacking in warmth and sympathy, rapping out advice with no humility.

You quote Dr. Pusey to me but after reading part of his life, I should not be guided by him, he did not strike me as an amiable character, only self-opinionated and heedless of the feelings of others. He was obstinate more than able. Reading between the lines in that life the halo which shone for a time about his name enabled him to lead some far abler than himself, but he remained calling himself a member of the Church of England while he well knew he was teaching those who had a conscience to leave her for the Church of Rome.

In a letter to Rosslyn's father Dr. Pusey advised him how to treat one of his parishioners.

Dear Mr. Bruce,

I should fear absolving would do her harm and communicating more. I suppose she has been so long accustomed to her sin that she thinks very little of it. Could you not frighten her by saying that our Lord's words 'blessed are the pure in heart, for they shall see God' imply that those not pure in heart will not see God . . . and unless she repents she is going the way to Hell? and that it has been a great mercy from God that she is not insane, for that many have become insane with less perseverance in sin?

And that unless she breaks off the sin she must go to the workhouse, for those ones who do those things are not fit inmates for a home? I should think that very possibly the rough ways of the workhouse would be better for her, but before you mention this you must know that you can carry it out, for workhouse guardians often make difficulties about admitting people. But anyhow I would not absolve or communicate her until after some decided token of penitence.

As his later life in the ministry showed, such advice as the foregoing would not have appealed to Rosslyn's warm and understanding heart.

CHAPTER SIX

Honourable Member for Dogs

Probably the Oxonian who had the most lasting influence over Rosslyn was Dr. Walter Pater, Dean of Brasenose. With his large pale face, heavy moustaches and stoop, he was often reserved, baffling and mysterious, even with his intimate friends. Yet to those who asked for it he gave help eagerly, patiently and generously, particularly about work or choice of a profession and above all he tried to clear away the scruples of men who intended to enter the Church. He never thought of himself as a schoolmaster to make men work. 'The fact is,' he said, 'most of our men are fairly well to do and it is not necessary that they should learn very much. At some colleges I am told that certain of the young men have a genuine love for learning. If that were so here it would be quite too dreadful.' He sighed and turned away.

Rosslyn was drawn towards the whimsical sage, with whom he felt he had much in common. Pater's father too had died when he was at school. Rosslyn had wept over his novel *The Child and the House* in which Pater showed a boy, whom he could not help identifying as himself, deeply sensitive, and touched by sorrow. Fifi remembered when his *Studies in the Renaissance* scandalised Oxford twenty years before. Yet Rosslyn found it filled only with an endearing sense of beauty. It was Pater who instigated Rosslyn's life-long interest and delight in Dante.

Dr. Pater had a reputation for writing words and sentences on cards. Then when he had accumulated a pack of them, he was said to bring them out as though he were playing patience and make them into a kind of mosaic. In fact, he said that when he took notes he made them on slips of paper for the greater convenience of sorting them. 'If I live long enough,' he added with a sigh, 'no doubt I shall learn quite to like writing.'

Pater's unwilling efforts to take part in college discipline were almost farcical. Once when he was called upon to quell an outbreak of rowdyism he turned a hose into an undergraduate's bedroom window and, having soaked his bed, had then to give him leave to sleep out of college. Another time at a dinner party in the house he shared with his two sisters, he drove some of their guests away after what he called 'being pressed controversially beyond the point of wisdom' into saying that 'No reasonable person can govern his life by the opinions or actions of a man who died eighteen centuries ago.' Pater relinquished all Christian beliefs for a while but later Christianity flowed gently and almost imperceptibly back in a different, less conventional form. Yet when it was suggested to him that he would live to see orthodoxy break down, he shook his head and said 'I don't think so. There are such mysterious things. Take that saying "Come unto me all ye that are weary and heavy laden." There is a mystery in it that is something supernatural.'

This was something with which Rosslyn agreed, and which he continued to teach throughout his own life.

Of other more conventional theologians Rosslyn heard at this time he said: 'There is nothing in their utterances I don't hear over and over again in the schools of theology and lectures. So long as men are wrangling about points of intellectual dispute, the true progress of the Church is merely marking time,' and 'Hang theology, the worthless medley of most human chattering! The love of God is broader than the measure of man's mind.'

During Rosslyn's first Christmas vacation, his uncle the Archbishop finished his ordinations, dined with his chaplain, dictated his letters and observing that these were the happiest days in his life, fell into a coma and died on Christmas Day. During his last few days his terrier, Scamp, hardly left him, staying on his bed and 'showing great affection'.

The family funeral, which was quiet and unostentatious, took place in the little churchyard adjoining the palace at Bishopthorpe, where his own nine children and his brother's eleven (many of whom were present) had spent much of their earliest and most memorable childhood. A commemorative service was held the same day in York Minster. Afterwards a marble monument was put up in the Minster with the figure of Scamp at the feet of his recumbent master. The working people of Sheffield erected a bust in their parish church, with inscribed beneath it: 'The People's Archbishop'.

The Queen offered Aunt Zoe a grace and favour apartment in Hampton Court Palace, but for the moment she refused it, feeling that she could be more use to her large extended family if she lived in London. The family had always teased her affectionately about the many Prime Ministers she had to stay at Bishopthorpe. Now, to everyone's astonishment (not least of all his own) her own son, Basil, not long down from New College, Oxford, found himself Prime Minister of Tonga. He had held a small official appointment in the South Pacific Islands, when old King George, father of Queen Salote, found himself in trouble and Basil was told tactfully to sort it out. 'In your twenties,' he commented, 'to be elder brother to a monarch of ninety-two is an unusual experience.'

At Oxford Rosslyn began to submit sacred verse to competitions, and light-hearted quips to the frivolous undergraduate weekly *The Rattle*. Later he became joint editor announcing that 'Last year's *Rattles* published at 1/6d. are now fetching 10/6d. No comment.'

An Illustrious Order of the 'New Rattle' was introduced and the first list of knight companions was published. Among the letters of thanks from recipients was Sir Henry Irving's:

Thank you for your great graces
heaped upon me, poor deserver, I
Can nothing render but allegiant thanks and
remain accordingly Yours faithfully.

Lord Ampthill wrote from the Union, whose President he had just become: 'Gentlemen, many thanks. Fearfully busy. No time to be funny. Yours faithfully.'

It was just over a decade since Dr. W. A. Spooner had announced the hymn in New College chapel, 'Kinkering Kongs their titles take'. Now *The Rattle* offered a prize for the 'neatest and best spoonerism. It must be effectually set as well as intrinsically sound.' Needless to say the entries soon became quoted as having come from the reverent lips of Dr. Spooner himself, including: 'You have tasted two whole worms, you have hissed all my mystery lectures and been caught fighting a liar in the quad. You will leave Oxford by the next town drain.'

Rosslyn came by accident on some valuable private tuition from Dr. Spooner who wrote to him from New College on black-edged paper: 'Dear Sir, I found only a couple of men were waiting to attend my lectures on St. John this term, so I adjourned to my own rooms. If you will come at 11 tomorrow I will give you a lecture on the early part of the subject. Yours truly W. A. Spooner.'

'The cream of university life is in the first summer term,' wrote Andrew Lang in his *Oxford historical and picturesque notes* of the time. 'Schools are too far off to cast their shadow. There are many things to do. There are drags at every college gate to take college teams down to Cowley. There is the beautiful scenery of the stripling Thames to explore.'

For Rosslyn there were the plays to act in, instigated by his Dean's wife. He took the parts of Lord Alfred Lindsay in *The Dowager or Why did you Die?* and Mr. Buster in *Oor Geordie or The Horrid Barbarian*, and acted steward at many of Mrs. Daniel's productions.

Once he got to know the Daniels he became a close friend of the whole family. Emily Daniel was much younger than her husband, and turned out not to be formidable at all. She was an extremely good water-colourist and expert bookbinder. Their two exceptionally pretty and amusing little girls, Rachel and Ruth, (called by Rosslyn Thrisby,) were ten and eight when he first lent them his white mice to play in their doll's house. He told them stories and they illustrated them. 'Dear Brucey,' wrote Rachel, 'I have kept my promise and drawn you a little bird but it is so shamefully scribbled that I am also sending you some pansies which are nearly as bad.'

There were summer picnics on the river with more mature young ladies, specially the two Misses Horsfall, one of whom, Truda, fell irrevocably in love with him. 'At a fancy dress dance,' it was reported, 'the Misses Horsfall went as flowers, and Mr. Bruce as a fugitive from Worcester. Dancing was kept up till 4 a.m.' Possibly there were some harsh words over the fugitive's feet, for Rosslyn was brushing up his dancing before Eights Week with Mr. Wood in Hollywell Street, where a lady partner taught the waltz and other ballroom dances.

Groups taken at the time show that Rosslyn had a touch of the dandy, a trace of the bizarre about his toilette. His tie was looser and a little more flamboyant than the others. In one group he was the the only man wearing a stock. In a group of Freemasons, his Masonic apron and cuffs were worn with much the same air as his eighteenth-century ancestor, the Earl-Bishop, was said to wear in Italy 'a white hat edged with purple, a coat of crimson silk or velvet, a black sash spangled with silver and purple stockings'.

There was a certain distinctive panâche about Rosslyn's dress, whether in rowing gear, or after a commemoration ball, when as a 'Two collar man' (one who carried a spare for when the first had been worn limp) he danced every dance with tremendous vigour. By dawn, his low-cut white waistcoat had slipped lower than ever and, whereas most of his fellow undergraduates had retained their buttonholes, his had been given away in exchange for a lady's fan.

Rosslyn described the last night of Eights Week:

The raft of the Varsity Barge was crowded with youth, beauty, and charm, garbed in the exquisite satins, silks, and feathers of that happy occasion. On the Barge itself stood the gigantic and universally honoured Captain of the Boats, President of the Union, Senior Scholar of his College and an admitted Master of English, pure and undefiled. At the supreme moment of the last race for the 'Headship of the River,' the excitement was so intense that the crowd surged forward to the edge of the overloaded raft. Only to the Princeps Juventutis watching from the top of the barge was it apparent that a terrible disaster was imminent. Above the indescribable hubbub proper to bumping races, resounded as from the heavens his stentorian voice, 'Damn you, ladies, get off that blasted barge, AT ONCE!' and they did.

It was said that even the Dean himself soliloquised, 'Clarity covered a multitude of swims.'

The festivities at Worcester, after the success of their 'Clinker for the third time,' were mentioned in *Isis* as being

of a thorough, if riotous, nature. The bonfire, inaugurated by a surreptitiously smuggled tar barrel of alarming proportions, attracted a fire engine and 28 sleepy firemen, a fire escape and several policemen, beside the vast crowd of inquisitive sight-seers, who received an animated address by a Union orator from a top window on the importance of the occasion and the mysteriousness of certain movements.

One of the defeated crew, who with various coaches were the guests of the college, brilliantly coerced 'on the light fantastic' and his combination with the Worcester captain, which was generally voted a *pas de quatre* (an expression which he corrected to 'mama of the kittens') really recalled empirical experiences.

A subscription list to defray expenses for damage and to meet the demands for satisfaction from the authorities reached the required fifty pounds.

But for all the delights and deviations of his first year, including Rona's having puppies one night under his bed, Rosslyn had studied hard and his results in schools were sufficiently gratifying for him to receive a telegram from Harrogate, where Fifi was staying with his Great-Uncle William:

CONGRATULATIONS. UNCLE AND I DELIGHTED WITH YOU. FIFI.

In the Bruce family, props were gradually being withdrawn. Rosslyn's aunt, Lady Bruce, died at Downhill and, in May 1892, Elma, who, more than anyone had mothered her younger brothers and sisters, wrote from Inverleith Row:

My dear Rosslyn,

I have a piece of news for you which will astonish you I guess, only please don't say anything about it for a little while. I am going to be married and probably before long. Can you guess who? Only Hilda could of the others. I suppose I must tell you—

I hope you won't mind having Canon Keating as a brother-in-law?'

The news of Elma's engagement was not so astonishing, for she had inherited her mother's fine features and was intelligent, accomplished and charming. Her twin sister had been married long enough to have three children. It was Canon Keating who was the surprise. He was Principal of the Episcopal Church of Scotland's Theological College and a Canon of Edinburgh Cathedral. He came from County Cork, via Truro Cathedral, wore pince-nez and was considerably older than any of the Bruces.

Within weeks of the announcement Uncle William died, aged eighty-four.

The Edinburgh house was dismantled and put up for sale and the proceeds spread among his fifty-four nephews and nieces and greats. The same summer Rosslyn's stepmother died in Geneva. Her remains were returned to Sheffield for a grand funeral. Her will, proved in Geneva in September 1892 revealed that her personal estate amounted to twenty-nine thousand pounds, of which she bequeathed two thousand five hundred each and her jewellery to her already rich sisters and the rest to her maid. But nothing to the Bruces.

Douglas, the eldest, now twenty-five, took control and sent his two youngest sisters to boarding school. Kathleen, the youngest, had a love-hate relationship with St. Michael's, Bognor, which she complained was 'like a convent with sisters in nuns' habits and the girls were forced to bath in chemises. There was chapel three times a day and five times on Sundays and processions in veils.' She became fanatically religious and had a vision of the infant Jesus coming down from his mother's knee 'and snuggling warmly in my yearning arms'. She used this as an excuse for being late for supper, which was not understood. 'My breasts were still warm where the babe had lain. I could still feel his fingers on my lips.'

From then on the little house in Scarborough became the main Bruce base, from which visits were paid to the newly widowed uncle at Downhill and to Aunt Zoe in London.

At Oxford Rosslyn was making his mark.

There is something irresistible about Mr. Bruce of Worcester,
[*Isis* reported on a Union debate]. Whether he is heckling the
officers at question time or making one of his angel-visit speeches
he has always so evidently set before him a determination to
amuse the house, that the house could be hardly human if it refused to be amused. Thursday's debate was no exception to the
general rule. There are very few of the Union who could rise to
move that 'This house would welcome the adjournment of the
House of Commons for 20 years' without experiencing the pain
of seeing their audience slowly departing throughout their speech.
But hardly any one stirred till Mr. Bruce had finished and his
triumphant cheeriness of manner carried him unscathed through a
succession of daring alliterations, execrable puns, paradoxical
commonplaces, uncommon paradoxes which could have wrecked
any less buoyant a speaker. A perfect crescendo of Cs led up to a
horrible declaration that 'the Commons is the rookery of the
country with their *cause* as the prevailing note.' Mr. Hilaire Belloc of
Balliol came in for some chaff as 'the honourable member for
France'.

And a fortnight later:

Mr. Bruce was more flippant and funny than usual and his mis-
quotations were more bare-faced than ever. Mr. Liversidge was not
so good as he used to be but he doubtless suffered as anyone of a
more sober temperament would have suffered in comparison with
the previous speaker. Mr. Bruce's rhetorical fireworks blazed away
as merrily as ever: 'a jelly-fish gaining vitality by compound
division', 'above the tinkering hand of your political jerrymander',
'shadow of a shimmering church', 'a mere mirage of a nobility',
were some of his phrases. His speech was irresistible and
forcible.

And then there was the day

when Mr. Belloc so far forgot himself to move that 'This house de-
plores the worthlessness of the English novel of today.' The debate

77

had the rare advantage of actually interesting orators and oratees alike. The mover brought tears to the eyes even of the unbelieving and was powerful in his pathos but lugubrious in his length. Mr. Bruce who was brilliant, immortalised himself in his epigram 'The pedigree of the hero in a modern religious novel having a long lineal descent of maiden aunts.'

Isis said that Mr. Bruce objected to all modern novels. He did not think they were doggy enough. 'Now Scott knew a good dog when he saw one. Pepper and Mustard were the finest characters in fiction.' He liked dog-eared books, and always made a point of procuring them in that condition. He thought novels were going to the dogs, and he was sorry for the dogs' sake. Mr. Stride rose and asked if the last speaker were in order in pulling two puppies out of his pocket.

This, with his most memorable sally, about his perfect Skye terrier—'The A1 K9'—won him the title of 'the honourable member for dogs.'

Belloc and Bruce complemented each other well on the platform and remained good friends off it. Many of Rosslyn's lasting friends were made at the Union as well as the inevitable passing friendships with his fellow lights of the time. It was a golden age in the newly decorated Union, with such stars as R. C. Phillimore, Earl Beauchamp and Lord Balcarres following each other as Secretaries, and then Presidents with, in their wake, John Simon, H. A. Morrah, A. A. Roche and F. E. Smith (with shades of things to come when, as Lord Birkenhead, he became Lord Chancellor).

F. E. Smith, the Liverpool boy who delayed speaking at the Union till he had adjusted his accent for the fashionable drawl of the time, made his maiden speech at a Cambridge night in opposition to a total abstinence movement. 'F. E.' ended with the revelation that an earlier speaker that evening had, on succeeding to his baronetcy nearly a quarter of a century before destroyed his father's entire carefully laid down cellar: 'I tell you, Sir, that if in years to come the honourable gentleman comes to me when I am nestling in Abraham's bosom and asks me for a drop of water I shall say to him "No, not a drop! you dissipated greater liquor".' It was his first rhetorical triumph.

Among Rosslyn's closest friends made then was Percy Dearmer also destined to wield a pen in the church. Harry Brittain was befriended at once over the eternal problem of trying to keep a dog in college. Harry's was a bulldog which eventually earned the name of 'Worcester Jim'.

Nigel Playfair became another lifelong friend. Nigel only spoke once at the Union. His heart was more deeply in the O.U.D.S. and his soul already dedicated to the stage, though his father was then determined that he should become a barrister.

Nigel was small and very funny, with fierce passions burning in his breast. The play had just been put on in America of du Maurier's immortal novel, *Trilby*, with Tree playing Svengali. Nigel had managed to persuade the management that a young Oxford actress, Dorothea Baird, was more like du Maurier's familiar illustrations of Trilby than any other young girl who could be found.

Most of Rosslyn's friends made through Nigel were artistic and a little unusual. Particularly so was Paul Rubens who began the day with breakfast about two in the afternoon and had dinner at midnight and would then sit at the piano happily composing for the rest of the night. 'I hate going to bed but I love staying there,' he explained. His early compositions, written on envelopes, were invariably lost and had to be recomposed, but this never seemed to trouble him in the least and he tossed off overtures for amateur dramatics, te deums and love songs as easily, Rosslyn said, as though he were playing noughts and crosses.

Rosslyn served on several Union committees with Harry Irving, son of the 'Arch Mummer', Sir Henry. Harry kept open house in Radcliffe Square with a perpetual supply of porter and chops and cigars provided by his talented father. His rooms were filled with crime stories and he used the Old Bailey as a Club.

On the athletic side was C. B. Fry, 'a magnificent Greek-god-like young man who was enormously popular wherever he went and yet hardly seemed to notice it'. Rosslyn also knew the more delicate-looking Lord Alfred Douglas whom Oscar Wilde described as 'quite like a narcissus—so white and gold.' Bosie, as his family called him, was a good footballer but liable to appear on the playing fields wearing a wreath of flowers and on his feet a pair of patent leather shoes. Rosslyn met Oscar Wilde while on a dog walk with Fifi. The fact that Wilde's play *Lady Windermere's Fan* had just been banned by the Lord Chamberlain was of no consequence to Fifi, as no doubt his prison sentence later was of no consequence either. Fifi had as many friends inside as she had out. On this occasion they discussed Walter Pater.

Rosslyn only just missed getting a blue. If he had stuck to one game, he was told, he would have easily succeeded, but his activities in sport, as in everything else, were widely diverse. By his third year he had won his college rugby colours and his rowing cap. He was President of Worcester College Athletics and had a good many all-round wins himself.

In college he was also President of the College Church Society, and President of the de Quincey Society, founded the year before he came up and now a thriving dining club with, among its officers, his cousin Johnnie Delabere, A. G. H. Gurney (who was to become his cousin by marriage) and Percy Buck, already an aspiring serious musical composer, whose sad brown eyes, Rosslyn said, he would notice looking up from below him when he was trying to make one of his more frivolous speeches.

He followed Percy Buck as President of the Worcester College Debating Society, having served his term as Treasurer and then Secretary.

Out of college he was a member of the Apollo Masonic Lodge and of the Christian Social Union. He followed Hugo Law as Secretary of the Irish Dinner, with Lord Basil Blackwood, the Earls of Kerry and Westmeath and a handful of other Irish enthusiasts as committee. Viscount Suirdale, whom he had also met in Ireland, followed him as President.

He was also Secretary of the St. Edward's Old Boys' football team and its annual dinner.

> To see some forty men, [he wrote at the time] solemn clergymen, staid county magistrates, strict schoolmasters, studious undergraduates, and severe professional men, some of whom had not met each other for a dozen years, chaffing one another as 'Cabby', 'Puppet', 'Abie' or 'Trundles' brought it home that

the fetters of friendship formed at fourteen are fully as firm at forty.'

Rosslyn was President of the Strafford Club which met 'in memory of Sir Thomas Wentworth, Bart., K.G., Baron Raby and Earl of Strafford, executed May 1641, age 47'. The Strafford Club met in undergraduates' rooms to discuss such subjects as political retrospect, quixotic anarchy, gambling and the Privy Council. In Rosslyn's rooms, now 11, Walton Street, it discussed Anglo-Saxon federation. On special occasions the members dined in the costume of Charles I's time. Rosslyn, in a flaxen curly wig, was said to look more angelic than cavalier.

Clearly his angel tendencies were not in abeyance. He was never too absorbed by his heady new 'public' life to fail to answer calls from Fifi and her friends to conduct Bible classes or a Sunday School outing or to run the Daniel children's sports on the lines of College athletics. His compassion was not restricted to the very young. When his Rev. Uncle George Skene, who had been so distressed by the marriage of his beloved sister (Rosslyn's mother), had a nervous breakdown, an appeal was launched on his behalf and Rosslyn replied at once. Poor George, known at Eton and Oxford as 'Mammoth Skene', never fully recovered from his wounds inflicted both at the Crimea and from his sister. The methods adopted by the committee formed to help him seemed hardly the best cure for a nervous breakdown. 'Since February I have written 29,490 letters. It has been very exhausting as I have never ceased writing before 4 a.m. and it is often later,' he wrote and returned Rosslyn's five shillings adding: 'I am very touched by your generous kindness. I am just as pleased with your liberal act as though I kept it.' Rosslyn sent it back again addressed in a disguised hand.

CHAPTER SEVEN

Bruce v. Belloc

Rosslyn was showing his dogs in earnest now and breeding Skyes that were to become well-known all over the world. He had already sent a niece of Rona's to the Greek court in Athens. H.R.H. Prince Napoleon had also bought a dog puppy for eight pounds.

John Simon introduced Rosslyn as 'Bruce, who breeds bitches for all the crowned heads of Europe'. Now Queen Victoria wanted a bitch puppy of Rona's, a full sister of the Queen of Greece's Skye. When the day came, the bitch was on heat, so instead Rosslyn took her sire, Lord Lennox, intending to explain that his daughters were very like him. Just before the audience on the Castle terrace, Rosslyn was told that he must bow but must not speak to Her Majesty till she spoke to him.

The little old lady came slowly out and Rosslyn bowed and let Lennie off the lead so that she could see him better. She smiled, nodded approvingly but said not a word. Lennie trotted up to her and she bent down to pat him in a proprietary way. Rosslyn was bursting to explain that this was not the bitch puppy Her Majesty was to have. And then, to his acute embarrassment, he saw Lennie trot off down the path and sniff at one flower pot after another. The moment of suspense was almost unbearable when he stopped beside one. To Rosslyn's intense relief, however, he kept all four legs on the ground and returned to his master. The Queen thanked him and said she would like to have 'her' very much. It was too late to explain now. Rosslyn had already been dismissed. But in the train on the way back to Oxford he could not help wondering whether the Queen had noticed 'and was too much of a lady to say so'.

Lord Lennox's daughter was in due course sent to Windsor 'The

Queen', wrote her secretary, 'has named her puppy Rona II as she
thought Rona a pretty name and wished the puppy to be called
the same.' Rona II appeared in a print of a popular silhouette
of the Queen that hung for several decades in many a loyal front
parlour.

Rosslyn was at this time learning German, reading the prophet
Jeremiah in Luther's translation, Xenophon, Ben Jonson, the cate-
gories of Aristotle, Hailer's *Holy Living*, Hume's *Essays*, Hook's
Church Dictionary and the Gospels in the original Greek.

His tutor reported well to his great-aunt Fifi and stressed 'his
undiminished love for the study of logic and philosophy', adding that
'to the fact that the great portion of his reading time is devoted to the
works of Plato and Aristotle can be attributed his remarkable
comprehensive ability, and incisive power of reasoning, shown in his
subsequent utterances.'

In the Union Rosslyn was as frivolous as ever. 'Mr. Bruce's speech
proved the most entertaining of the evening. The breathless impetu-
osity of his predecessor now gave place to a series of daring attacks,
delivered with the utmost faith and bristling with effective points.'

At a debate referred to in the house a month afterwards as 'The
Revolting Daughters', Rosslyn said that he had no daughters but he
had cousins. What was one man's cousin was another man's daughter.
'He gave an original translation of Honi Soit, etc. If you think a
thing's not nice don't say so,' reported *Isis*. 'Mr. Bruce kept the
house in roars of laughter all the time and it is the best I have ever
heard from him. It was the speech of the evening.'

At the end of the summer term 1893, Howard Liversidge wrote
from 2 Ship Street:

Dear Bruce,
    You will no doubt know that I am running for the Presidency
at the end of this term. It would give me much pleasure if
I might include your name in my standing committee. May I do
so?

Rosslyn accepted.
The standing committee consisted of President, Librarian,

Treasurer, Secretary and ex-Presidents, who agreed to serve with five elected members.

Rosslyn served on the standing committee throughout the Michaelmas term, with Howard Liversidge as President. The next election was arranged for Saturday, November 25th, 1893. It was held in the Steward's office at the Union, in which warning was given, as usual, of a fine of five pounds for canvassing.

The candidates standing were:

Mr. F. R. C. Bruce, Worcester (proposed by the President)
Mr. H. Belloc, Balliol (proposed by Earl Beauchamp, ex-President)
Mr. W. G. Howard-Gritten, B.N.C. (proposed by Mr. F. E. Smith, junior Treasurer)

Voting was keen and results were announced from the chair in the debating hall at 10.30 p.m. that night and were repeated in the *Morning Post* next day:

Mr. F. R. C. Bruce, 203, Mr. H. Belloc, 123, Mr. Gritten, 72. Mr. Bruce was accordingly elected Secretary.

'Congratters—F. E.' F. E. Smith scrawled across a piece of Oxford Union Society paper.

'My dear Bruce, I beg to offer hearty congratters on your success. I did my best in the matter. I am so very glad at the results. I will behold thee on Wednesday at the hour of 7. I am yours ever, Philip King.'

'Dear Bruce, Heartiest of gratters! I win half a crown and am glad to think that my one little vote just brought the majority up to 80. Did the hounds poll? Ever yours, W. K. Stud.'

Lord Beauchamp and H. A. Morrah added invitations to dine with their congratulations.

Within a week another achievement of Rosslyn's was recorded in the *Morning Post*. With his Skye, Rona, Rosslyn had won his first terrier championship at Crufts.

The *Octopus* picked up his twin successes and included Rosslyn in a Pepysian skit on a typical Oxford day of the time:

'Not before ten of the clock it being a very sunny morning and with

my wife in a new frock, which methinks becomes her well, to breakfast with Mr. Bruce of Worcester who is known to my cozen.'

In the spring term of 1894 Rosslyn took his place as Secretary of
the Union. 'It was fairly crowded' the *Oxford Magazine* reported on
the second evening.

> The attractions of our Cambridge visitors are evidently as great as
> ever, but the principal feature of the early part of the evening was
> the total eclipse of question time. Presently a feeling of alarm
> spread abroad through the meeting. The President was there. The
> junior Treasurer was there but—there was no Secretary. It was
> appalling to behold his empty chair. The President was appealed
> to, but he could only say vaguely that the Member for Dogs was
> not in his usual state of health. His friends, who had seen him in
> the afternoon manifested signs of alarm. At length another filled
> the empty chair.

Rosslyn, in his rooms, was forced to nurse a fever and sore throat
that made it impossible for him to speak at all. However, he was
there to speak in a debate on foreign policy of which *Isis* said:

> Influenza made no difference to Mr. Bruce's fluency. His flow of
> humour was as abundant as ever.

As Secretary Rosslyn was among the representatives invited to
festivities at Lyons, which had to be postponed owing to the murder
there of President Carnot. The letter conveying this information
concluded by complimenting the Secretary on his mastery of the
language and saying that it had caused the recipient much amused
pleasure and that he wished he could be as humourous but the English
language 'was outside him'.

Rosslyn was one of the select party of the Oxford Union who met
at the Grand Hotel, Birmingham, to join in a debate against the
Edgbaston Debating Society. 'Mr. Bruce's speech proved the most
entertaining of the evening.'

That spring his elder sister, Zoe, and her husband were leaving

England with their four young children for Australia. Rosslyn went with them to say goodbye to their Uncle Hervey. It was Good Friday and the Rev. Mr. Newham made the unfortunate mistake of referring to the crosses on the hot cross buns provided for the children as being 'symbols of High Churchery'.

'So you really think that a few currants and a little sugar would tempt the evil one?' Sir Hervey stormed and from then on any mention of the Newhams sent him off into an oration on the suggested evils of a hot cross bun.

Rosslyn went to the boat to see his sister off. He knew he might never see her again and the desire to go too was almost too much for him. 'Don't be ridiculous,' she said. 'You're only just starting to be sensible. Think of your career.'

Their eldest brother Douglas was now in his first curacy. He was about to marry Margaret Lord, daughter of a barrister and principal Registrar of Probate at the High Court of Justice.

Lloydie was also engaged, but the thought of abandoning his sisters, particularly his twin, Gwen, lay heavily on his gentle handsome head, and he did not hurry the ceremony. Eventually his young lady came and asked him fairly and squarely to name the day. But still he could not, and angrily she snapped off their engagement, leaving him puzzled. Gwen went with him to his first curacy. Neither of this pair of twins ever married. Gwen remained with him to act as 'parson's wife' in his parish and to housekeep on the lines of Allie at Scarborough.

None of the seven sisters had learnt to cook; there had been too much moving from one house to another. Nor did any of them learn to dust. All had a share of their parents and great-uncle's Victorian furniture and pictures, the frames of which had crossed corners in the 'Oxford' fashion. Over each otherwise clean and tidy home lay a characteristic half-inch layer of velvety dust that gently blurred outlines and rounded corners, particularly so at Scarborough, now their holiday house.

The two elder unmarried sisters, Irene and clever precocious Hilda were teaching in girls' schools. Wilfrid was at sea in the Merchant Navy. 'He was home from China', was the last report, 'broader than ever.'—broad, beaming and cheerful, with always a weather eye for the girls. Podge had trained as a nursery nurse and was one of the first qualified Norland nannies. On and off duty, she wore, like a nun's habit, the Brown Norland uniform with the apron and its Irish lace insertion. As she grew more and more up to her nickname, so it became harder to find other clothes that would fit her. Her first post was to care, in secret, for the illegitimate child of an anonymous peer. Later she was able to turn the Scarborough house into a home for noble orphans and illegitimates, for whom, with her many Scarborough friends she became 'the sun and the moon'.

Kathleen, the youngest, passed her examinations well enough for Douglas to start looking for a teacher's place for her when she left school. But Kathleen refused to be bossed, particularly by her elder brother. Rosslyn's more diverting and unpredictable advice however, she sought, visiting him at Oxford whenever she could persuade anyone to take her there. She was now sixteen and 'thought she looked older'. Over her school uniform she pinned a disguising collar borrowed from the hem of a lace curtain. Her curly brown hair she put up with ribbons, for hair pins were not allowed at school. She was bright, questioning, original and very pretty indeed. The first time she went out to dinner in a restaurant she bought a few pennyworth of coarse unbleached workhouse sheeting, a square of dye and a bottle of gold ink and cut out a cloak, dyed it, painted a magnificent design on it, and felt 'quite à la mode'.

Rosslyn's friends were enchanted by her, and she, collectively, by them, because they were 'strong and young and beautiful and intelligent' as she was.

Encouraged by her claims that her brother could converse with the birds, they added d'Assisi to Rosslyn's first name, Francis. From then on he frequently appeared in print as F. d'A. R. C. Bruce.

Gabriel Gillet, poet and dilettante wrote, after Rosslyn had shaved off his blonde moustaches:

'My dear St. Francis, *Now* you are worthy of the name. He didn't wear an upper beard. I enclose the photograph I promised you. Will you come to the Bach concert tomorrow week? Also will you lunch at the Union on Sunday at 1 o'clock. Yours ever, Gabriel Gillet.'

There followed a drawing of Mephistopheles, after the style of Aubrey Beardsley with curling waxed moustaches, carrying a cross and wearing a cloak embroidered with a curled tulip and one lit candle.

Alan Stanley, as he called himself, enclosing a copy of his 'Love Lyrics' dedicated 'To G——', wrote from Pembroke College:

My dear Bruce,

I herewith send you a copy of The Lyrics—it flatters me that you see anything to admire in them. Will you quote a few passages in your next sermon to the birds and fishes?

Yours ever,
Stanley Addleshaw.

The summer term of 1894 was immortalised for Worcester College by the production in its romantic garden of *Alice in Wonderland*. Rehearsals were reminiscent of Wonderland itself with actors and little actresses resting on the grass beside Rosslyn's tame white rabbit, brought to inspire the other. 'In the afternoon they came into a land,' Rosslyn quoted from *The Lotos-Eaters*, 'in which it seemed always afternoon.'

Permission had been sought and was given by the author, the Rev. Charles L. Dodgson, the elderly Christchurch don who nearly twenty years before had written under the pseudonym of Lewis Carroll his whimsical fancy which he had at first pretended to disown. The little girls it was intended to amuse were now, according to Nigel Playfair, 'middle-aged females who continued to come and stay in Oxford and skittishly accept the toys and packets of pear drops that Mr. Dodgson still produced for them from his pockets'. Though he appeared to take no interest in the Worcester College production, he was sometimes seen shuffling about the rhododendrons during rehearsals. Nigel Playfair produced the play, using only lines from the original books *Alice in Wonderland* and *Alice Through the Looking Glass*, without any rewriting as in the London production. The costumes were taken from Tenniel's illustrations. Paul Rubens composed special music and Emily Daniel printed the posters and programmes, which years later became auction room treasures.

Rachel Daniel, now twelve years old, had the appropriate long ripply hair to play the part of Alice. Her little sister Ruth played the Dormouse. Paul Rubens played the Mad Hatter, doubling as Tweedledum to Nigel's Tweedledee. Nigel's sister, Audrey, played the cook. Hugo Law played the Cheshire Cat, Lord Suirdale played Humpty Dumpty and Rosslyn both the White Rabbit and the March Hare.

The day before *Alice* was to be put on, the Vice-Chancellor of the University announced that no money could be taken for this kind of charity performance. After some quick thinking it was decided that the audience would be allowed to come in free, but would have to pay to go out.

On the back of an *Alice in Wonderland* programme is scribbled a note from Baron von Born of Austria, a fellow commoner of Worcester and keen breeder of English pointers and, what he called 'whire hard setters'. 'Will you come to have tea with me at Magdalen Saturday next at 4.30. Some of last night's dogs will be there. Yours sincerely C. Born.' He later induced Rosslyn to become a member of the Kennel Club. Rosslyn had arranged for Kathleen to come up and stay with the Daniels for *Alice in Wonderland* and she was invited again for Eights Week. The Daniel girls, though younger, adored her and she, though privately envying their much better opportunities for education and meeting interesting people, was a little patronising of them.

Rosslyn and Nigel took her to see Holman Hunt's picture in Keble College chapel. They were shown round by a shy clergyman. Kathleen, being of an inquiring nature wanted to know whom Holman Hunt had married. To Rosslyn and Nigel's surprise their guide's cheeks turned from ochre to crimson and he changed the subject. As they went out he drew Rosslyn aside and whispered, 'My dear fellow, did you observe the terribly embarrassing circumstance that occurred just now in the chapel? I could hardly tell a young lady that Mr. Holman Hunt had married his deceased wife's sister.' From then on a Deceased Wife's Sister became, between the three of them, a simile for the unmentionable.

Walking beside Rosslyn in his clean white flannels, Kathleen wanted to know what O.U.B.C. on his cap meant.

'Oxford usually beats Cambridge,' he replied instantly.

Kathleen heard Rosslyn speak at the Union on a subject already dear to her heart—education for women.

The Oxford Association for the Education of Women had made

considerable headway in their efforts to obtain a B.A. degree and diploma for lady students. Their memorials, signed by over a hundred members of the congregation were now laid before the head Hebdomadal Council, and *The Times* reported:

The motion was discussed in the Oxford Union in favour of the admission of the fair sex to University degrees. It was an Eights Week debate and the feminine motion, specially laid to ensnare a large and overflowing gallery, thoroughly appreciated the witty sallies of Mr. Bruce of Worcester.

Isis reported:

The Eights Week debate was emphatically a success. Fine weather and a distinctly feminine motion had attracted a large, even overflowing gallery and an unusually crowded house. At one time the debating hall was about as full as I should think it could possibly be. Wit and humour flowed abundantly during the private business and most of the 'stars' in that time-honoured farce were well to the fore. Mr. Bruce introduced a new element.

Mr. Bruce had been in evidence several times that evening already [reported the *Oxford Review*] and he at once disclaimed all intention of being serious and he carried out his proposal thoroughly. Not that anyone ever dreamt he would be serious. He gave the house an interesting reading from Aristotle—the chief good is a thing of degree—garbled, I fear, Mr. Bruce, but be thankful that the house does not know its Ethics as well as you do.

Quotations followed, thick as peas, 'Women' he went on to tell us, 'women students must submit to regulations.' There was a scathing description of a girls' school where they said Dominus Domini Dominum, 'learning in fact to decline a lord'. It was a model Eights Week and the house laughed and applauded vigorously. At this point in the debate a large exodus occurred, fully a third of the house going out. This was scarcely polite to the next speaker.

At a debate moved by Hilaire Belloc in favour of the abolition of the peerage, Rosslyn had opposed him and won. When put to the poll only 65 voted for the abolition, and 107 against it. The golden gates of Presidency of the Union seemed almost within Rosslyn's grasp. A note came from the future Lord Birkenhead: 'Dear Bruce, Is it any use offering to nominate you for the standing committee next term? Yours ever, F. E.'

Simultaneously R. C. Phillimore, Secretary, wrote from 36, Eaton Place:

Dear Bruce,

I shall be delighted to propose you for the Presidency next term and am honoured by your asking me. I think that if I do, I had better for your sake not speak this time. It might have a bad effect on your chances! I shall be taking a degree on the 11th but I can get my cousin to put me up and he'll be quite willing to speak to the Union on the 10th on almost any subject, but I seriously think that you'd better not ask me. I shall be glad if you let me know early what is decided.

Yours R. C. P.

'The Union is in a state of great trepidation,' reported *Isis*. 'Its elections take place today Saturday, and I fancy Mr. Bruce's chances.'

Standing against Rosslyn was only one candidate, Hilaire Belloc, proposed by the President, A. J. Morrah.

Rosslyn was proposed by Lord Balcarres who also proposed John Simon as Librarian. Viscount Suirdale was proposed by F. E. Smith as Secretary.

None of the three friends, Bruce, Simon nor Suirdale was elected. Hilaire Belloc's success over Rosslyn came as a surprise.

'It was a remarkable thing,' said J. S. Phillimore of Christchurch, who later became Liberal M.P. for Ripon, 'that the Union could prefer a foreigner to a justly prized and celebrated native dog and quip fancier.' Rosslyn wrote congratulating Belloc who replied:

Dear Bruce,

Thank you very much. What am I to say? You know how impossible it is to predict future at any time in the Union and you must know how convinced I am that you would have made an infinitely better President than myself. Naturally I am proud of the Union's action but I must own that it would have given me a less mixed pleasure to have felt the result of that action, in a case where it would have affected any one but yourself.

My very sincerest thanks for your congratulations. I have no doubt that I may have much better reasons to return them.

Affectionately yours, Hilaire Belloc.

Rosslyn asked Belloc for his nomination for Presidency next term. To his further disappointment, Belloc had already given it away to P. J. Macdonnell. On November 28th, 1894, he wrote from Balliol:

My dear Bruce,

If I had thought it at all possible that I should be elected, or even in the event of my election, my nomination could have been the least value, I might have consulted you before giving it away. In that case I might admit I should have had an especial pleasure in helping to retrieve what you must call flattery in me, on hearing the accidental result of Saturday. Unfortunately I am unable to do anything in that direction. I have been asked for and have promised my nomination simply upon the principle that it was difficult to refuse anyone who happened to ask me first, out of those with whom I have so long and so pleasant an acquaintance at the Union. I was prompted, perhaps, to this in promising my nomination, because I generally believed that nomination to be worth very little, if anything at all. Members do not, so far as I know, vote by the nominations and if they do you know how many names are written to you as supporters which carry far more weight, and deservedly so, than my own. May I ask you to believe that I am sincerely sorry that even in this, as I believe, small matter, I cannot act at the moment as it would most please me to do.

Very sincerely, yours, Hilaire Belloc.

Bruce and Belloc continued to goad each other in debate.
Meanwhile three months before Hilaire's first book of sonnets appeared, 'Oxford Verses, edited by Rosslyn Bruce,' was published by B. H. Blackwell.

The collection ended modestly on Rosslyn's own sonnet 'A fragment on Raphael's Holy Family'.

Later he preached on the miracle of the Renaissance painters being able to envisage the face of Christ, since there were no known contemporary pictures of Him.

> Lo! When the picture first appeared to men,
> They gazed,—and thought,—then mutely gazed again;
> But radiant angels, borne on silvery wing,
> Dropped from high heaven, all too glad to sing
> Their joyous welcome to the work complete,
> Then heavenward sped, their tidings to repeat
> Of art's new offering:—how the gentle Muse
> Had breathed such fragrance on the glowing hues,
> That dazzling symbols, bathed in splendour bright,
> Figured in floods of faintly mellowed light.
> While thus they made the courts of Heaven ring,
> Rose, like the sounds that throbbing echoes bring,
> A song of praise, less loud, but not less clear,
> Telling how art in heaven was held more dear,
> Bidding sweet Raphael mid the saints appear.

Fifty copies of *Oxford Verses* were printed on large pages of Dutch handmade paper, numbered and signed and sold for seven and sixpence. There was also a much larger printing on smaller paper at two shillings each. Copies of *Oxford Verses* edited by Rosslyn Bruce, appear from time to time in the sale rooms among rare books, with a fifteenfold increase in price.

Into Rosslyn's own large copy he bound letters from his contributors.

Isis headed its review THE PICK OF THE BASKET

An excellent selection of Varsity rhymes is that contained in the neat little volume of Oxford verses which has just been issued under the Editorship of Mr. Rosslyn Bruce. From the Foreword by Mr. P. J. Macdonnell, written in the best *Spectator* manner and calculated to awaken the interest of readers and to disarm the captiousness of critics—as soon as they understand it—to the fragment of the editor's which closes the collection, its pages are characteristic of the Oxford of today. Of the pieces that are new to us, we must single out 'An April Day' by Mr. Lawrence Binyon while Lord Rosslyn's sonnet in the style of Petrarch is admirable.

Mr. Gillett's 'Love Songs' and Mr. Addleshaw's 'Love at Hinksey' are sufficiently erotic and erratic to satisfy the most up-to-date and decadent among us and it is refreshing to turn from them to the dainty verse of Mr. Morrah. If we must judge the book by the standard whereby other books stand or fall, we can fairly say that the ideal of collecting the cream of the Oxford verse of the earlier 1890s deserves to succeed and that it has met with the success it deserves.

The Scotsman said:
'Mr. Rosslyn Bruce will doubtless please young Oxford men by the collection. It is very refined and might be better if there were more fun in it but the whole is readable, fresh and pleasing.'

'Humour is excellently represented in this volume,' said the *Manchester Guardian*.

'This is a neatly printed volume of poems,' praised the *Oxford Review*. 'The book contains some really charming pieces. Many more pretentious volumes have less in them that is truly attractive.'

'The printing is tasteful and the pretty white wrapper is artistic in its very simplicity,' said a publisher's circular.

'It is always interesting to see how the youth of Oxford is getting on in its aspirations towards poetry,' observed *The Times*. 'The collection will instruct as to this and do little more, because some of the pieces are good enough not to be included in a collection of this kind.'

Rosslyn asked contributors and friends to annotate his copy with their opinions of certain pages.

'Very quaint,' wrote H. A. Morrah of P. J. Macdonnell's Foreword, and others added, 'Truly Macdonellian', 'Archaism irregular', 'People wonder at it', and 'Both foolish and in bad taste.'

Of one of Gabriel Gillet's more inspired love songs, Nigel Play-rair wrote: 'Rather cold in "The keen windy weather" for "his lithe white limbs"' and K. L. wrote: 'Rather warm.'

Rosslyn dedicated the book to Mrs. C. H. O. Daniel which dedication page Nigel noted was the best in the book. She herself said: 'Very nice indeed. I am very proud of it.'

A week after publication Rosslyn received a slim volume inscribed; 'To Rosslyn Bruce from the Printers, Christmas 1894', with a letter in it from Emily Daniel 'enclosing a little edition of Milton's Ode on The Nativity. I had intended to give it to you the other night but it got crowded out. It is the only copy that has as yet been given away.' There were only two hundred copies printed by her and her husband, 'The Daniel Press, Oxford', for Christmas 1894. The print was very small and not very even and the wrapper was hand stuck.

The Daniel children wrote to Rosslyn often, sometimes in code. Rosslyn replied playfully in poems and anagrams and funny little drawings of cherubim and animals. He never learnt to draw in an adult way but the ideas were always there.

Dear Brucie, [Rachel wrote at Christmas]

Thank you for the splendid paint box. Ruthie sends you her very best love and is going to thank you for the chocolates. We are going out to six dances and two parties as well I am going to another lovely dance I expect it will be about the best. It rains nearly every day here and it doesn't seem that we are going to have that glorious skating I am longing for, but with loads of love and hoping you will have a simply more than lovely Christmas.

I am yours affectionately, Rachel Daniel.

However both hopes were fulfilled. The Christmas vacation began for Rosslyn with Harry Brittain's twenty-first birthday ball in Sheffield. Rosslyn and three other Worcester College undergraduates arrived from the station on the top of a hansom cab. They returned to Oxford to find their lake several inches thick with ice and not an ounce of snow to spoil it for skating. It was the year of the great frost. Rosslyn, Harry and half a dozen others wasted not a moment in issuing invitations to a Grand Gala. It was described in *The Queen* under SKATING AT OXFORD.

Mr. Bruce, of Worcester College, organised a charming Ice Carnival a few evenings ago. Skating was carried on to the strains of a band stationed amongst the trees on the banks. The light from the moon, and numerous lanterns and Bengal lights—to say nothing of the torches carried by the skaters—was quite brilliant. Professors and students turned out in great force, and many of the former showed remarkable agility in executing difficult turns.

The Gala was voted such a success that an encore was demanded quickly before the thaw came. The thaw held off till Worcester College had run out of funds and friends from other colleges came to their assistance to keep the thing going. One party after another was given with refreshments served under the illuminated trees. Probably nobody enjoyed these parties so much as the two little Daniel girls, whose company and laughter undergraduates could enjoy without being accused of waltzing too often with the same girl.

In Rosslyn's last year at Oxford he got his B.A. in Classics but did badly in Theology. His treatise on David had ended on: 'Not withstanding the tribute which we should assiduously lay at the shrine of the great Hebraic king, he was essentially a man one could not introduce to one's sisters.'

Queen Victoria, by William Nicholson, with her Skye terrier, which Rosslyn (*right*) bred and sold to her.

Bicycling in County Derry, with solid tyres and front brakes only. Toe-steps were provided to keep the feet clear of the pedals while spinning downhill.

Oxford Union Society Committee, 1895, composed entirely of ex- or current Presidents and Secretaries, and a Librarian. *Back row:* Hammond, Gill, W. K. Stride, Bruce (later Rev. Dr.), J. S. Phillimore (later Professor). *Second row:* J. Bradbury (later Lord Bradbury), F. E. Smith (later Earl of Birkenhead), P. J. Macdonnell, Hilaire Belloc, John Simon (later Lord Simon). *Front row:* A. Boyd Carpenter (later Sir Archibald) and Bradby Burt.

CHAPTER EIGHT

The Curate's Egg

In the summer vacation, Rosslyn went off to Downhill, from whose gale-swept colonnades he, the Bruce twins, Hugo Law and four sporting young ladies of County Derry headed inland for two week's bicycling tour. All tyres were solid and all pedals fixed, allowing no free-wheeling. The girls, wearing knickerbocker suits and outsize cloth caps secured by hatpins, let rip downhill with their toes resting on the steps each side of their front wheels. The only means of stopping was the sharp application of a front-wheel brake which could well result in the rider going over the handlebars. The gayest, wildest, prettiest and most universally adored of the four was Lota Stuart, whom Hugo soon afterwards married.

It was somewhat typical of Rosslyn's uncle, having invited him to stay in his marbled palace, bursting with priceless treasures and rich food, and having himself in his youth raced his four-in-hand against Hugo's grandfather along the same roads, to send the very small bill for the hire of Rosslyn's bicycle on to him after he left.

Rosslyn returned to Oxford to work for and retake his theology exam at a higher grade.

Harry Brittain's parents invited Rosslyn and his sister Kathleen to Sheffield for the Master Cutlers' Ball, attended by the Duke and Duchess of York. Rosslyn's programme showed that he danced more than the necessary duty dance with his hostess's daughter. Gabriel Gillet was also there. Kathleen danced frantically and then succumbed to flu. Gabriel Gillet wrote on December 30th, 1895:

My dear Rosslyn,

So glad to hear that your sister is better. It was stupid of you to stay in Oxford all that time without a maid or a wife. What are you to do? Leeds for a term? Yes, if you have really settled to enter the Ministry. But I still hope you may repent and turn to some lowly career in which marriage is not a crime or absence of any religious principles rather a help than a hindrance. Is Oxford House a night school? No, you've done enough philanthropy in your time. Holiday in town? Probably you're there by this time so should be useless to object if one wished to do so and in any case you pass Grantham both ways, a fact I would bid you to remember. Mildred H. is getting visibly and daily fatter all for the love of you. Don't be the hopeless chap known as Rosslyn Bruce any longer but imitate that combination of sound common sense, Catholicism and drum stick virtue which subscribes itself, Gabriel Gillett.

Other friends and well-wishers had already made suggestions for Rosslyn pursuing careers in politics, literature and the stage. What, however, he intended to do next was to put to the test his family's faith in his ability to follow the more selfless vocation of priesthood by working full time in a Bethnal Green settlement. In his vacations he and J. S. Phillimore, of Christchurch, had already helped with boys' clubs at Oxford House under Dr. Winnington Ingram, Bishop of London. Now he moved in and soon became surprisingly proficient at washing babies in buckets with carbolic soap and nursing their sick mothers in slum tenements. When the Bishop of London said that the largest number he had ever seen sleeping in one room was twelve, Rosslyn was able to cap it by taking him off to see a room where there were fifteen. It was not unusual for him to dine at 2 a.m. on soup from the Salvation Army shelter and sleep in a fourpenny doss house on the Embankment and then get up to comfort children brought to court for stealing food. He learnt that a friendly helping hand at this stage often decided whether a boy would become a confirmed criminal or a useful citizen.

When St. Paul's Mission Cocoa House was opened, Rosslyn was put in charge of it. His duties included helping to prepare the cocoa and bread and butter and going out into the docks to bring wanderers in. One night he made a haul of two very drunk blue-jackets. They were such a handful that when he met another rescue party he exchanged one of his intoxicated men for a sober one in their charge, who helped him to lay out the drunk in a school classroom being used as an overflow that night. Men lay about the floor 'curled up like the letter Z' Rosslyn said, 'all ready for a Ziz.' His own bed was invariably a marble-topped table in the corner of the coffee room from which he rose early to see the men off in the mornings.

From the squalor of Bethnal Green Rosslyn took time off in the drawing rooms and ballrooms of Belgravia, sometimes taking with him teams of Bethnal Green boys to perform for the rich to raise funds to open more clubs. Through committees concerning these clubs Rosslyn re-met Noel Buxton, not long down from Cambridge, who persuaded him to act in fund-raising plays himself with a group of Knightsbridgians at 15 Wilton Crescent. This led to more social gaieties, but Rosslyn was equally happy dancing at a hop in an obscure Dockland parish hall or in the gas-lit streets to a barrel organ, as he was at a coming out ball beneath the chandeliers of a stately home. At either he would search out the shy and lonely and draw them into a group, only abandoning them when assured they had as much attention as himself.

He continued to meet his Oxford friends and through them others who had an indirect effect on his life and his family's. Through Gabriel Gillett he met Aubrey Beardsley, who was a year younger than himself. Aubrey regarded himself as a writer and man of letters, and his brilliant book illustrations merely as a means of livelihood. Rosslyn observed to Aubrey's sister Mabel of his *Le Morte d'Arthur* illustrations 'The odd thing about Aubrey is he doesn't really *believe* in fairies.' Mabel who had little of her brother's fastidious elegance remained a friend of Rosslyn's and later of his sister Kathleen's, after Aubrey's tragic death of consumption, aged twenty-five.

After eight months at Oxford House, Rosslyn was invited to stay for a summer holiday at Clifton, the estate near Nottingham that his cousin had recently inherited through Sir Hervey Bruce's late wife, Marianne, née Clifton.

After the bleak splendour of Downhill, Clifton Hall, although an outsize mansion by most standards, seemed to the Bruces like 'a comfortable domestic egg laid in the cosy nest of Clifton's thatched village'. This cosy domesticity included a Renaissance 'pages' hall', redecorated with Dutch painted panels by the current Sir Gervase

Clifton before a visit from Charles I, a Georgian octagonal hall almost the height of the whole house, a Chinese drawing room the width of the house and a scaled-down copy of the Crystal Palace for potted palms. A mighty staircase led up to two dozen bedrooms. Comforts did not at that time include a bathroom though later baths began to appear like cast-off boats in some of the bedrooms.

In the garden peacocks were strutting among ancient yew trees and statued balustrades leading down to the seven terraces 'the most famous examples of their kind in England'.

Below the house on the river side, the Trent wound fiercely between high banks. On the other, a garden door led to the church in whose charnel chamber skulls and bones of the Clifton family had rested since Domesday, with the aisle paved with tiles initialled J. C., not, as might be expected, in memory of the founder of the Christian Church, but of one of the many Sir Juckes Cliftons. One, ancestor, mentioned by Queen Elizabeth, as 'Gervase the gentle' had fought at the Battle of Bosworth Field, and another had raised a memorial in the church in 1631 to the memory of his seven wives, three of whom were daughters of earls. Sir Hervey now spent six months of the year at Clifton with his son, Hervey J. L. Bruce, and daughter-in-law Nellie, whom Rosslyn found 'beautiful, kind and like a mother to me'. She was one of the lovely Ricardo sisters of Bramley Park, Guildford; another had married the future 7th Duke of Richmond and Gordon.

Her twin sons, Ronnie and Percy Bruce, both now in the army, were engrossed with their first young ladies and Rosslyn was left to explore the surrounding country with Benjie, their younger brother who was still at Eton. They walked to Nottingham through the cathedral-like avenue of trees, Clifton Grove, that stood then on the cliff high above the race of the Trent. They looked at a statue of the last of the Cliftons, Sir Robert, M.P., showing 'the ugliest pair of trousers ever sculptured' Benjie said. 'The people's idol' he was called, though later he was described by Cecil Roberts as 'a mid-nineteenth-century rake who, having squandered his fortune on the turf, opened Clifton colliery hoping to recover his wealth'.

Rosslyn and Benjie then took the towpath from Clifton a mile upstream to Barton, Rosslyn's birthplace, almost unchanged since his family had left its rectory.

Rosslyn returned to the slums, still not entirely sure that he might not be able to serve the world better through politics. However, by the following summer he had decided to apply for a place for Michaelmas term 1897 at Leeds Clergy School, where his two brothers Douglas and Lloyd had been before him.

Working in the East End there had been little time for dogs and birds and other 'beastly delights'. Now, when he returned to his sisters at Scarborough for a four-month vacation he was at last able to realise his ambition of opening his own zoo, in which he pointed out in his introductory leaflet 'powerful disinfectant would be used and animals would be liberated for exercise after show hours'. To ensure further approval, he invited a list of imposing local dignitaries to lend their names to the zoo, the Mayor of Scarborough, Lord Bishop of Hull, Sir George Sitwell and other baronets, J.P.s and M.A.s, and local ladies with charming names. 'The Amateur Zoo, Foreshore Road, Scarborough near the pier, organised by Rosslyn Bruce, Esq., B.A. was open during July, August, and September from 11 a.m. to 7 p.m. Admission was 3d. Schools and parties by arrangement. Profits to the R.S.P.C.A.'

The objects of the collection, Rosslyn said were:

1. To increase the interest taken in domestic animals generally.
2. To introduce many curious animals not usually tamed.
3. To show how cleanliness and attention render them happy and attractive.

Besides the animals he had kept at Oxford and lent or given to friends, Rosslyn begged, borrowed or bought enough to offer on exhibition:

over 200 beautiful and curious live pets including a magnificent Golden Eagle (said to have captured a child!); the Smallest Shetland Pony in England (33 inches); the largest Rabbit (17 lbs); Four horned Hebrides Ram; Flying Fox with wings twice as long as his body; Champion Rona, the best Skye Terrier living; Silver

Prince, the Crystal Palace Challenge Cup Winner; Cavy with 8 inches of hair; Chicken without feathers; Opossums, Raccoons, Owl-headed Lovis, Salamanders, Lizards, Combassoos, Quails, Doves, Jackdaws, Partridges, Cockatoos, Rats, Mice, Ferrets, Owls, Hawks, wild-eyed Kitten, Frogs, Silkworms, Dr. Jameson's famous Brown Bird, all tame and labelled.

An incubator will be hatching goslings, ducklings, guinea fowl and pheasants, with Baby Farm attached.

The public hatchings produced a pang of sympathy for the exhibits which gave rise to Rosslyn's verse:

> I am a lone unfathered chick,
> Of artificial hatching;
> A pilgrim in a desert wild,
> By happier mothered chicks reviled,
> From all my relationships exiled,
> To do my own lone hatching.
>
> Fair science smiled upon my birth
> One raw and gusty morning,
> And now the sounds of barnyard mirth
> To lonely me have little worth;
> I am alone in all the earth
> An orphan without warning.
>
> Seek I my mother? I would find
> A heartless personater;
> A thing brass-hided, man-designed
> With steampipe arteries intermined
> And pulseless cotton batting lined
> A patent incubator.
>
> And when to earth I bid adieu, to seek a greater,
> I will not do as others do,
> Who go to join the ancestral crew,
> For I will just be gathered to
> My incubator.

Rosslyn said he made more friends through his animals at Scarborough than at any time before in his life. Admiring girls and reptile-struck boys were always in attendance to help him. After the show was over, the exercise began, not only for the animals but for the helpers who, accompanied by their charges, bathed, played games, rowed out to catch fish for them and for years afterwards wrote reminding Rosslyn of those wonderful days at Scarborough and Robin Hood's Bay with girls with names like Winifred and Grace and Daisy.

The zoo drew the sporting and animal press, for some of whom Rosslyn had already written at school. Now his happy and original replies to their questionings produced invitations to write regular columns, which he reluctantly declined.

He had hoped to disperse all the animals before proceeding to Leeds, but willing as his young helpers were to take home their new-found friends, several were made by their parents to return them, and there was no time to set about finding them new homes.

Leeds Clergy School was then 71 Clarendon Road, about a quarter of a mile from the main buildings of Leeds University. The house is now part of the Albert Mansbridge College, centre for hospital and health studies. Into this large red-brick building, dignified by four vast pillars and a chapel, stepped the new student with two dogs on leads, several bird cages and a chipmunk peeping from his pocket. The young Principal, the Rev. W. A. Burrows was reassured that homes would be found for the leftovers from the zoo and the vice-principal, the Rev. J. B. Seaton, helped Rosslyn to house them for the night.

The Rev. J. B. Seaton wrote of the time: 'Numbers up to 27, our utmost capacity. Everything goes on much as usual. The poor old idolater's lecturers are being trundled out again. We have 12 freshers. The beautiful looking-glass on the stairs, alas, has had feet put through it. Compline bell has just rung, and as you know, even a vice Principal may not cut that.'

Leeds Clergy School was small and homely. Principal and lecturers all lived together as a family and the atmosphere was exceptionally warm and lively. Rosslyn's brothers had left a family reputation for quiet, studious reliability; however reports of Rosslyn's independent distinction as 'an irresistible speaker and dynamic. performer' had gone along before him, and he was sent at once by Dr. Patten to preach at Wigan. 'Go to Lancashire and tell the people about the Resurrection,' said Dr. Patten. 'Go with my blessing, Lancashire's waiting for you.'

Full of fire and enthusiasm, Rosslyn set off for the Lancashire that was waiting for him. Arriving in Wigan, the message was still ringing in his ears but when he reached the hall where the meeting was to be held, no audience was to be seen. Still repeating the Bishop's message, he inquired where it had been moved to and was gently informed by a lady that this was the place all right but the meeting would not be a very large one, adding 'But we have asked some members of the Mothers' Union to stay behind.' There were fifteen members, twelve gone home and three left.

This was his first lesson in the unpredictability of congregations. 'When two or three are gathered together,' he began, and gave the same rousing talk he had prepared for the whole of Lancashire.

At Leeds Rosslyn filled stacks of notebooks on theology, knowing that they were there if he needed them, though he rarely consulted them, preferring to go straight to the source if needed.

In the summer term he went up to Oxford for his M.A.

John Simon wrote asking him to speak at the Union:

> You have not forgotten your promise to assist a distressed President and to delight a jaded house by a visit this term, I hope. 'Sweet are the uses of advertisement' was my suggestion. Now about dates. Would Thursday, last meeting in term, suit you or would you prefer the one before? The later date would probably suit Croker King best and the idea of hearing him denouncing advertisement would be funny indeed. Let me have your choice and *don't don't* disappoint me. Will you be a reverent senior or Seigneur by then? I want you for another purpose also to come down—to give me some hints and material for ideas for Stride for *Isis*. Hastily yours ever,
>
> J. Allsbrook Simon.

'With the newly dight M.A., Mr. Bruce of Worcester, again in our midst, it was quite like old times,' reported the *Oxford Review*.

Back in Leeds, Hugo and Lota's letters were the brightest spots in an otherwise dull patch. Now came a letter from Hugo from Dublin announcing the birth of his son. 'Lota wishes me to ask if you would consent to become Godfather to the little one. She says there is no-one whom she would so much like to have for her son, as Godfather.' Typically, Hugo, (no doubt goaded by Lota) crossed out the 'son' and put it in various other places in the sentence. Rosslyn was suddenly desperately homesick for Dublin and the dear, loving, laughing Laws. He wrote joyfully accepting and Lota replied herself on paper on which she had stitched a tiny lock of auburn hair and embroidered a silk shamrock beside it.

My dearest bruvver, [she wrote in mock baby language],
'Fank 'oo for 'oor ravver tweet wee teary nocturne and for ve wee practical sonata 'oo sented me before church today.
I'se sendin' 'oo a love lock from ve fird side of vis triangle, and a good wish about 'oor 'zamination, and a big hug from us.
Hugo is not doin' out on vat long steep windin' path, at ve end and summit of which sits a chancellor all lorded & proper, on a woolsack patient. Je pense a toi et Je t'aime! A Dieu.
Ta soeur, Lota.

The new baby was christened Hugh after his father, and Francis d'Assisi after his godfather, when he was at Oxford, (which curious name did not prevent him from rising to a high rank in the army and keeping the silver christening bowl that Rosslyn gave him for over seventy years to give to his first grandson).

Lota was so touched by little things Rosslyn had let fall about his own childhood that she wrote asking him what would happen if she and Hugo died. Rosslyn assured her he would care for the boy and asked them to put a codicil in Hugo's will to that effect. Lota replied greatly relieved, saying nothing could be more terrible for a father and mother than to die not knowing what was to become of their child. When she next came to London, where they had a house in Kensington Square, she went over a hospital in Whitechapel looking for children without parents. 'But Hugo would not let me adopt them, only pray for them.'

Rosslyn passed the necessary exam before being ordained as a deacon, and started to look for his first curacy. Advice was given to look out for a preferment in the newspapers and follow the chain reaction back to the empty curacy left at the root. Rosslyn knew from his father's experience it was often just a case of general post. One parson wanted a change and all the others moved round in a concerted heap, leaving no space.

Fifi wrote: 'My dear Rosslyn, Thank you for telling me of your ordination. I am very glad to hear that it is to be so soon and that you have settled for a curacy.' She knew the Bishop of Southwell who would be ordaining him. She hoped it would not stop him staying with her in Oxford for the St. Edward's Old Boys' dinner. Fifi was still going twice daily to the prison and continuing to write her stories and pamphlets and letters to the press signed 'Oxonensis'.

Rosslyn combed the papers and applied to 'Curate wanted, graduate, liberal, evangelical, mission work, manufacturing district, good preacher, semi-rural, bracing north Derbyshire. Deacon £120 p.a. Priest £130 p.a. Vicar, Dinting, near Manchester.'

The vicar, the Rev. E. C. Collyer, M.A., invited him for an interview explaining that he was severely handicapped by the peculiar geographical character of the parish. Part of it was a vast extension of Manchester suburbs. The rest consisted of outlying farms and villages on the Derbyshire moors stretching almost up to the Devil's Elbow. A young, physically energetic curate was desperately needed to walk the fifteen miles a day or more on visits and to meetings as well as being able to stand up to the Sunday services and weekday weddings, funerals and meetings.

Rosslyn arrived at Dinting station, a halt on a single line from Manchester to Glossop which is still carried across the valley on a sky-high viaduct known as Dinting Arches. The vicarage, a heavy neo-Gothic, smoke-grimed brick box, was perched on the almost perpendicular side of the valley, alone but for the signalman's house, and a level-crossing at which, if the gates were closed for a train, the driver of a cart had to jump quickly out with wheel-blocks to prevent the cart dragging its horse backwards. Below it, the tall chimneys of the cotton mills belched smoke and blackened the spire of the church. The steeply-slanting roofs of the back-to-back houses lay at the foot of this beautiful valley, like tea-leaves in the bottom of a fine Dresden teapot. The parish was unlike any Rosslyn had ever known before. There was none of the lush green of Carlton or the gentleness of Stokesley, and yet the rugged beauty of the surrounding hills instantly enchanted him.

He was offered the job. The church was only twenty-five years old. The Rev. E. C. Collyer was only the third vicar and Rosslyn would be the first curate.

He would be paid thirty pounds quarterly and, as lodgings would consume most of this, Mr. Collyer suggested he might like to live at the vicarage where he, a bachelor still, had a cook.

Rosslyn was publicly declared curate of Dinting on December 18th, 1897, and arrived in time to make his debut at the Sunday School Christmas party. He asked the children to greet him in the street by name till he knew theirs. 'It's all right for a little girl to smile or give a bow of her head, but it's a little effeminate for a boy to pass anyone with a grin on his mouth. He might not be smoking a pipe that he could take out of his mouth, but he could give a proper manly salute with his hand when he met his elders.' There were a few effeminate smiles and they all burst out laughing.

Rosslyn soon became known as a character in Dinting. He was put in charge of a new mission room in High Street West, and was not afraid to round up men from the neighbouring pubs to attend. He was described as 'very handsome with blonde hair, blue eyes, and great charm'. He usually carried or led some kind of a pet and always wore a top hat. When calling on one family he started larking with the children and the eldest's dinner, waiting in a pudding basin for her to take to the mill where she worked, was knocked off the kitchen table. Later that morning he turned up at the mill and surreptitiously produced from his top hat another dinner in a pudding basin.

One of his first sermons to be reported at Dinting was after Gladstone died. 'The ember of that bright light which has flickered so long is at last extinguished,' he began.

At this time he still wrote his sermons out in longhand, marking on the back where he preached them, which was never twice within a year. Later, though he gave as much time to their preparation, he reduced all sermons, speeches and lectures to a list of monosyllabic notes jotted down on a postcard or possibly half a jumble-sale programme or a dog's stud card. Later he never preached the same sermon more than once, but one which he preached first at Dinting in 1898, became well-known as the 'Remember Jesus' sermon. It ended up 'Remember Jesus. Remember again that he was God, became man. Remember that he died for you, remember that he has risen and then, remembering Jesus whenever you eat or whenever you drink or whatever you do—do all to the glory of God.' The message was so essentially simple. The sermon took ten minutes to preach but lasted, at any rate in one case recalled, for seventy years. Throughout his own life Rosslyn never forgot to say grace before and after every meal, and to give thanks after every journey.

Reports of his talks circulated and people came to Dinting out of curiosity to hear this young deacon with a golden voice proclaiming Christianity in the simplest terms. Soon he was being asked to preach in other parishes entailing complicated railway journeys which he enjoyed because of the friends he made on them. But for all his youth and energy, he was often tired and sometimes ill. Being unused to so much public speaking his throat was affected.

> You really ought not to preach so often [wrote J. B. Seaton from Leeds Clergy School]. A hundred and eight sermons for a deacon in eight months is perfectly monstrous. Dr. Liddon used to preach very very occasionally. He refused ruthlessly often and stayed at home and studied and stored his mind with thought. By the way, I heard of you in Liverpool. A young chap in a Manchester shop said you had been in and he had taken a great fancy to you and would never forget you.

(Dr. Liddon, a Residentiary Canon of St. Paul's Cathedral, was generally recognised as being the most eloquent preacher of his day.)

Another cause for Rosslyn's tiredness, he suspected, was the poor food at the vicarage. The vicar had a small appetite and took much less exercise than his curate. Rosslyn was not fussy about what he ate but he found the vicarage macaroni not only left him hungry long before the next meal but was not even satisfying at the time.

He laid out Uncle William's modest inheritance on custard pies from the little stone-built village of Charlesworth, when his visiting took him that way. But it was the long lonely walks on the moor that really made him ravenous.

In August he took a few days off to visit his sisters at Scarborough and 'Oh the fun! News!' of custard ices in glass dishes with the girls in a tea shop, with the rattle in the background of chipped ice being turned in the churn for the next batch. Rosslyn forgot the macaroni, the funerals and the surly miners. Hilda had had a fit. Which Hilda? Sister or dog? Chloe had got married. Which Chloe? Well she was expecting puppies. The human Chloe sat beside him, wriggling and laughing with delight, pretty, curly-haired and vivacious, knowing she was a favourite. She was just fourteen. The night before the big Scarborough Ball, sailor brother Wilfrid 'dropped in from China', broader, jollier, more amiable than ever, though still not very tall. It was hard to return to Dinting.

Rosslyn's first job as a curate, like the rotten egg served to the curate at the bishop's breakfast table, could only, with the best will in the world be described, as in *Punch*, as 'good in parts'.

By September he was ready for the month's holiday he had been promised. 'September 12th prepared to go to Ireland,' he made one of the rare entries in his diary other than forthcoming engagements, 'leaving my work after 8 months of fuss and labour. Has it made any difference to anyone? God only knows. Over 1,500 visits—1,362 recorded and 113 sermons, 89 of them in the parish and much daily prayer and some agony. Cui bono?'

CHAPTER NINE

St. Anne's, Soho

Rosslyn crossed to Dublin, went to the Abbey Theatre and drove next day to Marble Hill, forty miles drive from the station, arriving at midnight where dear, ecstatic, garrulous motherly-sisterly Lota, exclaimed at his thinness and started to coddle him right away— Hugo was 'charming as ever'. Francis 'a lovely boy'. The food at Marble Hill was always exceptional and Lota proceeded to feed him up with special titbits. When his throat was bad again she even made him stay in bed for a day or two. But it was her dear dotty take-it-or-leave-it zest for life that Rosslyn found most reviving.

'Is it very difficult to cook a dish like this?' he asked her and she replied:

'The easiest thing in the world. Y'use a clever boy. You could get it done in a twinkling.'

When Rosslyn went on to Downhill Lota wrote:

My very dear bruvver,

We were very doleful after you left us and no wee birds sang. And now us is dolefuller. Very doleful, not just only rather doleful but very, for there are only three of us now. Boo Hoo. Hopes you got your greatcoat in time for going to cold old England. Hopes you likes your uncle. Hopes you plays billiards very well with your big cousin and beated him. Hopes you admires all the dogs enough. Hopes most you a good happy wee boy. Amen to you.

There was no one at Downhill but Sir Hervey. Rosslyn told him he was to be ordained as a priest just before Christmas. Uncle Hervey grunted 'Then you will be the 12th of my father's grandsons to take Holy Orders and you can preach the sermon on Sunday.' Afterwards he wrote:

> I did not look how long your sermon lasted when you were here. I should say about twenty minutes. Your father's time used to be twelve. You can put a good deal in twelve minutes if you go the right way but I never object to twenty or twenty-five if there is anything in it. Our vicar rolls away for twenty-seven minutes preparation and there is nothing left to remember except occasionally a familiar crochet. In regard to holding up the plate, I do not know whether there is anything doctrinal in it but I cannot see how it helps. I have always thought it looked silly.
>
> Your affectionate uncle.

Sir Hervey's contribution to the plate was said to vary inversely with the length of the sermon—a sovereign for ten minutes—half a sovereign for twenty.

Rosslyn returned to Dinting to 'give magic lantern lectures and stop choir ladies from fighting'. He had formed a children's temperance club called The Happy Band, 'a kind of cross between a Sunday School and Concert Party'. The average attendance was 277, with 308 maximum; seventeen boys and fourteen girls took the pledge and the rest recited and sang songs mostly written by Rosslyn, one of which the vicar thought questionable:

> Don't you think that Charlie's right?
> He wants to marry the lot of 'em.
> But his ways you can't condem
> Cos he's gone to be a Mormonite
> In new Jerusalem.

Rosslyn also came in for some criticism over the playful jokes he made about the Wood family, whose Glossop-made fortune had helped to build the church and furnish it with an organ and a peal of bells. In a concert programme he quoted the text from Timothy II 'in a great house there are not only vessels of gold and silver but also of wood'. Then there was the affair of the piglet that he dressed up in baby clothes and carried into a bazaar, asking the lady who opened it whether she thought the dear vicar's new baby was prettier than most. The confused and short-sighted lady glanced first at the vicar then at the piglet to see if there was any resemblance. The vicar's patience finally wore thin when Rosslyn, coming home hungry from the hills, asked if the meagre stew was composed of Devil's Elbow.

Rosslyn started to devise a plan whereby he could live in rooms by himself and eat adequately on his tiny stipend. Once a week he sneaked secretly off into Glossop to attend Cookery Classes, and one night he astonished the vicar, when the cook was out, by producing a tolerable meal.

Meanwhile Rosslyn was writing letters to learned ecclesiastics on theological subjects, asking for advice and sometimes expressing his own adverse opinions in the press.

'I do not doubt the legality of a choral communion but on spiritual grounds I exceedingly dislike it and think it most inferior to a non-communicating choir,' replied the Bishop of Oxford testily.

The letters did not really help to resolve his doubts and fears so much as the sudden moments that came to him of certainty and delight in a promise of a Ministry.

A week before his ordination he was laid up with a high temperature but managed to recover in time to start for Thurgaton Vicarage, where he spent a quiet day with 'soup for lunch in spite of macaroni'. His hostess was kind to him but he was severely reprimanded by the father in charge over his correspondence and threatened with a postponement of his ordination. Now his powers of persuasion were put to the full test in his explanations. Only when he returned from a walk with the other candidates was he assured of a reprieve.

On Sunday, December 18th, 1898, he was ordained as a priest by Bishop Southwell in Southwell Cathedral. Next day he went to London to pay calls, in his new capacity, on the people he loved most. He had a long talk with Aunt Zoe and then dined and spent the night with the Laws. Next day he visited his sister Kathleen at Windsor and brought her back to Kensington Square for lunch, where she said: 'two pretty nieces would talk only of bustles and lace and gloves.'

Rosslyn returned to Dinting in time for Boys' Brigade, choir practice and a funeral tea.

The vicar was away, and though Rosslyn preached on Christmas morning, a visiting clergyman took the Evensong he had expected to be the first service he would take alone. In a notebook he recorded what he hoped he would never allow to happen when he was in charge. 'Ferial responses, wrong second lesson, jumbled anthem, interminable prayer, doleful hymns and a read sermon.'

Kathleen and Hilda came to stay after Christmas. Rosslyn took them to the pantomime in Manchester and on to the platform with him at a meeting with five thousand present. They were much impressed.

Kathleen deeply regretted that women were not allowed to take university degrees and asked Rosslyn to 'pass on anything that he had picked up there himself'. He laughed at her but introduced her to Homer and then Walt Whitman. She had inherited her mother's talent for drawing and now persuaded Douglas to let her go to the Slade School of Art in London.

After his sisters left, Rosslyn excused himself as tactfully as he could from living at the vicarage. He needed more room for his animals, he said, and moved on to the opposite side of the valley to the little hamlet of Simmondley, from which he could see the vicarage clinging to its perch with the church below. 'You can see the goods trains crossing the viaduct looking like beetles waddling along the top of a garden rake,' he wrote to Hilda. Behind the hamlet lay the little outlying villages of Charlesworth, Chural and Sitch with picturesque Hayfield, like an alpine village beyond.

Now he was able to keep several dogs and as many birds as he liked. He made friends with other fanciers and became a member of the Hayfield flying club, which had an annual show of racing homing pigeons with classes for birds that had flown five hundred miles or over, or three hundred miles or a hundred and eighty. He started gatherings for fanciers in a working men's club and founded a fanciers' annual church service with suitable lessons and addresses.

During Lent, he gave a series of lantern lectures under the general heading of 'The Man of Sorrows' billed as:

His foreboding of suffering (how Jesus knew he must die.)
His determined purpose (how brave he was)
His agony (how sad he was)
The rigor of love (how he died for us)
His victory (how he saves us from sin)
Fellowship with his sufferings (how we are one with him)

The talks were illustrated with reproductions from the Old Masters. Even in the days before cinema and television it was rare to attract big audiences for such a series, but the hall was always packed, mostly with cotton operatives.

During a period of local disturbance, Rosslyn was asked to take over the headmastership of the National School for six weeks while a new headmaster was being found.

Now that he and Mr. Collyer were under separate roofs their mutual admiration returned. Rosslyn felt less restricted and was able to make his own friends and go on expeditions in his free time without having to describe them at the next meagre meal. Week-ends being the high peak of his business he was never able to go away from a 'Saturday to Monday' but quite often he took a day off in the week and bicycled the sixty miles to the beautiful park round Chatsworth or 'dined and slept' at Clifton or Thrumpton for tennis and duck-shooting or a dance. When his friends came to stay he managed to borrow a dog-cart to meet them at the station. Hugo, when addressing political meetings in the district, visited Rosslyn 'to recover'.

The younger of the Irish twins, Percy Bruce, had recently married Aletheia Paget and wrote with joy of the pleasures of the condition. Rosslyn was beginning to wish for the same pleasure. There are references here and there to a great love with half-torn-up sonnets, and several weeks of pages torn from an engagement diary of this period in which a later entry appears: 'Burnt old letters. Ghastly!' It was rumoured that she was the daughter of a rich Yorkshire landowner whose parents refused to allow her to share the poverty of a curate's life

Nellie, the Bruce twins' mother, wrote asking 'How are your private affairs progressing? Is it on or off?'

Rosslyn's next visit to Oxford seemed likely to be his last to beloved Great-Aunt Fifi. She had already said she had received her last payment for literary work though in fact she wrote two more articles. Her heart was bad and she suffered a good deal but was grateful to the doctor for telling her quite plainly that she might go at any minute. 'No long illness, no nurses and friends troubling themselves but just a stoppage of breath and a passing away to trouble no one,' she said hopefully, and then delighted in telling how the doctor had said to her: 'If you had been a bad woman you would have been one of the worst.' She signed herself in her next letter to him 'the poor old evil liver'. She continued to go to the prison and to church but people were always finding excuses to walk home with her, for she looked so frail. Tatters had already 'gone before'.

Rosslyn reminded her that his mother had said to him with a sigh one day when he was a little boy: 'I would give a very large sixpence to see Fifi.'

He received news of Fifi's death on October 6th, 1899, three days after her last visit to the prison. An obituary in *The Times* referred to her as 'a personality which between childhood and old age had become associated with the children of royalty, leaders of literature and the outcasts of the street and prison. Of noble and striking presence, the index of a character permeated by culture and accomplishments, by warm and Christian love and profound and humble religion.'

Nellie wrote to Rosslyn sympathising and telling him how sorry she was that he could not spend Christmas at Downhill. Kathleen had been invited and had accepted. Nellie described the splendid grandeur of the guests she would meet. Kathleen's version of the house party came later. Hylda Paget soon afterwards married Bill Tilney.

My dear boy, I expect now that the party has dispersed you may be amused to hear about it. I don't know how many of them you know. Lord Euston is a huge big man with a red face and fair moustache and squeezes my hand so hard and so long on every possible occasion that I didn't know at all what to do! However he's gone. He's a good shot. Then the Pagets, of course you know Sir Ernest. Do you know Hylda? If not you must at once. She's most sweet. She's thirty-three but looks about twenty-three and is awfully pretty. We spent many times stroking one another. I like her. Then the St. Mawes. I didn't like her at all at first but latterly I liked her much better. He is more or less a cypher and has a twin. Sir Ernest St. Luke, just the same as he is. He has only been married a few months. Percy and Aletheia are nice and very fond of one another. She's very married and rather tweet. Sir Hervey is quite nice to me and of course Benjie is quite charming. On the whole it's been ripping. Hylda and Lord Euston being the most amusing items. We're worn out with the guns all day and in the evening we play roulette. Everyone has gone except Bruces now.

Later she said that Sir Hervey had taken her to the churchyard and showed her his wife's grave. 'I miss her my dear.' And that evening he said, 'My dear, would you like to live here? You could pour out the tea and mend the china and things and there's no one here to get into mischief with. You wouldn't be in my way.' Half of her thought how relieved all her brothers and sisters and uncle and aunts would be. The other half decided she wanted to get into mischief.

Rosslyn's two years at Dinting were nearly up. The next advertisement he answered was: 'Experienced priest wanted, stipend £180 p.a. Rector, 28 Soho Square.'

The result was that the rector, the Rev. J. H. Cardwell, came down from London to spend a week-end during his holidays to see if Rosslyn would do for Soho. He arrived late and they were just sitting down to supper after brief courtesies when Rosslyn was called out to a distant dying parishioner.

The next day they met at communion. Rosslyn confessed to some internal disquiet at preaching when his future life work depended on the impression he made. His visitor's reply was characteristic. 'It is a most improper position for you. If you will allow it I will preach the sermon.' And he did, not only then but in the evening too. As the hill up from the church was steep, Rosslyn suggested that his guest should stay at home while he himself took the children's service. At tea-time, when he told of some of the quaint replies of his children he realised that Mr. Cardwell knew them already. He had gone for a little walk and passing the church had dropped in, but in case Rosslyn would be self-conscious had chosen a seat where he was not visible.

Next day Rosslyn was offered the senior curacy of St. Anne's, Soho, which he accepted with delight after thirty-six hours in which his 'whole heart was set upon learning the secret of this good strong man's powers'.

Rosslyn left Dinting in a glory of presentation parties including a drawing-room dance. The church club gave him what the local paper described as 'a silver ink stand of chaste design' and the Boys' Brigade gave him a send-off from the station.

His new rector had warned him he would 'go out like a lark and come in like a mole', and like a mole he would start digging right away, preaching on his first morning at St. Anne's and taking the youth club in the afternoon. Changes were so usual and everyone so busy he must not expect anyone to look up, even on his arrival. The ritual of St. Anne's, the rector explained was 'dignified and solemn with signs of an evangelical distrust of external ceremony, while conforming to the usages of modern churchmanship'.

Thus Rosslyn was a little disconcerted to hear from the cabbie on his way from the station, 'Not 'igh! I tell ye it's the 'ighest church in England, reglar cattylic. Hincense, not 'arf! Why, there is a thunder cloud of it hev'ry day, and sacrileges 'anging from the ceiling.'

London was still rumbling with horse-buses, tinkling with hansoms and shrilling with cab whistles. A few electric broughams whimpered softly through the streets where motor cars honked like geese. It was a wet night and drivers of carts, buses, horse-trams and cabs were all exposed to the rain. Horse muck was thrown up on shop windows. A crossing sweeper or two still lurked at the corners to earn a copper clearing a way for long-skirted ladies. In the porch of 28 Soho Square, was a much-needed boot-scraper with brushes.

Again Rosslyn was to be paid quarterly and the rector invited him to live at the rectory—28 Soho Square, which rambling house was joined to 1 Soho Square. There were six other curates and here comments and criticisms on the daily food were not restrained. Mr. Cardwell would listen in apparent rapt interest and then rejoin smilingly but emphatically, 'Get it eaten! Get it eaten.'

In fact the food was much better than at Dinting Vicarage and was backed by frequent meals and presents of food from the many Soho parishioners in the catering business.

When the Rector was made a prebendary, the curates clung obstinately to the cherished name of Mr. Cardwell.

'Prebendary sounds too much like a cross between a perambulator and a dromedary,' Rosslyn objected. Finally they settled affectionately on the name 'the Saint'.

Rosslyn had hardly been in London a week when he was accosted at the door by a young man who alleged he had advised him to emigrate. It had been good advice for he had become very prosperous in Canada and was effusive in his thanks. Rosslyn explained that it must have been another curate but so overwhelming was the stranger's appreciation he accepted the story. The stranger, in gratitude had brought back the head of the most magnificent caribou ever shot in Canada which was on its way from the docks. Finding he had left his money with his luggage, the stranger asked for a loan of a few shillings for his cab back. Needless to say, the head of the most magnificent North American reindeer ever shot never arrived and the other curates took the greatest delight in teasing Rosslyn about it. There was more fun over the new senior curate of St. Anne's appearing as a 'weedy soup-plate-hatted curate' in a cartoon in the evening paper. A reporter went to the rectory to follow the cartoon up and found, far from the weedy curate he had expected 'the Rev. gentleman in his study in his shirt sleeves with a large bull dog looking suspiciously at me from the hearth-rug. A pair of foils hung over a bookcase. Some seven-pound dumb-bells lay on the floor with a gun-case under the settee. A curate militant indeed!'

Soho was the toughest corner of the West End. Street brawls and knifings were even more common then than now. It was also the most cosmopolitan district in London. It was not uncommon for one of the clergy to interview representatives of seven or eight nations during one morning, most of them in distress. The church school's staff included one Indo-German priest and another part-Greek, but parishioners got the same reception, Rosslyn said, 'whether they were descended from Shem, Ham or Japheth.'

The choir of St. Anne's consisted largely of boys with nominally R.C. parents. Disagreements among the lady choristers at Dinting were nothing to the outbreaks of violence among the more belligerent St. Anne's choirboys. One particular menace was the grandson of an old-time world-renowned fighter. One night when returning with him from the bedside of a dying man in Newport Street, with the boy carrying his robes, Rosslyn came upon a policeman being beaten up by a mob. Clergyman and choirboy weighed in with their fists and were able to keep the crowd at bay till more police arrived.

The day of the senior curate began by producing printer's copy for the church bill-posting, interviewing young mothers who came for advice about clothing and feeding their babies, taking communion at the heart hospital, of which he was chaplain, and a wedding. An Italian who had been married three weeks previously came back with 'I not like me vife—will you no unmarry me?' Except for the occasional formal lunch with the ecclesiastical dignitaries, Rosslyn usually snatched lunch with a journalist or actor friend. If he was not giving one of the lunch-time addresses, there were old soldiers' pension sheets to be filled, with the ancient heroes fighting their battles all over again. Then came parish visiting, seeing emigrating families off from stations or docks, choir practice, evensong, confirmation candidates and lantern lectures and temperance meetings. He had a Bible class at Swan and Edgar's for the assistants.

Dearest of all his jobs was his Sunday School which often extended to weekdays when he was to be seen striding about London trailing twenty or more boys or girls on some outing to the zoo or museums.

In the summer Rosslyn took part of the Boys' Club down to Windsor to camp and learn to row on the river. Several boys in their first jobs were unable to come so Rosslyn formed the St. Anne's Cricket Club out of the left-behinds and arranged for them to join the others for a cricket match over the week-end. Several of these boys signed a letter with the campers telling them when they would arrive. 'It seems to be that Soho is nearly dead without you to make jokes about the chaps,' wrote their captain. 'We tried to horn them up last night but it was not much use.'

Rosslyn's first sermon at St. Anne's to draw a full church was billed as 'Do Animals live after Death?'. Remembering Fifi's beliefs he said he was perfectly satisfied that a human soul, such as a man, was not and could not be complete without the knowedge, memory and association of animals. If animals were entirely eliminated from the sphere in which he, Rosslyn, was present, he lost his identity. If there were no animals in heaven, only a fraction of him could go to heaven. If he loved an animal enough to make his love immortal then that animal, being the object of his love, became immortalised by it. Any creature that was loved enough, became love.

Rosslyn gave a series of lectures 'Towards The Citizens' Influence' from which quotations appeared in Sayings of the Week. He took the citizen each week in a different role: as voter at elections, talker among his friends, reader of newspapers, spender of money, joint owner of public property, and finally as a member of the church. 'Priests are an exceedingly dangerous lot and if they once get out of hand with the laity, clericism is a real enemy to the country' he was quoted, and: 'A parson is supposed to be as clever as Socrates and as eloquent as Demosthenes. Looking holy is practised far too much and what is wanted was more naturalism.'

On one occasion he bewildered his congregation by threatening them with 'an incoherent medley of metaphysical obscurities veiled with semiconscious subtlety calculated to mystify the comprehension of the sophisticated intellectual, and to humiliate the aspirations of the unpretentious, by a cumulative complex of inferiority to a state of insanity.' He then proceeded to preach his sermon in words of not more than two syllables.

One day Rosslyn thought he saw Sir Hervey Bruce in St. Anne's congregation, but his uncle wrote that he had long known that he had a double in London as he was told by people that they saw him in London and got no response. 'Either I have the power of being in two places at the same time or making myself invisible when miles away. It is forty years since I was in Soho.' However, next time he was in London he turned up in the congregation just to watch the effect on Rosslyn of his supposed astral spirit appearing. He left without a word and wrote telling Rosslyn what he thought of the service, ending: 'I saw some marvellously brilliant hats on some female members of your congregation not far from the pulpit.'

Rosslyn wrote back asking him, as a member of the congregation, to subscribe to a fund of things needed by his parish. Sir Hervey replied with a postal order covering exactly a parish magazine and its postage to him for a year.

Besides needing stretches of quiet in which to prepare his sermons,

Rosslyn was also working for his B.D. The poetry he wrote at this time was mostly jotted down wherever he happened to be, often on a park bench after walking several miles.

Monday was regarded as the clergy's day of rest, so Rosslyn would dash off on dog or bird ventures or on some outing with Benjie, who was at a diplomatic crammers in Garrick Street. Though Benjie's allowance was exactly a hundred pounds a year, board and tuition found, he was determined to see every play on in London, as were Kathleen, who was still at the Slade, Nigel Playfair, who was vainly trying to realise his father's ambition of practising as a barrister, and Rosslyn himself. Benjie's interest in the drama was, he admitted, 'tinged with the desire to meet a real live actress'.

In the eight acres of Soho there were eight theatres, fourteen music halls and a hundred and twenty-two pubs. The church warden was the chairman of directors of the Empire Music Hall. The London Underground having only just begun to be built, stage people still made a point of living as near to their theatres as was convenient. Moreover, many of them continued the Victorian habit—or took to it for respectability—of going to church.

Soon Rosslyn's popularity in church was transferred to the theatre and there was hardly a London stage in which he had not delivered an address from behind the footlights. In one music hall he was given four minutes and was told if he was not finished at the end of that time the curtain would come down—a useful lesson he never forgot.

John Drinkwater took Sir Frank Benson to view Rosslyn on the stage and Sir Frank instantly offered to take him on tour in the provinces with his Repertory Company 'a training ground for young men from university who wanted to become actors'.

But Rosslyn was content with his four-minute stints.

As usual Rosslyn was attracted by the children he met in his work and now he chatted to them while they were waiting to go on. He soon found a new following of friends who crowded round him to ask if he had a mouse or a squirrel in his pocket. He was amazed to find how little these children knew about anything outside the theatre. Now he could be seen trailing groups of fussily-dressed little girls behind him on the way to see the ducks in the park or following him into the children's service. Most of them could read and write a little but few ever had time to go to school. Soon he had quite a following of stage children in the Sunday School and had started his great campaign for enforced education for theatre children. Meanwhile he was allowed to set up special classes in St. Anne's school at hours that fitted in with rehearsals and performances. He himself taught the children with volunteers to help him. The *Referee* reported 'A novel announcement in the Garrick programme! The Rev. Rosslyn Bruce of St. Anne's, Soho, has very kindly undertaken the education of the children engaged at this theatre. Who will say now that talk of the reconciliation between the church and stage is all humbug?'

In a letter published in *The Times* against the employment of children on the pantomime stage he wrote:

A chorus girl's life is hard enough but a child under fourteen has to be on duty seven hours a day when there are two performances, in addition to the five hours spent at school and one hour on average spent on train or omnibus. Children like the excitement but this difficult employment needs careful adjustment.

Rosslyn kept many of the children's letters. Madge Titheradge wrote to him on pink embossed paper with three Japanese children on a bicycle made for three, carrying lanterns and fans:

Dear Mr. Bruce,

I am sending you a little card, also one for Miss Bruce which I hope you won't mind giving her. They are not really gorgeous but still they wish you a Merry Christmas just the same. When you come to the theatre do come round and see me. Find your way through the stalls and come through the pass door on the left. Am longing to see you

With love Madge.

Marie Löhr was another of his favourite child actresses. He gave her a white mouse.

Marie wrote from Lupus Street:

Thank you for sending me that dear little mouse. I will take care of it and I think I shall call it Bruce, as you gave it to me. I am getting a lot of snaps and Christmas cards together for some of your poor children. We are rehearsing every day at the Cavendish Rooms. I do hope I shall see you before I go.

Once he asked the theatre children to think of all the other ways a woman could earn her living. One little girl submitted a list of two hundred ending up with Sunday School mistress, 'these are all I can think of now'. They included ten kinds of maids, lady pawn broker (a sort of intermediate between buyer and seller), envelope folder, artificial flower maker, rag and bone picker from the dustbins, organ grinder, street singer and player, street dancer, artist's model—in fact all that Rosslyn was trying to get the children away from. Tailor's trotter (she has to run backwards and forwards on all sorts of errands), bugle and head trimmer (bugles are long beads generally used to trim ladies' mantles), military and naval cap peak embroiderer, street doorstep cleaner, fishwife (fried fish and she works very hard at it too, poor thing), walnut and pea sheller, artificial teeth sorter and matcher. All of which were in the ken of his Soho children. Another wrote that she did not approve of Ruskin, who had drawn up a list of rules for young ladies:

I think Ruskin is too particular about the way he wishes girls to behave. He does not seem to realise how hard it is for some girls to be quiet and keep out of mischief, especially at school. Besides I think that very quiet and apparently good girls are generally rather deceitful and sly, whereas when a girl is noisy and mischievous, it's all on the surface.

Rosslyn met James Barrie through a beggar-boy who came to one of his classes and then made a door-to-door collection for himself in the name of one of Rosslyn's charities. J. M. Barrie afterwards described him as 'tawny haired and more audacious than ordinary. He called again an hour or less after and was told that I was writing to you on the subject.' The incident led to an exchange of letters and Rosslyn's calling to sort out the trouble.

Barrie was then living at the old countrified Georgian house in Bayswater Road called Leinster Corner that was later to become an important home in Rosslyn's family. Barrie made himself a comfortable writing room in the sunny loft of the coach house at the bottom of the small garden and here, when Rosslyn first met him, he was writing the rather whimsical novel, *The Little White Bird*, inspired by his walks in Kensington Gardens across the Bayswater Road. It was from this book that he later wrote the play of *Peter Pan* for charity performances for the Children's Hospital.

Rosslyn brought his own white bird, Purity, a dove. Barrie was delighted to hear how, when dining out with the Bishop of Hull the conversation had turned to Nansen and birds' wings. To settle the point Rosslyn had produced Purity from his pocket. As the bird walked up to the dignitary, the latter held his hands over the bird and said 'Oh, the dear little thing! Bless you!' and Rosslyn claimed that his bird had been ordained.

A friendship grew between Rosslyn and James Barrie who, according to Cecil Roberts, 'may have found in Rosslyn Bruce—always so full of fun and mischief—the boy who never grew up.'

CHAPTER TEN

Young Londoner

In Soho, in the heart of London's West End, Rosslyn became part of the national events of his time. He had been at St. Anne's just over a year when he took a bunch of his young actresses to see Lord Roberts' triumphant return on January 3rd, 1901. On the 21st, he took Kathleen to a party Madge Titheradge gave. Afterwards they went on to supper with the cast of the play at the Garrick Theatre, with Nigel Playfair and Hugo Law. The next day he gave his annual tea party for all his godchildren and took them on afterwards to see the show at the Garrick. That night Queen Victoria died. There was a great hush over the city and many people went about weeping, so deep was the emotion. That Sunday, the sermon which Rosslyn preached was billed as 'A Widow Indeed'.

Ten days later he watched Queen Victoria's funeral from Noel Buxton's window and attended a crowded service at St. Paul's in the evening. He was on the committee for raising the Queen Victoria National Memorial in St. Anne's ward, Westminster, most of whose committee members were theatre people or restaurateurs.

Rosslyn wrote to his uncle in Ireland saying that seeing friends in the hurly-burly of St. Anne's Rectory was like trying to catch a train in a crowded railway station. He had his own rooms in the large rambling house combining numbers 1 and 28 in Soho Square but invariably his friends or their messages were misdirected and never reached him.

Sir Hervey advised him to join a West End club:

Undoubtedly, living in London, a club is a desirable handmaid. The Carlton is £10.10s. You might find the University clubs too stupid for you and I do not know their prices. Some people like the Union; the situation is lively and it is much nearer to you. The Bath is in a quiet situation and, I am told, admits men and women. I know nothing more but the fact that the swimming bath is a luxury. I suppose they do not all swim together as is the fashion now at some sea places.

Rosslyn asked to be put up for the Bath club by his Oxford Union friend, Lord Suirdale's father, the Earl of Donoughmore, who replied from 84, Sloane Street, 'Dear Bruce, Very glad to see your writing again. I have done all that is needful at the Bath club and have been very glad to do so.'

The Bath club had been opened five years before in the Marquis of Abergavenny's house in Dover Street as a result of Lord Desborough and Sir John Henniker Heaton saying that, apart from public baths, there was nowhere to swim in London. The ballroom was turned into a swimming pool, and squash courts and Turkish baths were added. Unlike Bexhill-on-Sea, which had announced the year before that mixed bathing was permitted, bathing at the Bath was strictly for its all male members. Nigel Playfair also joined the club and he and Rosslyn met regularly 'to Turk', a combination of taking a Turkish bath and talking over the problems of the world, which later became almost exclusively the Turkish atrocities.

Soon after joining, Rosslyn took Kathleen, and Nigel took another girl, to lunch at the Bath hoping to see Lord Donoughmore to thank him. Kathleen took them all on afterwards to 'a pinafore dance', in a studio that ended at 5 a.m. and next day Rosslyn took a boys' outing to Hampton Court, leaving them to play under the supervision of his young helpers while he visited Aunt Zoe.

Aunt Zoe had now accepted a Grace and Favour apartment at Hampton Court which Queen Victoria had again offered, just before she died. The large attractive rooms overlooking the lawns and distant lake had been the nursery of King Edward VI.

One of the most usual requests made of Rosslyn by members of the Bath club was to defy the Bishop of London and marry divorced parties in church. One wrote that it was 'impossible to get any clergyman in London to marry us and as I dislike the idea of a

Registry Office I ask if you could see your way to perform the ceremony please. Any advice as to not marrying or meeting will not avail because my mind is made up. I must be married not later than the 7th of March.'

Rosslyn could not, of course, acquiesce but he was happier than most to give a church blessing after the Registry Office ceremony, with wedding hymns.

Rosslyn and Nigel were often to be seen at the Garrick club looking for talent for charity shows, and persuading resting actors and actresses to give their services, which could be backed by smart young people with time on their hands. Rehearsals took place in Rosslyn's rooms at St. Anne's Rectory and in Nigel's in Lincoln's Inn which, decorated by Walter Crane, he kept on after he gave up the bar for the stage.

Rosslyn often succeeded in enticing rich young playgirls into parish activities, to show them that they could have just as much fun searching poor chidren's heads for lice as playing parlour games. Those followers who thought it was fun to be wherever he was, entirely agreed.

When Rosslyn was invited to translate Bach's Oratorio from the German for St. Anne's choir to sing at Christmas, he took two weeks off and joined night with day to get it finished. Back in the world again, he felt too disorientated even to go to a dance with Kathleen. Next day he tried to preach but his voice disappeared and the rector had to take over in the middle of the service. The Saint himself took him to recover at Tunbridge Wells.

The first performance of his version of the Christmas Oratorio was sung on December 20th, 1901. Aunt Zoe came from Hampton Court to hear it and Rosslyn lunched with her afterwards. Next day the *Morning Post* said that 'the choir of St. Anne's was remarkable for the clear enunciation and reverend interpretation of the apt new words of the Rev. Rosslyn Bruce's translation.'

The Times said:

Translations of words for which, in a foreign language the music has been composed, present difficulties but the feat is doubly hard with Bach or Handel. To choose a phrase that will not only fit into the rhythm but will include a word that is at once expressive and adaptable to a florid passage or suitable for a sustained note, taxes the vocabulary of any master of the English language. Mr. Bruce had completed his task with distinction.

From then on Rosslyn's translation was sung regularly. A ticket survives, on the back of which he scribbled in pencil 'This card was held by Queen Alexandra at a service at St. Anne's, Soho, during the Oratorio, left in her seat and subsequently brought to me by an observant (or inattentive?) choir boy. R. B.'

Queen Alexandra took a great liking to St. Anne's and came there from time to time, usually without being noticed until the press drew attention to her attendance afterwards. Sir Hervey wrote from Downhill, 'I hear that you have been reading the lessons to Her Majesty. I hope you read them carefully, quietly and left a good impression.'

In his next letter he wrote:

I suppose you will soon be seen in the lobbies of the House, as I see your young friend Hugo Law in his ambitions for parliament, is prepared to take a seat for the Nationalists and of course must so swallow the rebel pill. I daresay when the time comes for it, you will find the petticoats and strawberry teas on the terrace pleasant and the company perhaps amusing though not loyal or select. I shall not be there to look on and spoil your sport.

On Sunday, April 6th, 1902, Rosslyn missed evensong to go to Paris with Nigel to visit Kathleen, who was studying sculpture at Colarossi's studios. They took their bicycles and slept on the boat during the night and then bicycled to Abbeville, stopping off to look at pottery to take to Kathleen, who had once said she only had one mug in the room where she lived. At Amiens they put their bicycles on the train for Paris, where they slept in a small smelly hotel near the station. Kathleen was amazed to see them but immediately stopped work and arranged a day at Chantilly with a handful of other art students.

Kathleen's friends were unlike any Rosslyn had met before. In London, artists were outwardly staid and strove to look and be-

Portrait of Frederick, 4th Earl of Bristol and eccentric Bishop of Derry, painted by Madame Vigée Le Brun in 1790. He built two great houses at Downhill and Ickworth.

Rosslyn as senior curate at St. Anne's, Soho. His expression was often likened to his ancestor, the Earl-Bishop's, particularly after either had made a borderline remark.

Small cousin with large collie at Clifton, 1905. Gervase Bruce, who was killed in action as a midshipman at fifteen.

With Noel Buxton Rosslyn travelled in Macedonia in the wake of the Turkish atrocities.

have like lords and ladies. Kathleen's Paris friends all looked and behaved according to their individual outlooks. To Rosslyn it was balm to find others like himself who went about their lives talking as they liked, dressed as they felt and oblivious to comment. This was the first of many visits he and Nigel made to Paris while Kathleen was studying there. Among her friends whom they met were 'an energetic young Spaniard, Pablo Picasso', for whom Rosslyn procured a fox terrier, whose muscles the great master, Rodin, compared with Haniko, the Japanese dancer, who was his model. 'She is strong and stands as though rooted to the ground like a tree. Her anatomy is very beautiful in its singular power and her muscles stand out as prominently as a fox terrier's.' Later Rosslyn met Rodin himself in his studio where Kathleen was a pupil. It was surprising to find how inelegantly he had been made compared with his own statues. He was short, top-heavy and hairy and spoke with a husky stammer. In his studio nude models moved naturally about to supply him constantly with studies of nudity in various attitudes. Rodin believed that there was not a muscle of the body that did not reveal thought and feeling, as in the face. 'Follow nature,' was his watchword. He oscillated between Christianity and Atheism and Kathleen followed him. He warned his students against believing in inspiration. They could achieve nothing except by hard work. At a picnic to celebrate Rodin's birthday, he put Kathleen's hand into the hands of Isadora Duncan and told them they should help each other. Rosslyn said Isadora was a young lady 'who could dance in her petticoat without seeming to be improper'. He also met her brother's endearing young wife, Penelope, who was both pregnant and penniless at the time. Gertrude Stein wrote in her *Autobiography of Alice B. Toklas*: 'Kathleen Bruce, a very beautiful very athletic English girl, a kind of Sculptress, had at that time no money to speak of either but she used to bring a half portion of her dinner every evening for Penelope. Kathleen Bruce was learning to model figures of children and asked to do a figure of Gertrude Stein's nephew.'

Rosslyn described Miss Stein as 'a bookish American lady writer who talks and writes any way she likes, mixing her tenses and first and third persons at will, with her odd companion and sounding-board Alice B. Toklas.'

On their first visit to Kathleen, Nigel was so charmed with the life that he stayed on, but Rosslyn had to be back for duty on Saturday. He missed the train to Calais and finally left Paris at 9 p.m. with his bicycle in the guard's van. At 3 a.m. the boat reached Dover and he climbed on to his bicycle and rode most of the way back to London, stopping at Canterbury for breakfast. He was back in time to take the morning service. When asked if he had enjoyed his holiday he replied, with some discretion: 'I learnt how to eat for 95 centimes a day including tips.'

In May, a special service was held at St. Anne's in thanksgiving for Mafeking. Rosslyn took some of his young people into the streets to watch the celebrations; Londoners played mouth organs and concertinas trimmed with red, white and blue rosettes.

The coronation of Edward VII was scheduled for the following month but the king's sudden illness caused it to be postponed till August. There was a Canadian arch beside Whitehall made of straw and grain grown on Canadian farms. Rosslyn took his birds along next day for a feed.

He went to Clifton in September and was there when Ronnie, the elder twin, came home from the South African war. Arches were put up in the village and flags were flown from every cottage. The church bells rang and the horses were taken out of the shafts of the carriage which was drawn in by willing hands. Mr. Haines, the agent, presented him with a silver cigarette case inscribed by the inhabitants. The servants and workmen gave him a silver cup which was filled and his health was drunk with loud cheers. All the villagers were invited to the hall for a tea party in honour of Ronnie's return and they danced to a quadrille band.

Later Rosslyn married him in London to Ruth Okeover.

Kathleen returned from Paris to Soho Square on December 12th in time for the Slade Arts Ball to which she had invited Rosslyn and Nigel. Rosslyn and Kathleen set out for the ball together, promising to creep in quietly and not wake the other exhausted curates. At the ball, Rosslyn was so engrossed with another girl that he was quite unaware that Kathleen had slipped and hurt her leg and been carried off by Nigel and some girl students to be revived in his chambers. Rosslyn arrived there to find doctor in attendance who announced that her leg was broken and she must go to hospital. Nigel refused to allow what he called this breach of hospitality and insisted on Kathleen staying where she was. The leg was duly set after the manner of the time and a young French student, Mademoiselle Macord, was chosen to stay the night as a nurse and chaperone. Rosslyn crept in to St. Anne's rectory alone without waking the curates.

Next day he went back to Nigel's chambers where he found Kathleen considerably more lively. It was a Saturday and he refereed that afternoon at a boys' football match in Regent's Park. At the Bath club he found a message asking him to tea with an uncle and aunt, Admiral Sir James and Lady Bruce. Here he learnt that Kathleen's accident had been reported to the family and Mademoiselle Macord considered a quite inadequate chaperone. If Kathleen would not go to hospital, he, Rosslyn, must stay in Nigel's chambers too.

So, after a dinner party in his parish, he collected his toothbrush from Soho Square and moved into Nigel's chambers. Mademoiselle Macord had by this time left (possibly dismissed by Uncle James who had hurried to Kathleen's side).

Kathleen had been invited to Downhill for Christmas, which grandeur, in fact, she cared for less than ever since finding her new life in Paris. Nigel felt bound to offer some form of alternative formal entertainment and it was decided to give a dinner party on Christmas Eve. Unfortunately the only guest available at such short notice was Mabel Beardsley. So Rosslyn and Nigel sat down and composed for the personal column of the *Morning Post* an open invitation:

> A brother and sister living in rather pleasant rooms near the Temple invite any ladies or gentlemen who may be lonely to dine with them on Christmas Day. All ladies must prefer Lewis Carroll to Marie Corelli and the gentlemen must not wear made-up ties. Reply Box XXX.

The sensation was immediate and tremendous. The *Daily Telegraph* had a leading article on the subject and even *The Times* could not refrain from comment. They had over four hundred replies, written with varying wit, and they chose ten who promised to be most amusing, writing polite regrets to the others. A meeting place was indicated with the ten accepted guests in the gardens at the top of Chancery Lane.

So numerous was the correspondence that they forgot to order the dinner till Christmas Eve and frantic efforts had to be made to persuade their local Café Roche to send one in with its attendant waiters. When the moment arrived to meet the guests Nigel began to wish they had never taken this horrible risk; however, Kathleen, Rosslyn and Mabel were ready for anything.

Even though Rosslyn had been in church from 6 a.m. till 5.30 p.m. he went out to receive the guests alighting from hansoms to lurk somewhat hesitantly under the faintly lamplit trees. He then escorted them back to Nigel's chambers where they had a most amusing evening. They played snapdragon and charades. The party included another brother and sister, a French actress, a lively general, two American students and an Indian civil service grass widow who, it was agreed afterwards, was perhaps the only near risk. 'You can tell at once,' Nigel said. 'The yellow dress! a sure sign of an underlying streak of fastness.'

They parted with vows of eternal friendship at two o'clock in the morning. With the exception of the French actress, who became a great friend and invited them to lunch the next day, none of them knew or guessed the names of their hosts and hostess.

On New Year's Eve Rosslyn totted up that he had paid 2,208 parish visits that year.

It was a great time for causes. After twice 'missing them by minutes' Rosslyn met the Webbs at tea with the Pankhursts. His two great social causes were for the education of stage children and for better conditions for mothers and babies living in slum conditions. He had warm human experience of both, touched with loving humour. The Webbs had cold dry statistics. Neither seemed to complement the other and he left feeling disheartened. Later they exchanged letters to no avail.

However, over Kathleen's immobile leg, his own young set backed each other's causes with enthusiasm. Nigel's was for the National Theatre. Isadora Duncan's was for the world to learn to dance like falling leaves. 'Look at the way couples dance at a ball,' she said.

'They look as though they would all much rather be horizontal.'
Harry Brittain wanted closer Anglo-American understanding and had
already invited Rosslyn to the first Pilgrim Dinner in London. He was
now organising the first Dinner in the U.S.A. Noel Buxton's current
cry was for help for the Bulgarians on whom the Turks continued
to perpetrate atrocities. Rosslyn, with a sympathy stemming from the
tales he heard at his mother's knee, wrote to Sir Louis Mallett at the
Foreign Office asking for advice on organising popular meetings to help
to remedy the trouble in Macedonia. Sir Louis replied encourag-
ingly, which is more than the Prime Minister did when Rosslyn wrote
to him. His letter, headed Private, from 10 Downing Street was written
in longhand by a secretary and signed A. W. James Balfour:

Dear Sir,

I should hesitate to give any general advice on the subject mentioned in your letter yesterday because I think the propriety of
holding meetings in particular districts must largely depend upon
local conditions. If there is a strong desire to find a safety valve for
what are certainly most legitimate feelings I would not repress it.
On the other hand I do not know that much practical good would
come of it, for the Government needs no stimulus to their anxiety
to put an end to the present state of things in Macedonia; and
Foreign Countries are little likely to be affected one way or the
other by what they would regard as only more British sentimen-
tality. I can hardly therefore go further than I did in my letter to
the Archbishop and leave the question an open one to be decided
in each case on special grounds but on no general principles.

I remain, Yours faithfully

Another cause that Rosslyn threw himself into with enthusiasm
was the R.S.P.C.A. He was widely quoted in a sermon as saying that
a horse had no amusements, no theatres and went on working with
little relaxations. 'He should be sent to the country for a fortnight
of blessed life scampering about the fields and really enjoying himself.
One has to be careful not to be mawkish or namby-pamby in regard to
animals, but every horse should be given some time picking his own
grass and playing with his own daisies every year.'

When Kathleen recovered Rosslyn took her to see his beloved Lota and Hugo. They were enchanted by her, Lota volubly and Hugo showing a slow smile. When they took their children to Spain they took Kathleen too and Hugo taught her to drive a motor car. She sent an excited postcard '*and* I'm learning Greek and I've got two things in the Salon'.

The next one said: 'Just come in from a swim. It's getting warmer. Hugo is back. The papers have given me some rather nice notices for my Salon thing. What they really appreciate was done in three hours so I think I shall give up working very hard. Ruth Daniel's little friend is coming to stay with me. Goodbye dear boy, I hope you're as comf as I am.'

As there was no instant reply the next said: 'Are you all dead? I've been in bed with a fever and haven't heard a word from a soul for weeks. Lota is the beautifulest woman at all. Guess you know that as well as I do. Ruthie Daniel is posing for me (funny little soul) or was before I fell ill, and will again. Good luck to you. Please write to me. Kathleen.'

Later Kathleen brought Isadora Duncan to stay at Soho Square. After Isadora's illegitimate baby was born in Belgium, Rosslyn came home to find Kathleen in his rooms in a state of shock after assisting at the birth. She begged him to return with her to help Isadora in her trouble. Rosslyn could not go at once so suggested Kathleen should bring Isadora and the baby back to Soho Square. By the time Kathleen reached her Isadora was on the top of the world.

Donald Read wrote in the *Daily Mail*: 'I hold no brief for the clergy but the following extract from my diary proves men and women can be attracted to the church even in a place like Soho. "Friday. Went to St. Anne's in the evening. The church was crammed. It was very impressive."'

The congregation at St. Anne's after the report was the largest its sidesmen remember on a summer evening. There were not any empty seats on the floor of the church. Rosslyn was preaching on childhood. People were becoming child conscious. It was the dawn of the Peter Pan era and the end of the green baize door that segregated the children of the well-to-do from their parents, was in sight.

Extracts from his sermon were quoted in the press and used as captions for pictures on calenders.

> Anything that is little and fresh, all that is small and helpless appeals to us, not only in childhood but in the animal world. One sees this love of the young shown in the highest part of our being. We are all reflections of that which is best. We are made in the very image of God—that which we see expressed in the admiration for young animals is reflected in the very highest and most spiritual part of our nature.

> Art has never tired of representing childhood in all its beauty.

> Childhood demands our reverence and our love to protect it from the fiends of evil, from those twin fiends drink and gambling. Children require our care and protection from the evils of sweating, from the cruelties of child labour.

> Unless ye be converted and become as little children ye cannot enter into the kingdom of Heaven. Unless, that is, the feeling for childhood and for all that is beautiful in it can be brought into our own heart.

Rosslyn's lantern lectures for children were described as 'a pantomime in themselves. Many famous little actresses were there.'

The *Daily Mail* said: 'Mr. Bruce treats the animals with his usual vivacity, fun and wisdom. Chaff and pathos hurtle from his lips with astonishing buoyancy and he keeps it up too, for there is not a dull moment throughout.'

The *Scotsman* said: 'He will always please the young. The lecture is full of instruction. The fun is refined, fresh and pleasing. No one could fail to be interested.'

The *Globe* said: 'He had established a great reputation as a lecturer which he bids fair to enhance.'

The *Coster Gazette* wrote: 'Parson Bruce is a bit of a knock out, the buster's sides are aching still. If he ever laughs as much again he'll burst right away.'

A series of articles Rosslyn wrote called 'Every Day Topics' included one on luck, discussing walking under ladders and seeing magpies on Fridays. Rosslyn provoked a series of letters to the *Westminster Gazette* ending on: 'the Divine will over-rule all these curious superstitions'.

He prepared a set of sermons round the poets and another, with which he used lantern slides, which he called 'Birds, Beasts and Clergymen'.

There was hardly a church in central London Rosslyn had not ministered in, with as many again out of London.

It was the fashion for popular preachers to have their profiles, mostly three-quarter, reproduced on postcards already signed like film stars, but with room to be signed in person for the purchaser fortunate enough to catch the prelate, dean or humble curate on his way out of church. Some were taken full figure and fully robed and, in the case of a bishop, carrying his pastoral staff. Prebendary Carlile of the Church Army could be bought for a penny-halfpenny in sepia, in action in the pulpit with his trombone. Rosslyn's picture was a discreet Elliott and Fry copyright, looking dreamily fey into the camera. But for the clerical collar it might have been a young ballet dancer or a faun in the woods.

Rosslyn's lantern lectures on Dante were so popular that they were repeated the following year and were said to have brought about the new wave of Danteism as a great force 'which brings every humble earnest follower to the seat of Dante's master, the incarnate son of the living God'. To reproductions of the Pre-Raphaelites he added his own strange, almost Blake-like drawings with diagrams explaining Dante's conception of the path of the spirit. The lecture describing Dante's *Inferno* was packed out. Rosslyn's introduction to Dante appeared in the evening press:

Dante was the greatest of all *poets*, not of the fashion in which the word is generally pictured, but in its original meaning of worker or performer. He was the greatest of the performers the world has ever seen. Dante was sketched as a citizen. But for him there would have been no Florence and but for Florence no Dante. He enjoyed talk with all the great men of the time whatever they were, great merchants, powerful bankers and writers. All who had influence over the hearts, the souls and the affairs of men were the friends of Dante. He was soldier, scientist, scholar, who had all the knowledge of his day and generation centred on his mathematics, chemistry, philosophy and theology. He was the Shakespeare of his time. At thirty-five he was Prime Minister, at thirty-seven an exile, banished for ever from Florence, to be buried alive if he returned. By his exile he became the most divine, the greatest worker, the greatest thinker and the greatest speaker that ever lived—a man intoxicated with the spirit of self-sacrifice.

Rosslyn was thirty-two, flattered, indulged and left with all too little time for quiet and prayer. Might exile be the key to his own salvation? Fired by his own ecstatic interpretation of Dante's thirteenth-century exile, he began to consider it.

CHAPTER ELEVEN

Thatch and Feudalism

Rosslyn's material for his B.D. had been accepted by the Dean of Christchurch, who asked him to come to Oxford for the final part of the degree. 'The dissertations show marks full of study and thought. As a matter of taste I cannot say that I admire such flowery rhetorical style as you use in the essay on neo-Platonism, scarcely appropriate to the seriousness of the subject.'

Rosslyn continued to back Noel Buxton's work for the Bulgarians and wrote a prayer for the cause which was circulated throughout the churches of Britain.

> Receive O most loving God and Father, the tribute of our humble and most hearty thanks for thy great mercy bestowed on the oppressed in the Turkish Empire; forbid by thy most mighty power, the renewal of oppression and wrong and bless with the abundance of thy divine favour, the hearts and minds of all those who are striving for thy glory and for the reign of peace and good-will amongst men.

Noel visited Kathleen in Paris and described in stirring language the terrible conditions of disease, torture, cold and starvation in Macedonia.

Young, active, loving people were needed on the spot to distribute food and clothes and to organise relief of the awful plight for the Macedonian Relief Fund, for the benefit of some hundred villages burnt by the Turks.

It was the youths and babies, Kathleen's two favourite subjects for sculpting, that touched her heart and decided her to abandon art and go off to Macedonia with Lady Thompson at very short notice.

Noel begged her to write him as often as possible, but in spite of her self-confident attitude to life she admitted she was so shocked by things that could only be confided to a brother, that it was to Rosslyn that she wrote almost daily. 'One woman in the worst plight brought here today,' she wrote. 'She herself has gone mad with horror and the doctor does not know what course to adopt. If her child is allowed to be born the people of the village will kill it.'

'We have both stoutly refused to stay in the harem, the women are such beasts—beasts, dear boy, there is no other word for them. So we are living in the men's quarters which has its painful side too.'

They visited burnt villages and at the house of a Bey were sent for half an hour to his harem. 'You can't imagine what these women are like, bright scarlet hair and absolutely black teeth and all fat and bare-footed and their conversation was the most vile I have ever yet come in contact with. The mud was very bad too.' But she was unperturbed by being shown a wound where a bullet had gone through an old man's neck.

She was hungry for letters from home and sure that the postman tore up any that came whenever there were enough to make it worth while his carrying them. 'Now that I have come to the nethermost part of the year, I found it the most godforsaken ga-ga country I ever knew and everyone has smallpox.' In spite of her Bohemian life in Paris, Kathleen was deeply shocked by a sick girl lying in her clothes—having nothing else—on the floor, covered by one blanket instead of properly in a white nightgown in a bed with sheets or, like her, in a Jaegar sleeping sack, three blankets, a wool cape, a fur coat and two hot-water bottles. 'Giving medicines and being nice to people is all very fine but killing the beasties is the great work. For myself I'm as fit as a violin and getting absolutely accustomed to the folk with smallpox. I watched a boy with tuberculosis and meningitis all day. At last about 8 he died and I just had to shut his eyes, cover him up and go for a man to make a box.'

Though the time seemed to Kathleen like weeks and months she had only been in Macedonia just over three weeks before she herself caught typhoid fever and passed into a delirium of high fever.

More than ever Rosslyn felt the need to withdraw from the

excitement of success and adulation in the city. He had already discussed his Uncle Hervey's suggestion that he might one day accept the quiet backwater of Clifton when the present incumbent retired. The Rev. Mr. Ffolkes lived in the village in a small house called The Glebe. The large Georgian rectory itself, with its extensive stabling and vast gardens behind a high wall was let to a well-off young couple, the Kerle-Smiths.

On February 1st, 1904, came an urgent letter from Sir Hervey on the familiar paper headed CLIFTON HALL, NOTTINGHAM.

My dear Rosslyn,

I got a telegram this morning telling me of Mr. Ffolkes' death. It is now for you to decide whether you will take the living or not. I expect I shall have plenty of applications for it as soon as it is known. If you accept it, I don't know what are the necessary steps to take. When I spoke to you before you thought you could not live in the Rectory and I don't think you could. I think you had better let me know about that. I could mention it to the people who are in it now. It might relieve their minds but if they made arrangements to go, it might be some little time before you let it again. Please yourself about coming. Whether it would be desirable or not under existing circumstances, I don't know. You please yourself. Nellie thinks it would not be. Yours most sincerely.

The day Rosslyn received his uncle's letter he lunched with the Bishop of London who advised him to accept the offer of Clifton by return of post. Here in London he was thrown into too much activity with too little time to think and read and write and study. The Bishop had hopes of his gaining a Doctorate of Divinity, and was not sure that this would be possible with so much time spent in the company of the theatre and the press.

Rosslyn returned to Soho Square to find a telegram from Lady Thompson saying Kathleen was dangerously ill. The alarm he felt over this news had the effect of deciding him instantly to accept Clifton. A few days later came a letter from Lady Thompson saying how seriously ill Kathleen still was. At first she had been nursed by a local carpenter. Lady Thompson wrote again on January 29th from Castora.

Dear Mr. Bruce,

I am very thankful to send you a good account of your sister. She has had no return of the fever and though extremely weak I trust all the bad symptoms are disappearing. Her spirits are good and she takes her nourishment well. They all say it was touch and go when the temperature was so very high and it seems that the wet sheets alone saved her . . . I am afraid it is a disappointment to her that she must go home. She herself is too sensible to let it distress her. I hope her relations will make her take care for conditions would be serious if she had another attack.

Benjie wrote from Calvados:

Just a few lines to say how *very* glad I am that you really *are* coming to Clifton. It will be delightful to have such a pal so close and I expect when I am at Clifton I shall spend half my time at your house. You could always kick me out. Further pleasant prospect for you. I know all the people are just *itching* for you to come, from confidences poured into my ear by the odd man, the head keeper and other high officials of state. Very sorry to hear about the child Kathleen. I hope she'll get back all right. I think, after all, perhaps sculpting in Paris is a safer though doubtless less exciting pastime than canoodling with bandits. Best of luck in your new office.

Your affectionate cousin, Benjie

Kathleen returned to her studies in Paris and Rosslyn wrote asking Noel's sister Mabel Buxton to make sure she was fit for work after her illness. Mabel was also studying art, but living in an hotel in much the same luxury as she enjoyed at home. Letters now increased between Mabel and Rosslyn, with less and less reference to Kathleen who shook off her convalescence like a tiresome old coat.

'Your attempts to propriety are nice,' wrote Mabel. 'I have to pretend to be proper at home. So would you, if you had a family like mine. I would like to tell you what they think (at least what I think they would think) about some things because you aren't like most people.'

A day in the life of a curate appeared in the *Daily Mail* in which Rosslyn played down the social life. His cousin, Colonel Hervey Juckes Lloyd Bruce, Benjie's father, wrote saying 'it leaves little time for sleep or to say your prayers before breakfast. I am sorry to see how much time you spend at the police courts and visiting public houses. I fear you will find Clifton very dull after it.'

On Thursday, March 17th, 1904, Rosslyn went to Oxford for his B.D. degree. Kathleen was back and lunching with Rosslyn at the Bath Club a week later. She stayed on with him till Easter. He took the three hours service at St. Philip's, Earls Court Road on Good Friday and preached his farewell sermon at St. Anne's on the first Sunday after Easter.

St. Anne's was normally seated for 900. There were 1,550 that evening. The sermon was taken down by one of the congregation and, to meet the wishes of many who were present, was printed with a green paper cover. It was little more than a thousand words of love from him to them. He spoke of the children whom he had asked in the afternoon what Jesus would be like when they saw him. One said 'He would be all glittering'— 'His face would be very brilliant'— 'His eyes would be like diamonds.' He explained that to see Jesus was to see a curled lip change to a smile, to hear a cruel word suddenly checked and to learn to be kind. All was simplicity. But the timing, the pauses, the rising and falling of Rosslyn's musical voice were art in its highest form.

Then came the presentation, a great mahogany roll-top desk with pigeon holes, secret hiding places, easily sliding drawers and ink pots and pen trays that swung out from secluded corners. A silver plate fixed to it was inscribed with his name with the gratitude of the parishioners, who also added a mahogany revolving chair. One parishioner, a greengrocer, said, 'We have been amply repaid for any little we have contributed to your happiness, by your friendship, simplicity of character and cheering personality.' The school-children gave him books and pictures, the Boys' Clubs made him bookshelves, the little actresses embroidered him countless pairs of slippers. The City and Suburban Canary Breeders gave him a terrific farewell and a gold-mounted fountain pen with which he said he would write about the ways of British birds. He used it, as he did the desk and chair, for the rest of his life.

Rosslyn arrived to find the village of Clifton wrapped in creepers with a little pinafored girl or sailor-suited boy at every gate and an old fellow sitting sideways on a blinkered and collared shire as it ambled through the broad street. Cottagers wore clean aprons and bonnets with ribbons under their chins.

At The Glebe, to his etymological delight, he was cared for by Mrs Cook, the garden was cared for by Mudd and his animals by Fox. In the choir sang A. Bird and D. Sharp and C. Triplets, with B. Reckless blowing the organ.

He wrote back to St. Anne's while his new gold pen was being inscribed, adding a postscript: 'I write this with a quill cut before breakfast which had spent last night suspended to the tail of my best peacock. That suggests something of the repose and leisure which is interspersed with parochialia.'

A Nottingham schoolmaster went to visit him and was surprised to find that the new rector from London had already acquired ferrets, a gundog and a horse called Audrey.

He was surrounded by dogs; in the stables there was also a Shetland pony that nuzzled sugar from the master's pocket. Some puppies that had just been born were 'introduced to him by the mother. She had already explained to them that their master was the centre of the universe and they must love, honour and obey him.'

He was taken to see the church which 'probably dated back as a place of worship long before Christianity was preached'. Of the peal of six bells his favourite was the third, cast in 1605 with the inscription 'MY roaring sound doth warning give that man cannot heare alway live.' He was shown the ancient oak chest with three locks so it could only be opened when the rector and both church wardens, each with a key, were present. In it were kept mortar boards for twelve singing maidens. The maidens themselves, clad in white robes, sat in the tower, segregated from the masculine choir in the chancel. Already the new rector had learnt all their Christian names and was planning a choir outing on the river.

The first guests were the two little sons, Toby and Geoffrey, of his old Oxford friends Percy and Mabel Dearmer. The boys helped to make rabbit hutches and aviaries in the garden.

Sixty-six years later Geoffrey wrote:

Rosslyn had the gift of making children in his care feel like guests. He certainly gave us a week we will never forget. I remember a large lake and fishing and catching roach and a man saying 'Splendid bait for pike'. Rosslyn saw us off by train from Nottingham and I could not think of words to thank him for our wonderful visit.

Their mother wrote two days afterwards:

I'm horrified to find that the cheque I sent couldn't possibly have covered the children's journey to and from Clifton. I feel as if I had sent you two parcels unstamped. You have given the boys a week that they will never forget. They were perfectly happy and it has been so good for them. Toby said 'I wish I hadn't to be told thrice before I do things. I forget sort of. If I lived with Mr. Bruce I should remember.'

Kathleen stayed for a few days before returning to France. He sent her off with more 'education'.

1904. Kathleen wrote:

Just to say bless you. Am still swimming in the nude and working and being content. I have read the little blue book, Plato, you sent me twice. Am frightfully cross that it's not much longer. I think I am going to have another go of typhoid. Make some news for me. Did you find my scarf, if so don't bind books with it or give it to the birds for nests.

From Orleans, again, 1904:

Dearest,

It was just rather dear of you to send me the Platos. I love and love and love him. Original of me? Oh dear, oh me I've just been having such a funny mushroom party with me and Rodin and a roast chicken and so few knives and plates but it's been a great success. He stayed three hours and I am going to his country house to-morrow. I am going to send to the International a bronze, that is if I sell what I've got in the Salon for £5 which I hope to do. That will pay for the casting.

Rosslyn was expected to lunch every Sunday at Clifton Hall, after which the family walked in the garden or leant against the two stone lions that flanked the terrace steps. He was also on call for dinner parties when a spare man was needed during the six months of the year that his uncle spent at Clifton with his son and daughter-in-law. Hervey J. L. Bruce, and Nellie. Then they moved off for the other half of the year to Downhill, followed, when available, by their sons and grandchildren.

One of the first funerals Rosslyn had to take at Clifton was of Percy's young wife Aletheia, who died when her second baby, Sheila, was born, leaving Percy with a five-year-old boy, Gervase.

Benjie scribbled a note in pencil on black-edged paper the night before:

Preach us a decent sermon, old boy, on the lines of Longfellow's poem, which I hope are nice and comforting. Not the cotton wool, heaven sort of thing which have not seemed like logic to me lately. Don't laugh, but don't see any reason why we should live afterwards any more than dogs and things.

This between ourselves, Benjie.

The next day he attended the bird show in Nottingham and on Sunday preached 'about and *from* Allie' in which he explained that animals and birds had their place in heaven too.

People soon began to hear of his sermons in Nottingham and walked out on Sundays to Clifton, to hear the man who carried birds and beasts under his coat or in his pocket, occasionally loosening a dove from the sleeve of his surplice from the pulpit to illustrate the flight of love.

The rather dreary Sunday School at Clifton became the service of the Ministering Children's League, which society with its motto of 'Every day a good deed', had preceded Scouts and Guides by thirty or forty years.

'Very old people can remember those bad old days when it used to be the fashion among boys to jeer at babies. Now the boys are chivalrous and courteous to people smaller and weaker than themselves and especially the smallest weakest of all, a human baby. Have you ever seen a newly hatched baby linnet or thrush all pink and wobbly with a large tumbly sort of blind-eyed head and a ridiculous fat middle adorned by would-be wing buds? They are the most ludicrous little people, but in three weeks there is hardly anything in the woods and fields more fascinating,' he told the children. 'I feel sure M. C. L.'s—I mean the Ministering Cock Linnets—consider their one-day-old babies are as beautiful as anything on earth.'

When flowers were in short supply Rosslyn announced that the church would be decorated with animals and birds. A farmer's daughter brought a garlanded cow to join in the procession of children carrying rabbits and guinea pigs, bird cages and kittens and leading dogs and lambs, singing 'All good gifts around us are sent from Heaven above'. On Rosslyn's shoulder was a Siberian owl.

When his eldest brother, Douglas, came to stay he complained about the damp of his rectory at Binton near Stratford-on-Avon. A stream ran almost through it and the only w.c. was perched in a little hut over the stream near the kitchen door. Rosslyn suggested that their uncle might find something better for him.

Douglas rose at the suggestion and reopened one of their old battles involving the loan of ten shillings. After a short ding-dong Douglas wrote: 'I think, Rosslyn, you and I must recognise this fact that however much we both want to be nice to one another, as I see you do to me, and more I do to you, we are so built that we cannot help jarring at times.'

He went on to say he did not think he could accept any of Sir Hervey's livings because he might make conditions which 'I might not be able to accept. You know that I claim to be an extreme High Churchman, who obeys the law and only believes in ritual in so far as it is an aid to devotion.'

Rosslyn wrote back that he was an extreme Broad Churchman and suggested that Douglas might like to go back to their own childhood home of Carlton, which was now empty. Douglas told Rosslyn not to take any steps on his behalf:

First I can't think that the Archbishop would be the least likely to give it. Secondly I don't suppose the people would much care for me. Thirdly I should probably be poorer than I am now and should in addition have much more worry. It is true that I need not keep it up but so Father thought and yet found it expensive. Father used to say, hyperbolically perhaps, that it cost £100 per annum to keep the roof in order.

Lastly the climate is the same or worse than Binton. I am sitting light to Binton because the damp climate is not good for the boys and is crippling Margaret with rheumatism.

Soon after Douglas was offered the incumbency of St. Anne's, Dunbar, on the east coast of Scotland. He accepted and their brother Lloydie went with his twin sister Gwen to Binton where this saintly pair were too engrossed with the church, village and birds in their garden to notice the damp. Douglas wrote from Dunbar that there was no school for little boys so he decided to get other pupils and teach them with his own. 'I am afraid that dear Aunt Zoe has never heard me preach' he went on. 'I am afraid that was merely hearsay evidence from an admirer, of which we all have *some*. I am *not* a good preacher because I have not the gift of speech, but some people like a man who is obviously trying to say what he thinks and that being my endeavour, is accepted as an excuse for my failure to really present it well.'

Rosslyn pointed out that for one who was about to start a school, his brother should watch his split infinitives.

Soon after this Rosslyn was himself asked to teach the fourteen-year-old son of Jesse Boot, the Nottingham tycoon who had carried on his father's chemist shop near Brucegate from the age of thirteen and opened branches all over the country, keeping down the prices of medicines by employing women. After he married the Jersey book-seller's daughter, Florence Rowe, he added the subscription libraries to the backs of all his chemist shops. As a Liberal he was much involved in local politics. Although he was a staunch Primitive Methofist Nonconformist, he and Rosslyn became good friends. Sometimes Rosslyn went to the Boots' large house in The Park, called St. Helier after their Jersey estate, and sometimes John Boot went to Clifton for the extra coaching he was having before he went to public school. Occasionally one of John's three pretty sisters went too to be shown the animals in the rectory garden.

The rural peace, with long days for thought and study and animal husbandry, was not to last. Within a year Rosslyn was being drawn into the city life of Nottingham. He could never refuse an invitation whether to preach at a funeral, judge at a dog show or dance a Highland fling. Now Sir Charles Seely, chairman of the Nottingham Hospital asked him to become its chaplain. 'Come over to the hospital and see the matron and the mortuary,' wrote the chairman, signing himself Charlie. Rosslyn accepted the post and they lunched together on hospital days, usually after playing a few sets of tennis first, most weeks, for some years. After Charlie Seely took Rosslyn to see a neglected workhouse Rosslyn declared in a speech that the system was antiquated and must go. 'We cannot continue to bring up children like a brood of rats. Others must be given the responsibility of their children, even if the mothers themselves have to be kept by the state.'

He said it was a disgrace that in our time of the world's history there should be any waifs and strays in the street and the way in which children were born or rather damned into the world had got to cease.

In a sermon in Nottingham billed as 'Hot Sand and Ginger' he urged the communities of Christian people to show a bold front, more guts and fight against selfishness, drunkenness, and gambling and lust, translating qualities that were admired in physical activities to the spiritual. It was extracts like this that the newspapers liked to report. They made good headlines and gave them a chance to refer to him as 'a fiery sporting gentleman'.

He took a special service for members and supporters of the football clubs of Leicester, instigated by the Tigers. He took for his text 'They went every one straight forward'. He referred to various sports and ended up with the 'straight forward pull of the oarsman.

Yet it's the little beggar who sits facing you who generally settles the destiny of the race.'

Rosslyn joined all the 'Fancy' clubs in Nottingham and started others. When asked in one what he would like in return for his actual hard manual work, he asked for a united attendance at a Fanciers' church service, at which he deprecated 'swindlers and fakers who reduced a beautiful hobby to a business full of temptation'.

When a coal strike broke out, Henry Bentiened asked Rosslyn to meet the miners' committee, as he already knew so many of the men through 'The Fancys' to try and persuade them to be reasonable. 'The only prospect I can think of getting them to agree to arbitration is to get a guarantee from the mine owners that a really impartial chairman would not be objected to by them.'

Rosslyn addressed the strikers at Clifton pit, where for nearly six months men and boys had struggled for what they felt were their rights. He attended numerous meetings and conferences and addressed them forcibly. He said the respect he gained for the collier at the age of four was something he retained to that day. He had the utmost respect for men who fed him by working with their hands as his audience respected any who worked with legs or brains. The people he did not respect were the idlers 'whether dukes or tramps. If a man will not work neither let him eat.' There was loud applause. Rosslyn then turned the accusation on the strikers, producing loud laughter. The men had made friends with Rosslyn in a way that made it possible for them to re-open discussions. When the strike was settled Henry Bentiened invited Rosslyn to side volubly with 'gondoliers against steamers for Venice', which cause he supported with enthusiasm.

Rosslyn was secretary of the Church Extension Society for Nottinghamshire and the Bishop wrote congratulating him on his report as being 'really quite exciting and I want you to understand how grateful I am to you for all that you have done so well and so willingly too'. Later he wrote: 'I will give you a medal if you can get every church in. You're not far off success.'

CHAPTER TWELVE

Macedonian Sorrow

Excitement ran high at Clifton Hall when Mary Murray, housekeeper
and general factotum also at Downhill, discovered in an attic a six-
foot-high sack crammed with crumpled papers and parchments that
had been undisturbed for at least a century. Rosslyn was there when
Nellie Bruce turned them out on to the floor. They seemed to have
been stuffed in as though for waste paper and many were affected
by damp and decay.

The letters were carefully ironed and read with fascination by the
whole family. There was a strange jumble covering a period of six
hundred years, including family deeds of the thirteenth, fourteenth
and fifteenth centuries, long memoranda of political events in Central
Europe in the seventeenth century, correspondence with Queen
Elizabeth and Charles I, and a translation of a chit from Cardinal
Richelieu recommending a footman.

There was a reference to Charles I's stay at Clifton in 1632, and
the great pleasure 'the kinge tooke in his intertainment was in your
barge and watermen'. There was a letter from the King himself
written from Hampton Court in 1634, addressed to 'Our Trustie
and wellbeloved' Sir Gervase Clifton, asking him to look into a
marriage arrangement to see whether the bride approved of the
choice of her father, Sir Henry Willoughby. Sir Gervase answered
that she 'affecteth Sir John Suckling above other men and doth love
him to marry him'.

The Bruces found a contemporary description of Sir John Suckling
by his friend Davenant:

The greatest gallant of his time, the greatest gamester both for
bowling and cards so that no shopkeeper would trust him for

6d, as today, for instance he might by winning be worth £200 and the next day he might not be worth half so much or perhaps be sometimes minus nihilo. He was of middle stature and slight strength, brisk, round-eyed, reddish face and red nosed. His head not very big, his hair a kind of sand colour.

In fact Lady Anne soon tired of him and appealed to another suitor to try to obtain Suckling's written renunciation of all claim to her hand. The rivals met in a London Street, argued, quarrelled and proceeded to blows. 'The unhappy Suckling was cudgelled into a handful' and died, unmarried, a man of broken fortunes.

As past president of the Strafford Society at Oxford, the greatest joy to Rosslyn was a series of letters beginning 'My dear brother,' to Sir Gervase from the Earl of Strafford, when he was Lord Lieutenant of Ireland, before he was impeached and finally, with the consent of King Charles I, beheaded.

Rosslyn helped with the sorting, and eventually the letters were sent to the Public Records Office and published as a command paper and presented to both Houses of Parliament by command of His Majesty in 1914.

Inspired by their discovery Rosslyn wrote a history of the parish and the family of the Cliftons of Clifton with extracts from the works of the two Clifton poets, Beaumont and Kirkenwhite. It was published in 1906, illustrated with drawings and photographs. In one, captioned 'The Author at Play', Rosslyn is seen with his wolfhound, a rabbit, a tortoise and Purity on his hand. He stands beneath a dovecote wearing a Norfolk jacket, a sporting tie with a loose collar and grey flannels.

The book was well received and reviewed, though with reservations from the Dean of Christchurch, Oxford, who wrote 'I think you have done a really valuable bit of work and cordially congratulate you upon it', but he ventured to hope that the author at play might look a little bit more clerical. 'Not necessarily a cassock but a somewhat *less aggressivly* lay costume,' he suggested. In fact this was only a restrained version of Rosslyn's country attire which sometimes included knickerbockers and thick woollen stockings and a huge broad-brimmed felt hat like a cowboy's, unlike his brothers Douglas and Lloydie's shallow black soup plates which were still sported by most Edwardian clergymen. Sometimes Rosslyn wore a dashing bow tie and, adorned with a parrot or two and his ring-tailed lemur would be seen about the village with the eager look of one ready for the next adventure.

Rosslyn spent a lively week-end at Dieppe with Nigel and some of his theatrical crowd. Merrily they all came down to breakfast in their dressing-gowns, the ladies' nightwear being as ornate as their evening dress—all except one. May Martyn, small, pretty and understudying Nina Boucicault as the original Peter in Barrie's *Peter Pan*, wore a simple childlike flannel night-gown with one prim button at the neck. Rosslyn said it was this one button that was Nigel's undoing. Nigel and May became engaged and asked Rosslyn to marry them at Tunbridge Wells, from Nigel's grandmother's house.

Nigel, Rosslyn and Arthur Hutchinson, who was to be best man, (later editor of the *Windsor Magazine*) stayed at the Spa Hotel. They had all been at Worcester College together. Next day they set off in an elderly hansom for the wedding. Nigel always said afterwards that the wheel came off, but Rosslyn insisted that the bottom fell out, and that Nigel arrived at his wedding 'his little legs running to keep up with the startled horse'. At the ceremony, Nigel was accused of taking the hand of the chief bridesmaid, Elfrida Clemens from force of habit, as he was nightly married to her on the stage in the play they were both in at the time.

Noel Buxton wrote saying he was standing for Parliament for Whitby: 'I wish you could stand politics because I must be at Tyne-mouth collecting canvases during the election. After that I am on for week-ends and any nights I am free.'

On a gaily flagged electioneering card Noel looked out, handsome and alert, his red hair and moustaches neat, and humour in his Buxton eyes. Though Rosslyn would not involve himself politically in public he helped Lota Law to compose an election song 'Vote vote for No(e)lio!' to be sung to the air of 'Oh, oh Antonio!'

> Vote, vote for Nolio!
> Tories ain't for me;
> Tariff's the dolio
> That they extolio.

We want the Staff of Life and our imports free
Then up we'll go to the pollio
And return N.B.

Work, work for Nolio!
He's the boy for me:
Their regmarolio
Don't attract my soulio:

We want the House of Lords to leave the people free
So up we go to the pollio
And return N.B.

Noel kept in touch throughout the 1905 election and on Election Day a telegram arrived at Clifton Rectory—BUXTON WINS MAJORITY 445.

Though Rosslyn would not make electioneering speeches, Noel had no difficulty in persuading him to become Secretary of the Macedonian Guild, whose object was to foster prayer and interest in the Christian subjects of the Turkish Empire.

Noel was frantically grinding his old axe, the Bulgarian atrocities. 'Do rub in the abominable conditions of the peasants of Macedonia in normal times and our responsibilities. Also that a fleet in the Bosporus does not mean war but protection.' Telegrams flew from Noel's home at Upshire, in Essex. WILL YOU TAKE OPPORTUNITY OF EXPLAINING APPEAL FOR PRAYERS. DO SEND SOMETHING FOR ME. QUOTE BISHOPS. NOEL.

Rosslyn wrote a piece founded on Kathleen's letters and Noel replied from 10, Adelphi Terrace. 'My dear Pater, *Well done*, I am delighted. Send 50 for the exhibition quickly. You are a brick and 2,000 slips about it. The personal messages are honey to my soul but must not appear please. They do harm. Ever yours, Noel.'

Rosslyn went up to the Lake District to speak on behalf of the Macedonian Guild at meetings at Keswick, Workington and Barrow. There was still a coach and horses running from Windermere to Keswick, which Rosslyn made delighted use of. He went on to preach at St. Anne's, Soho, and the Saint wrote:

My dear Bruce,

I was so sorry to miss you after the service. It was very touching and gratifying to see the welcome accorded to you by your friends of St. Anne's and not the least by your poorer friends. There has never been a larger congregation in St. Anne's at the week night except when Dean Garrett preached in 1892. I thank you sincerely for so generously putting into the offertory what I gave you for your travelling expenses. If you ever get a Sunday off I hope you will be able to come to St. Anne's and give us a sermon or two.

Affectionately yours, J. H. Cardwell.

Later that year Rosslyn agreed to visit Macedonia with Noel to see for himself.

Rosslyn, cherishing his Greek blood with pride, spent his last night in England appropriately at Thrumpton, the house of the Rev. Lord Byron whose romantic ancestor the poet had died fighting for liberty in Greece. Rosslyn wrote almost daily to Kathleen.

'Noel makes a most delightful and comfortable companion with his tireless capacity for sitting still under trying emergencies always bringing us to the top. His "forgettery" is sometimes even more valuable than his super memory especially when he "forgets every language except his own".'

They travelled with an Armenian who had only escaped from the massacre by pretending to be dead (which he demonstrated) by covering himself with corpses.

In Belgrade Rosslyn went to a wedding at the cathedral. 'It was like an English garden party. They were all standing in little knots talking. There was no music except the stentorian voice of a priest standing alone repeating prayers, who seemed to be entirely ignored by the whole party. It struck me as a cold and artificial ceremony!'

He was more pleased with the green frogs croaking along the banks of the Danube and the armies of bright green lizards in the old grey stone.

From Prilap, forty miles from a railway station, in spite of his wideawake hat and loose bow tie, he wrote:

Riding fourteen hours a day across mountain paths in sweltering
heat, you have to be thankful for having invested in a pale blue
cotton parasol. I wonder if you used what we call the 'Buxton
Teaser' at night? A calico bag, with no outlet whatever except a
space of some three inches for eyes, nose and mouth. This outlet
is protected by a layer of vaseline and Keatings powder, and one
sleeps serenely, sometimes hearing a thud, as one of the enemy drops
from the ceiling on to one's chest, hunts for an outlet, perhaps
discovers the Keatings and retires hurt.

The party to start with included Mr. and Mrs. Lothaire de
Bunsen and Jean MacNaughton, author of *The Lame Dogs Diary*.
The ladies, wearing topees, rode astride or followed in the baggage
cart, a medieval-looking tumbrel. Four poles had been roughly stuck
in the corners and a large rush mat fixed over them for shade. Noel,
in straw basher and Norfolk jacket attended them in the baggage
cart or led the horse.

They visited a dagger bazaar where a thriving business was done
in a primitive workshop, thatched on one side with leaves.

At one village Noel and Rosslyn were arrested by a Greek soldier.
Noel insisted on photographing Rosslyn sitting on a wall, hand-
cuffed and looking somewhat disconsolate. Beside him sat a soldier
with a rifle, looking perplexed and not sure whether he had done
right. The camera decided him and after questioning, in sign
language, he let them go.

It was all still on a bubbling almost holiday note. Suddenly the
tone changed.

We went to see the victims of an outrage in a village about five
hours from Monastir in which a band of 150, led by Turks,
attacked and destroyed the village of Smilevo. Till Sunday there
were about eighty families and now all but eight, we are told,
have fled to the towns. Among those we saw hidden in the Bulgarian cottages was one old woman, lying dying with a bullet
through her back who kissed my hand effusively, and murmured
blessings for having come to sympathise with her. Another old
couple had knife wounds. The old wife was lying groaning with

pain and high fever but the doctor brought with us injected morphine and she began to sing what we were told was a martial and rather bloodthirsty song. Saw a very beautiful young woman still in her gala clothes, with her head wounded. Her husband told us very realistically how she had been shot in his presence. We were able to provide a bottle for her baby, which since the accident had had no milk. The young man, aged eighteen had a terrible wound rapidly mortifying in his arm and hands. His fiancée sat with a set firm face beside him. His brother was brushing off the flies which were swarming round his only partially dressed wound. The doctor hesitated over amputation as death was inevitable any way. Round his bedside we heard disgusting accounts of devilry perpetrated on half-dead nude women and of tiny boys and girls who had been hacked to death in the most gruesome and unspeakable way.

Of these five not one was alive when we came back to Monastir four days later. Next day we started off at 4 a.m. riding without baggage for thirty miles and flattered ourselves we had escaped an escort, but wrongly; we were followed by mountain zaptieh. We arrived to find Smilevo in ruins with a few men only left who followed us round with dim eyes. No place was the wall more than ten feet high, mostly four feet. The graveyard contained the victims of Sunday's massacre, mostly foreshortened. Several children, including a girl of thirteen with five wounds in her breast. We saw the bullet holes perforating the walls and one cellar, where two visitors from another village hid themselves but were caught and killed, showed the marks of hatchet work outside the door, gruesome stains where they had finally been stabbed, and another house where four women had been bayoneted. There was a quaint little priest who had three times escaped after his house had been burnt to the ground. Already he was beginning to rebuild.

And so the letters continued, one after another of horrors.

On a fourteen-hour ride up the Baboona mountain, Rosslyn's grey pony kept up with the soldiers accompanying them, but when his escort suddenly left for the barracks behind them, the rest of the party, assuming that he was with the soldiers, went on.

My tired pony being unable to keep up I found myself alone and lost. Coming to four crossroads and myself thoroughly tired out, I think I've seldom felt more destitute. However I proved to be only two miles from the stopping place and for the last mile I found a guide on horseback. The combination of darkness, my own loneliness and the sudden absence of the elaborate escort combined with the assurance of the excessive danger of the country, both from brigands, komits and wild animals, made me thankful when I was joined by a Captain. When I asked the name of the village through which we passed he shrugged his shoulders and said 'Allah himself is glad to forget the name of these abominable villages. Can you expect me to remember?' Sought in vain for a gift for him and found at last a card case made, though I did not tell him so, of Russian leather which dear Jean had given me in Soho. I parted with it with the greatest regret, but felt bound to give him something for leading me in the right direction.

'On the next ride I was forming a little advance guard, riding on a grey with four soldiers, also on greys, on each side. Our party of nine had been marching for some hours in front unable to converse. To pass the time I began to whistle, and then to sing. I began with 'Lead Kindly Light' which I sang throughout but at the end a soldier said 'English musica' and proceeded to wave his hands slowly and gloomily in front of his very mournful face and 'Turk she musica' and waved his hands gladly, smiling brightly. Taking his hint I sang a very jaunty air, only the refrain of which I remembered – 'Her golden hair was hanging down her back.' There were many hours to spend marching over the dusty roads and when Noel reappeared to join us he was astonished to witness an English clergyman marching at the head of eight Mohammedan soldiers all vigorously singing words and tune of 'Onward Christian Soldiers marching as to War'.

Noel insisted on calling the dragoman we took with us 'the curate' chiefly, I think, because he wears long black skirts. They speak in many words but he is absolutely incapable of making himself intelligible in any tongue. He can kill chickens, pluck and cook them and in an incredibly short time, but always disappears into thin air if you attempt to rebuke or instruct him.

Rosslyn preached at Thessalonika in English with three interpreters, Bulgarian, Greek and Serbian and visited an orphanage to which no children were admitted unless both parents had been murdered. They were aged from five to fourteen, boys with their hair cropped and the girls with their hair scraped back. There was not a smile from any of them as they looked away from their visitors, lost, and, in the little boys' faces, hope only for revenge. A dark 'warder' stayed with them as though at the ready. Rosslyn tried to bring a smile from one little girl with plaits and for a moment she looked a little more alert, though still unsmiling.

In a tobacco factory Rosslyn thanked heaven for the Factory Laws at home. 'Child labour, ye Gods! cornea, rickets and every form of disease! Poor mites, they seemed hardly sufficiently human to extract one's full sympathy. There is no doubt one does get hardened here to the *slower* forms of murder!'

They went to the prisons—underground caves with no ventilation where untried prisoners were herded together—but they were not admitted. Visitors were only allowed to see those out for an hour's airing, on whose return, free fights took place for positions nearest the wall so that they may have something to lean on, for if a man lay on the floor he seldom rose again, so great was the overcrowding and starvation.

'Early in the morning we saw a wounded Bulgarian shot by a Turk in his own garden, as an act of reprisal. His father had been shot in the same place in the same way. The father was dead and for our victim there seemed little hope.'

At Drama they stayed at an historical little house where jackdaws, doves, cats and dogs peopled the roofs and inquisitively watched the strangers. 'Opposite the restaurant where the sensational bomb was thrown by the Bulgarians last month, the windows are still shattered.'

They spent a few days in Sofia, the capital of Bulgaria and there saw the whole army manoeuvring, some 40,000 men. They had a long interview with the Prime Minister who assured them that 400,000 soldiers could be put in the field at the shortest possible notice if need be!

They proceeded to Constantinople by train, travelling at about twenty miles an hour between a row of sentries, standing at attention every few hundred yards to keep watch for dynamite outrages. Here more complaints of the physical tortures in the Turkish prisons, were only hearsay. Rosslyn heard, on unimpeachable authority, of a western doctor being sent for late at night, to attend a Turkish palace; being taken in a curtained cab and driven he knew not where; being shown into a magnificent room where an expectant mother was waiting his services. The baby was successfully born and was taken from his hands by a Turk, apparently the head of the establishment, who, quickly and quite unconcernedly, broke its back across his knee and flung it on the floor and then calmly handed the doctor the sum of a hundred pounds and with a smile shook hands and bid him adieu. As he went out the doctor was warned that any inquiries would only cause 'trouble to himself'—indicating his throat would be cut.

Rosslyn did not go to see the Sultan at the Selamilim, as most Europeans do, partly due to his own feelings of the impropriety of joining in what appeared to be almost recognition of the Divine origin of his authority. But he did visit the Pope—'that is the Greek Ecumenical Patriarch'.

A letter arrived for the Rev. F. R. Bruce—'Rev. Sir, I am begged to inform you that His Holiness will be pleased to receive you tomorrow morning at about 9 o'clock. At a quarter before 9 I shall come to the hotel to accompany you, if you wish it, to the Patriarch at Fanor. I remain, Yours faithfully, Dr. Theotokas, *Avocat.*'

I spent nearly two hours tête-à-tête in an interview with the Greek Ecumenical Patriarch, conducted mostly in Greek, which I was largely able to understand. He also provided an English-speaking secretary. As the head of the Church he condemned strongly the action of any priest who took part in warlike organisations and assured me strict orders to that effect had been issued by the patriarchate. If these orders were disobeyed, he said, I must remember that priests were often peasants, closely related to those who had suffered. He denied in toto that orders had been given by any of the priests to the brigand bands but when I instanced episcopal warehousing of rifles, he reminded me that the Bulgarian episcopal palaces were full of rifles too. He thought that peace and goodwill amongst men was not for the present, when the Turk was doing nothing for reform and the Bulgarian trying to push the Greek into the sea. The King of England, he thought, was probably the only man sufficiently disinterested and powerful to relieve the miseries of Macedonia. His Holiness thought truth rather than love was the aspect of Christianity it was the duty of his church to emphasise. Before I left he bade me tell him something. 'Why the English are such friends of Bulgaria and why they have left their love of Greece.' I urged in answer that all our instincts were for sympathy with Greece; our classical system of education and love of the Greek romance; our conduct in the War of Independence and the memory of Byron and the modern policy associated with the memory of Mr. Gladstone. But the present attitude of Greece (the belligerent priesthood and cruelty to men and women) was constantly alienating sympathy. He shook hands with me warmly twice when I left and seemed to resist any attempt on my part to express physically the obeisance which I thought due. For this I was grateful to him.

On Rosslyn's way back to the hotel a man slipped a letter into his hand and disappeared. The letter was badly typed on squared paper headed Constantinople. It read:

Reverend:

If really you are interested for the victims of attrocities of Anchialos be so kind as to go this afternoon on board the S/S MICALI = of the Steamship Co, John Macdouall and Barbour, moored alongside the Galata Quay and sailing tomorrow for Piraeus. This steamer is the tenth that carries the remaining victims of Anchialos emigrating. They are hungry, naked and barefooted and penniless. Hundreds more are expected by the next steamers arriving from Bourgas, suffering from the Bulgarian authorities— persecution, and imprisoned and hindered to depart, succeeding to this only with bribery. Compassion ought to be impartial for the Christian, and it is hoped that you will kindly accede to our prayer and go on board the S/S MICALI. The agent or the Captain

'The hard-riding type of parson often showed hunting boots under his surplice.' Rosslyn on Aerial, on which he hunted regularly with the Rufford.

Clifton Hall in 1906, now a girls' secondary modern school.

The Glebe, Clifton, where Rosslyn lived before he moved to the Rectory.

we are sure will help you to this. You will then hear from the victims themselves what is true, so much so as they are of the poor ignorant and innocent mob the victims, and NOT DIPLOMATS MAY GOD HELP YOU

Thanking you sincerely,

we are,

CHRISTIAN FRIENDS

Rosslyn went at once with Noel and found everything as the letter had said. There in the pit of the ship were masses of half-clothed, struggling hungry women and tiny babies. 'There was nothing we could do but bear witness.'

National newspapers issued various accounts of Noel and Rosslyn in most complimentary terms calling them 'apostles of humanity' and representing them as being capable of far more benefit than they knew they could ever be. About a dozen national leaders came to see them off at the station, besides the British residents.

They went on to Berlin where the British Ambassador, Sir Francis Lascelles, and the Greek Ambassador, Cleon Rangabee, Rosslyn's cousin, were both exceedingly attentive to their needs. It was Cleon who had won the drama prize in the Olympics when Rosslyn was at Oxford, and who, with his mother, had sought refuge at Barton Rectory just before Rosslyn's birth. 'He is a delightful mixture of an enterprising Greek and a canny Scot and is recognised as a real literary and dramatic power as well as a diplomatic success,' Rosslyn said.

They saw many of the leading pressmen in Berlin and did what little they could to inspire interest in the depressed nations. Noel said: 'I am as convinced as ever that the only solution of the problem lies in the inevitable expulsion of the Turks, and the division of the country into Albanian, Greek, Servian and Bulgarian parts.'

Rosslyn and Kathleen's letters were published together on his return home as *Letters from Turkey, being glimpses of Macedonian misery by Rosslyn Bruce, and his sister Kathleen*. Rosslyn also toured the country lecturing on his experiences, backed by outlines of the political situation in Turkey as interpreted by Benjie. People were fired by the lectures, put money in the plate and promised to pray. They then went away and forgot.

CHAPTER THIRTEEN

Fall Upon Fall

It was now January 1907. Benjie Bruce, on diplomatic leave from Vienna, said that: 'Things will continue to dribble on in Turkey until we fight Germany which is absolutely inevitable though it may be 5 or even 10 years.'

'Benjie's views,' Rosslyn told Noel, 'were spasmodically interrupted by diatribes against these rascals who have made that miserable moth-eaten heaven-forsaken cub of a boundering earthworm, Bryce, into a British Ambassador. Benjie is a very dear fellow all the same.'

Rosslyn and Kathleen both now went through a period of the doldrums, following tremendous popularity and some fame, which both found dry in the mouth. Kathleen's work was being exhibited widely and selling well. Rosslyn's preaching, lecturing and writing was in great demand. People fêted them both wherever they went. But it was not enough. Both had a yearning now to settle, but neither had found a permanent mate. Kathleen said she wanted a father for her son. That was all. Rosslyn said he wanted a mother and baby all rolled into one. Bright clever letters poured in from Noel's sister Mabel. When they met she bubbled and enthused, but Rosslyn felt himself being gobbled up by her. He liked Mabel, he admired her, he looked forward to seeing her. When they parted he felt himself all over with relief that he was still safe. That applied to other good-looking, well-born young ladies. It was the little fluffy, childlike girls in the theatre or in the Nottingham shops or helping his sister Podge to nurse in Scarborough who really charmed him in the way that his newly-hatched baby chickens did. And yet he was still looking for his lost mother. Kathleen was very like her. Old photographs showed Janie Skene when a girl, with all Kathleen's strong good looks and charm. But Kathleen was now unique and anyway, though he loved her company, worried about her, taught her and discussed everything on God's earth with her, if another girl like her turned up she would not really make the right kind of wife for him. She was too independent, too eccentric, too unconventional, in fact too much like himself. And now, almost simultaneously, both went through periods of severe pain.

Kathleen was suddenly whisked into hospital with acute appendicitis. A nurse asked her if there was anyone she would like to see and thought she was delirious when she replied, 'No thanks, no one, except perhaps Bernard Shaw but he's out of London.' She was asked if she would like to see a clergyman and said 'God forbid!' whereupon Rosslyn turned up and would have been hustled away if she had not shown such relief. 'Sorry,' she said. 'He's my brother. I'd forgotten he was a clergyman.' On the way to the operating theatre she said, 'You *will* leave me enough inside to make a son one day?'

At Clifton Rosslyn had a new horse and hunted fairly regularly.

'The old-fashioned hard-riding type of parson who often showed hunting boots under his surplice is no longer with us,' the chairman of a Nottingham temperance meeting said, with Rosslyn on the platform beside him on his way back from hunting. Rosslyn's name appeared frequently among the great names of the field of the Earl of Harrington's pack, the Rufford.

On October 21st the Rufford met at Ruddington, where hounds drew a spinney near the churchyard. They found but the fox then took refuge in a drain. Most of the hunt left the spot, only to hear a few minutes later that the fox had bolted. Some of the followers accordingly turned back. A fairly stiff fence had to be negotiated and as the Rev. Rosslyn Bruce's mount was landing on the opposite side it pecked and the rider was shot over the animal's head, [reported the local paper under *Serious Accident to Popular Preacher*]. His foot caught in the stirrup and the horse lashed out, kicking Mr. Bruce on the thigh. Dr. Coughlan of Nottingham, who was riding alongside, saw at once that the injury was serious and a thorough examination showed that the bone was fractured.

He improvised splints from hunting crops and Mr. Bruce was conveyed to his home in the Earl of Harrington's motor car. The car then went on into Nottingham to fetch Dr. Stanley Tresseder, who came back with splints and set the limb properly.

The pain that Rosslyn endured was something he could not have imagined, even in Macedonia.

The *Daily Telegraph* reported: 'Misfortunes often seem to come in groups and the accident in the hunting field to the popular clergyman, always in great request in Nottingham and district, was followed by injury in a more vital part to Lord Manvers and on Saturday, with the Pytchley, Lord Chesham met a similar fate, though one of the best riders in England.'

Rosslyn's sister Gwen came at once from Binton, but one nurse was not enough for him. He slept badly and required attention by night as well as day. By now his little Scarborough friend, Chloe Hulton was a trained nurse and accordingly she was dispatched from Scarborough by his sister, Podge. The local papers gave a daily bulletin of Rosslyn's progress. 'The limbs have been subjected to the X-rays and the process revealed an acutely oblique fracture.' 'His general condition is about the same but no visitors are admitted.'

Lady Manvers wrote inquiring after him. Lord Manvers was recovering from concussion. Two Sunday School admirers wrote: 'Dear Mr. Bruce, Enid and I are so sorry you have had such a bad accident. We didn't mean anything unkind when we said "It serves Turther right". We only meant it for a joke. Perhaps Daddy will bring us to see you some day. Best love and kisses.'

His actress friends wrote with all-embracing sympathy, and Mabel Buxton wrote to cheer him:

The feeling of degradation and pain comes from all the unexpected and horrible feeble impatient petulant little bits of one's character which all come running uppermost when anything goes wrong which puts one out of love with oneself. I think perhaps that strong doses of R. L. Stevenson would help to pull oneself together. Such a tonic for all mental and moral croppers! I think we all ought to fall off our horses or be horse-whipped occasionally.

I know I ought and parsons, to be of any use to miserable people, must be the better for occasional bouts of pain.

This was the end of Mabel.

Hundreds of letters came from all his friends and admirers but dearest of all, as always, were Lota's loving, playful imaginative comforts.

Rosslyn was a poor patient, refusing treatment and often hysterical with pain and frustration. He soon cast aside the weights set up to apply traction to the leg. Even Chloe's pleadings that the shortening of the leg would ruin his beautiful physique, his athletics, and worst of all, his dancing, made no difference. He just could not or would not endure the extra pain of the stretching of the limb.

The surgeon wanted to re-break and set the leg, for his own professional honour if for no other reason, but the very idea of another operation turned Rosslyn faint. When his brothers and sisters, friends, parishioners and fans flocked to see him even when there were fifty letters in one day, he still felt neglected and alone. Noel sent frequent telegrams: 'HEAVEN BLESS AND RELIEVE YOU.' 'YOU CAN HARDLY FEEL IT IS GOD'S WILL YET.'

Just before Christmas, Sir Hervey Bruce died at Downhill, having previously explained to Rosslyn how he wished him to conduct his funeral when the day came. The fact that Rosslyn could not carry out this last wish in return for his eccentric old uncle's special affection and interest, only added to his feeling of ineffectual depression.

Early in the new year Noel wrote: 'My dear old R., I have been hoping to get more news in reply to my inquiry and was horrified to hear yesterday that you were worse again. I hope your secretary, when this meets his or her eye, will send me a line if you are not well enough to dictate. It is very sad to have you suffering and I long to hear it over. The agony of Macedonia is actually worse than last year. Let us give the guild a shove when you are about again,' and he made a whole list of excited suggestions for further work.

But Rosslyn could not bear to think of the suffering in Macedonia. It made him sick to be reminded of it. He tried to return to the work for his D.D. He had once playfully said only a broken leg would keep him at his desk long enough to deal with all his writing with ease. Now he was unable even to get near his desk and the pain and shock dulled his capacity for concentration. In an effort that completely failed to write a sacred poem he did, however, win a prize in *Football Post* with:

There were some proud Hotspurs of Tottenham
Whose backers once thought they'd put a lot on'm.
Now unless I'm a liar
They feel a bit shier,
Yes, shy'o'the shire of Nottingham.

Once he was on crutches he was able to demonstrate to Chloe that he could still dance in spite of two or three inches of shrinkage of the leg.

In March Noel wrote saying 'Would you use my ripping farm house near Cromer? My tenants let lodgings and I have jolliest rooms. I would come for week-ends. Tell me what sort of abode you contemplate? Sea? warmth? Yours ever N.'

On Ash Wednesday, nearly five months after the accident, he was walking again and Chloe returned home. Two days later Noel took him to Cromer and settled him into West Runton Old Hall while he went off to canvass for his brother Charles, at Teignmouth. Meanwhile he had alerted some of his relations in Norfolk and asked them to call on his incapacitated friend. Noel's grandmother, Lady Buxton of Colne House, Cromer, was first to arrive and offered her carriage whenever he needed it. Then from Northrepps Hall came Noel's aunt, while Rosslyn was out looking at wild fowl. Next day he accepted Lady Buxton's offer of the carriage to return the call, taking with him the aunt's visiting card, lightly embossed 'Mrs. Richard Gurney, Miss Rachel Gurney, Miss Richenda Gurney, Northrepps Hall.' Rosslyn asked the coachman whether they were three old ladies. The coachman gave a wheezy old chuckle and said they certainly were not. Rosslyn's spirits rose as the carriage lumbered along Northrepps Avenue with wood pigeons cooing in the oaks and elms whose buds were just beginning to burst. Ducks on the walled pond which they passed as they approached the house gave further encouragement.

In the drawing room at Northrepps Hall he met his hostess, a tall sweet-faced widow of middle age. She led him through the open french windows into the garden where he first saw her eldest daughter, Rachel, aged twenty-one, golden-haired and blue-eyed with a milk and roses complexion, elegantly dressed in scarlet silk and surrounded by dogs and little girls. Richenda, two years younger, was smaller, plumper and more shy, but their twelve-year-old sister Gladys, fair and frail, and her more robust schoolroom companion, Taffy, came bounding up to introduce themselves. There were aviaries in the garden and birds in huge cages in the hall, there was warmth and jollity. Sunday School hymnbooks and texts mixed with the luxury of this branch of the Gurney banking family.

Rosslyn recognised at once traits from Augustus Hare's *The Gurneys of Earlham*—bubbling, fashionably dressed, reckless-riding but Sunday-School-teaching young women, with less regard for convention than the daughters of the landowners in the shires he had hitherto visited. Mrs. Gurney's reaction to hearing that Noel had returned to London was characteristic. Noel's guest must stay to lunch and when lunch proved a riotous success, he must come back and stay for three days. Rachel went to fetch him next day from West Runton Old Hall in the dog cart.

In those three days Rosslyn endeared himself to the family and they to him. The special care that Rachel and her mother felt he needed—Rachel had recently had a hunting accident too—was cancelled out by the hardening-up process inflicted by the younger girls who stole his sticks and dared him to try to walk without them. To test his self-confessed ability to commune with the birds, a bantam cock was concealed overnight in his laundry basket to surprise him at dawn with its penetrating crow.

Rosslyn returned to Clifton a happier man and followed up his success in his usual way by sending, not flowers, but livestock.

Dear Mr. Bruce, [Rachel wrote on April 8th, 1908]
Many thanks for the rabbits which arrived quite safely last night. Gladys and Taffy are going to thank you. They seem to have so much to say that I shouldn't think the letter will be sent off before Sunday at least, and so they decided I must tell you they

have arrived. I have been reading your book on the Macedonians, what perfectly horrible accounts. Why didn't you tell us more about it when you were here? I believe I'm going to have a dachshund puppy. I have been craving for a dog of my own since my little terrier got shot.

Yours very sincerely, Rachel Gurney.

Dear Lady, [Rosslyn replied]

Four rabbits are well spent on four pages of nice letter and if les petites filles also write I shall have my interest in full. I didn't tell you about Macedonia because I wanted to see you cheerful and happy at first at any rate. And because it makes me feel ill. Noel wants me to give up Clifton and devote all my time preaching the need of English help for the Macedonians. I shall anyhow stay here this summer till I am strong again. Mrs. Wodehouse and her daughter are going to write and ask a Miss Gurney from Cromer way to come and spend a week with them at Gotham. I do hope she'll come because then I should see her perhaps. My naughty horse, Audrey, is being sold this morning. I still have Black Beauty. Unless you tell me not to I shall write to you again soon.

Yours very sincerely.

He returned to the pulpit six months after the accident. Wherever he went he was congratulated on his recovery though he walked, as he did for the rest of his days, with a very pronounced limp. After his accident he refused to ride a mare again.

On Easter Sunday he was five hours without leaving the church, with a hundred and twenty communicants and no help. It was hardly surprising that he collapsed during dinner at the hall that evening. 'He must have eaten something indigestible,' said his cousin, the new Sir Hervey, but his wife Nellie, whom Rosslyn referred to as 'My sort of mother' sent him off to bed in charge of a footman and he completely recovered after a good night's sleep.

'Dear Miss Gurney,' he wrote next, 'How splendid! You really are coming to Gotham! How often will it be becoming for me to come over? I shall want to be there all the time if you're there, except when you come and inspect my hutch.'

On June 1st, Rachel arrived at Gotham with her lady's maid in attendance to send her down to the drawing room looking well groomed, but she felt singularly out of place off her own home ground. It was the first time in her life she had not been backed up by hordes of Gurney, Buxton and Barclay relations. The Wodehouses were kind and thoughtful but the time dragged between Rosslyn's visits and yet when he came, she always seemed to be preoccupied with others. When somebody mentioned that he would be preaching at St. Anne's, Soho, the following week she said, trying to make it sound casual, that she would be in London with her family and might come and listen.

My dear Miss Gurney, [Rosslyn wrote from London after she had appeared at St. Anne's]

Of course I saw you in church and nearly invented some excuse to stop and speak to you before the service when I passed close to you on the way to the vestry, but feared you would feel a little uncomfy as there were so many St. Anne's people whom I didn't speak to. It was simply maddening not seeing you at all to speak to. After the service they took me away to conduct two meetings. Of course, course, course, I was very conscious of your presence all the time and thinking every moment whether you were approving.

Two days later he insisted:

Having your face down and being behind a pillar doesn't make it a bit harder to know what you are thinking about. We do not half understand wireless telepathy yet! If I have a particular sound and proper and rather quaint sort of thought in my mind, I know that it has come from you, because I don't keep that particular brand of thought in my own mind. Some minds give out thought circles of about the same size and when the circles fit one another in the air and vibrate against the other circles they affect the mind and let its owner know there are other such thoughts about. My dear lady did you ever know anyone who talked so much nonsense as this devoted lunatic?

Rachel then persuaded her mother to invite him to a relation's episcopal enthronement which, when it was postponed, was converted into tickets to the Horse Show in London.

Your last letter came in the afternoon, [he wrote], and after reading it I was singing just as loud and as happily as I possibly could and Triplets heard me and said very humbly: 'Excuse me but have you had any disturbing correspondence?' 'Very', I said, 'a letter that has done me good', and then, you will hardly believe it, he actually dared to say 'I shall have to ask Miss Gurney to write only in the mornings when no one is up.' Wasn't it frightful cheek? I have signed *Yours sincerely* without a *very* because there are not any degrees of sincerity. If I am sincere that's as much as I can be always. If the letter ends primly it is so much easier to say friendlier things inside without startling you. I am glad you were thrilled about the sweated labour. It is because of that that I get into trouble here with my very comfortable relations and am called a Radical and a Socialist and the cruelty of letting it go on while we, or some of us, eat and drink far too much makes me howl and howl with indignation and then I say so but it does no good. They only think I'm mad and then I have to learn that talk won't help but just go on simply helping others and fighting against one's own love and comfiness and luxury. Some days I want to burn my Sunday clothes, don't you?

This was a dig that did not go unnoticed in a young lady whose elegant clothes had hitherto occupied so much of her thoughts.

On May 19th Rosslyn went to Oxford for a week to take the final part of his D.D.—the last of a series of 'exercises' given orally by the University, partly based on his own published works which included his new book *Dr. Gore on Education*. He returned to Clifton at the end of the week a Doctor of Divinity. He was now Dr. Rosslyn Bruce but Rachel stuck to Mr. Bruce, though most of his friends who did not use his Christian name still called him Brucie.

In June he preached for his brother Lloydie at Binton. In Lloydie's and Gwen's twin hands the little rectory seemed anything but damp. Wreathed in creeper and proetcted by trees, its garden which strayed into the churchyard, was wild and lush. There were trout in the stream, the waterfall sang all night, the timbered barn was half full of hay and everything in the little rectory was soft with the velvety family dust. Kathleen was there too and went for a long walk with Rosslyn down by the River Avon, where wild forget-me-knots bloomed on the islands left after the spring floods. Rosslyn told Kathleen he was in love. So was she. But this time it was serious. So was hers. She had met him a few years before at a luncheon of Aubrey Beardsley's sister, Mabel's. Now Mabel had asked her to tea because he would be there—not that he was the kind of man to go out to tea. She had nothing suitable to wear so had turned two hats into one and cut up a handkerchief into a white collar and cuffs. Con walked her home after the tea party and they had seen each other every day for a fortnight. Her other admirers were distraught but she could think of no one but Con. He was not very handsome, nearly as old as Rosslyn himself and had been taught by a governess till he was eight. The family had lost all their money and since he grew up he and his brother contributed to their sister's education. His sisters had opened a hat shop in Beauchamp Place. One thing Kathleen omitted to mention till later was that he was the brilliant and courageous explorer Captain Robert Falcon Scott, who had re-turned from his first Antarctic expedition in the *Discovery* in September 1904 five years before. 'But it makes no difference.'

Con Scott had worshipped her from the moment he saw her but was anxious about stepping into marriage. He feared to cause her unhappiness by not proving worthy of her. Not knowing how else to handle it she was now going to Italy on a walking tour with Hugo, on Lota's advice. Con merely said: 'Take your time girl and write to me often.'

Kathleen's confidences made Rosslyn surer than ever that he loved Rachel but, like Scott, he feared his own inadequacy. Rachel, as daughter of a late High Sheriff, pampered with her own lady's maid, London season and rounds of gaiety, would find the life of a parson's wife dull, hard-going and perhaps disillusioning.

He and Scott were almost of an age, Kathleen was thirty, an es-tablished sculptor, with ten years or so of unusual independence behind her, and a wide assortment of admirers. Rachel was a very young and sheltered twenty-two, who, he had to admit, would hardly fail to be bowled over by any man taken into her tiny orbit with news of a bigger wider world outside. All the same he longed now to be assured of her love. It had begun as a jolly convalescent relationship with the whole of the Gurney family, with special regard for the eldest and most elegant with whom he had the kind of flirtation that was part of the pattern of his life. It was not till he talked to Kathleen that he thought seriously of marriage. And then came Rachel's bombshell. 'My dear Mr. Bruce, After August 10th my plans are rather vague. Did you know I've just had an invitation to New York for six or eight weeks at the end of September? Wouldn't it be glorious if I go? I've always longed to go to America.'

Rosslyn wrote by return of post:

How dreadful! I mean dreadfully exciting about America. Please, I don't quite approve? Two whole months! Oh, I must tell you about my kiddie sister. She has just made up her mind to be married quite quickly in August to a sailor, Captain Scott who led the South Pole *Discovery* expedition a few years ago. He was new to me and I am naturally inquisitive about him, because although I have hundreds of sisters, Kathleen (I call her Kiddie) has always been my special charge. She is the artist one, who lives in London. I am sending you her photograph.

Perhaps it was America (an invitation from Aunt Fanny of an American branch of the Buxton family in Boston, possibly incited by Rachel's mother expressing anxiety over the suit being paid by this eccentric ecclesiastic), perhaps it was Kathleen's engagement or Rosslyn's admission of his fondness for his sister. Whatever the cause, here came the rift, without which the course of true love never did run smooth. Rosslyn could detect a delicate withdrawal in the letters. It was enough to stiffen his determination and, cancelling engagements and jettisoning funerals, he sent a telegram accepting an invitation to Northrepps he had already refused. He followed it up in person without waiting for an answer.

Although he had a hilarious time with the younger members of the family, Rachel contrived to be so elusive that he was never for one moment alone with her. In fact she spent much of the day down at the nearby farm. When he followed she was off again into the woods. The three days of his stay ended with a rabbit hunt with her tall sporting brother Quintin, which went on half the night, with the girls sometimes hunting and at others being hunted.

I sort of believe you're rather cross with me [Rosslyn wrote] and it kind of feels as if it was my sort of fault. Is it really settled that you are going to go to America for two months? What on earth are *we* to do? Rather oddly all my relations and friends think it necessary to write and congratulate me on my sister Kathleen's engagement to Captain Scott! It is rather absurd really because of course I am the person who comes worst out of the deal, as she has always been my special pet lamb and I must expect to lose a good deal of her confidences of course and so it is not very pleasant work answering endless letters from gushing admirers of hers. Still I am very pleased about it for her sake and it is always what I have been hoping would happen some time or other. She is the sister I told you of, who thanks God seriously and constantly that she has no parents because so many of her friends have suffered from misunderstandings and restrictions and she remembers nothing at all of hers. It does not sound nice exactly but she is always determined to see good, good in everything and it really is from her point of view quite healthy. Love, love to dear Taffikins and little Turveydrop.

Taffy and 'Turveydrop', as he called Gladys, because her mother was always begging her to straighten her back, were, as go-betweens, his most important allies.

My dear Mr. Bruce, [Rachel wrote next day]
Why do you think I'm cross and especially with you? Is it because of America? Really I am in a most peaceful state of mind with everybody and I believe it's you who's rather annoyed. Please don't be. I shall make up my mind later whether I go or not. I'm sure you will agree with me it would be a pitty (*sic*) to let slip such an invitation without consideration.

Taffy was going to Oxford for a music exam the following week. It seemed that Rachel would be taking her, but would be staying with her Pelham relations who would want to organise her every moment.

Oxford is close to Nottingham [Rosslyn insisted] two hours by train and Oxford is so very nice if there is someone to show it to you, in little quiet bits at a time. And then I have a room always waiting for me at my old college. Isn't there some practical plan which would allow us to look at pictures and sit and talk about you and other nice things without being a nuisance to other people by demanding a chaperon?

From the Pelhams' house came a plaintive note:

My dear Mr. Bruce,

Do you really think you *will* come on Wednesday? It seems such a very long way out of your way but of course it would be very nice for us and I shall be very glad because I didn't know that cheering people at exams could be so difficult. Have you ever felt that your hostess almost disapproved of you if you smile even? If you *do* come on Wednesday meet us outside the school at 1 o'clock. Or I shall be in Magdalen Gardens after 2 o'clock if that is near at hand. I quite expect you will find the journey too long.

Miss Gurney dear, [came the prompt reply]

I shall come to Oxford from here, arriving 12·29, drive to the school and if the train isn't late ought to be there by 1 easily. Then I want you to see Worcester College gardens because that is my other home and I am wholly irrepressible on my home ground. So if you are feeling prim or distant you had better refuse to come to our garden, but you won't will you? I have to 'stay the night' in Oxford at Worcester College and have to 'return as far as Leicester' on Thursday any time. So if crowds of Pelhamite cousins come to see you off I shan't see you, or know you, till the train starts.

CHAPTER FOURTEEN

Bruces in Love

All went according to plan.

My dear Rachel, [Rosslyn wrote for the first time]
    What a visit to Oxford! I hope you will remember all of it and that you know, even better than I do, *where* we are. The Primrose League meeting here, addressed 100 conservatives on their duty to the country, bicycled into Nottingham, met Harry Lauder, addressed a factory men's meeting, slept in Nottingham and wrote a long letter to you at night beginning 'Adorable'. Read it through, burnt it carefully and went to bed and again dreamt of that round seat in Worcester Gardens and your white dress and whiter self inside. I am not going to post any compromising letters to you until I may. I have written to your mother and said that Oxford was very happy and thanking her for saying 'Go if you think well.' Oh you have been so wise and sensible and sweet so I must be sensible too.
    Now I am going to see the villagers and think all the time how much nicer it would be if you were there **too** to make it a real visit for them. I know they will think me more than usually lively and begin to ask where I have been and who I have seen and I shall have to be very very discreet. Goodbye Rachel dear,
        Yours affectionately.

And Rachel replied 'My dear Rosslyn,' for the first time.

I travelled miles and miles after you got out of the train. I am *so* glad we've had those two days and that we have had a good talk but you mustn't think there's any sort of even an understanding between us because I am not at all sure about anything yet. Really I am not. All the same I promise to play fair and let you know as soon as I can. I can't help thinking it is much harder for a girl to get married than a man. First, a girl has to leave her home. You only go on living at Clifton and you've never had a family home so you don't know what a wrench it would be to leave one's mother and brothers and sisters and one's *home*. Then when a girl is married she generally has to go through a lot of worry and pain and bother, and she must settle down quietly and not go flying about to glorious house parties, hunting, abroad, dances, London, etc. If I don't marry now I can go on being gay for another three or four years at least. All the same I'm not so silly as not to know that a happy marriage is the very highest ideal we have on earth. I believe you thought me horrid yesterday, talking so much about liking luxsury (*sic*) and horses and smart servants, etc. It was horried (*sic*) and I don't know why we talked about it but I know one thing. When I do marry I shall live like my husband does and like the things my husband likes and not be a brute about it.

Rosslyn wrote playfully:

If there is no understanding there must be a misunderstanding and if there is a misunderstanding it ought to be removed as soon as possible. But there is an understanding really. Rachel quite understands that Rosslyn loves her devotedly and absolutely and Rosslyn understands that dear Rachel talks a good deal about luxury and the things that she will miss because she's not at all sure that she loves him. There was a little stir in church this morning because the baillif's daughter had given me her banns to publish without letting anyone know, so it came as a mild surprise to the assembled villagers. It would have surprised them more if they had known that the sermon was all about you. I have written to Noel. Poor man, I do not know what he will make of it. I didn't mention your name but I spoke vaguely of 'your cousin'.

Noel replied to this letter: 'What *do* you mean? I began to jubilate but unless I'm certain, how can I be sure? I am not saying anything so you must be explicit.' Rosslyn sent the letter on to Rachel, with: 'Noel is right I must be explicit. So must Rachel.'

Three days later he was writing to Rachel:

Most curious things have happened very delightfully. This is far the most important letter I have ever written in my life. The tenants at the Rectory—the large house across the way—are going, probably in October, and have written to make it almost certain. I must see you almost immediately about this, mustn't I? Yes, please, I don't at all want to have to let it again, do I? Rachel dear, do you want awfully to go to America in October? I want you to very much and yet I rather dread it. A woman in the village here said she would as soon her husband were dead as to be in the Nottingham hospital. And that's only four miles away. Kathleen sends you such a lot of messages, such as do not let her be over anxious about its *importance*, because a big new lasting friend is not anything to be afraid of. People overdo the vastness of the change. 'My self, my character, my soul—and she means, but didn't say, and my God—are still to be the same.' But everything at present seems to be going to be so different for you. But Kiddie is a quaint child. For instance no power on earth will make her wear jewellery, not on any principle but because she thinks it unsuitable for her, so she has absolutely refused to have the conventional ring and has offered to give *me* a pearl necklace Nellie sent her. Isn't she mad? But she looks so much more beautiful than she ever did before, with a wonderful breadth of earnestness in her skyie sort of eyes. She is frighteningly in love I should think, but she tells me she never writes to him without saying let's put it all off again and forget and forgive! What odd things girls really are. I was rather glad though to hear her say that because it reminded me of 'There is not even an understanding' but I did not say anything. Of course 'Their terms' are very unusual.

'She even lets him brush her long hair,' Rosslyn added wistfully, having never more than 'touched, just very lightly', the top of Rachel's lovely golden hair. Sometimes daringly 'just to see her beautiful eyes' he would take away the delicate gold-rimmed spectacles, without which she, so endearingly to him, could not even see whether the roses were in bloom without peering into the rose bush. 'I am only trying to make you feel it would be happier to try and get to understand as soon as possible. I know you really can't till we meet again. May I come over for the middle of the day tomorrow?'

Rosslyn my dear, [she wrote as though with a deep sigh]

Do you know America *has* been getting rather small lately? It began to get small at Oxford and it's getting much smaller every day. Sometimes I'm longing for you to come here and yet when you arrive you will very likely find I've fled in a fright. How silly! I certainly hope you won't turn up today though, as the house is full and I am not at all fit with a bad cold and people are talking to me every five minutes and walking through the room. I wonder what their faces would be like if they could read this letter. It will be a bit of a shock to Norfolk I know, and I don't quite know how I am going to get round the American plan as those dear Boston Buxtons insist upon paying every penny from the minute I leave this house till I come back again, for me and my maid. Mother was delighted with being 'saintly' in one letter and 'mother' in another.

Rosslyn's reaction to Rachel's reference in her letter after their Oxford meeting to 'worry and pain' brought, he said, the deepest and truest bond of all. 'I believe now so much in the beauty and use in pain. Just a year ago I should not have understood. I remember the doctor saying men seldom have to suffer as you have, "but women nearly always do, don't they, nurse?" I look on women altogether so differently as I have never been taught to regard them in that light— as the pain bearers.'

Rachel's answer was, perhaps out of shyness, on a completely different wave-length. 'Don't think we don't possess pens in this house. We do. It is rather amusing to put the children on to write my letters for a change.'

Rosslyn replied to their frivolous letters with joke telegrams and letters written backwards while he continued to try to pin Rachel down to a serious decision. He brought out the 'and pain' again as meaning shyness 'I suppose the disappearance of that cannot be hoped for until the mutual trust in each other has become so perfect that the idea of being one flesh is fulfilled.'

Rachel replied she hadn't the faintest idea what he was talking about.

'You are wise and sensible and I can never quite guess how you see so clearly and so far' he wrote of his Beatrice-like image.

Rachel wrote: 'I told Eustace, who I always call my little brother because we tell each other most things, I had been thinking rather seriously about marriage lately. He said: "I can't quite imagine you being married but they say people generally quieten down after they are married so I dare say you won't be quite so wild."'

She said the children came thumping into her room every morning at about seven to know 'Are you feeling happy this morning? Have you had any letters this morning?' or if there was a letter from him they said it was only a bill and not worth fetching. 'Little beggars!'

'Hurrah,' Rosslyn wrote hopefully, 'you are just the dearest the most beautiful and most adorable and beautiful and reasonable and sensiblest girl in Europe or America.'

At last he was able to go to Northrepps again for three days. Surely in the next three days a decision could be made. It was all great fun again and the place was milling with relations. At 1 a.m. Rosslyn wrote from his room to hers, to tell her how he 'begrudged the description of Aunt Laura's dead baby'.

I expect even when I see Aunt Laura and her live baby I shall find them as delightful and as charming as all the nice people I've seen already. But I just want to be alone with you and your sweet mother and Gladys and the three other supporters. Love is just a little exacting and I shall be so jealous of the rest of the world till we are all alone for a long time. The vision of you tonight with your hair down was most unsettling and showed me a sort of glorious dream with all the whole world reflecting just you.

Rachel confided in her diary:

'I have never read *anything* more beautiful. He must love me. His inner soul must be beautiful.'

At last he was able to be alone with her in the front hall, but even now she kept walking away round the large circular table. He knew, and she knew, that until he actually physically caught her there could be no decision. It took her twenty minutes to come to a standstill.

By tea-time her mother had given her blessing, the younger ones were in uproar, telegrams were being sent and the engagement was to appear in *The Times* on Monday morning.

The American visit was cancelled and instead Aunt Fanny Buxton's daughter, Jessie Tredwell, was invited to come over to be a bridesmaid. Plans were made for the wedding to take place in October, by chance on the anniversary of Rosslyn's hunting accident.

He left Northrepps a happy if somewhat bewildered man.

Next came Rachel's explanation of her confusing behaviour, and from then on her bashfulness vanished. 'Do you remember telling me that Lloydie broke off his engagement because he never could bear to be alone?' she wrote. 'Did you realise it took absolutely all my strength of mind to make myself stop with you alone. I was simply terrified. Remember I can bear things best when people are not too nice to me.'

Rachel afterwards confessed that she had liked him after the first evening and knew that she was in love with him after the first week, yet when it came to say an everlasting 'Yes' she would have given anything to refuse him but daren't. She went down to the cliffs above Overstrand.

In front is the sea. That is the world to me. Where I am is the land, the bracken, the gorse and the woods to shout amidst. That is home. Often and often I have longed to go and have a good dip into that great sea world lying out there and yet I have always been glad to turn inland to the home woods. Now I really am going into that sea, right into an unknown married life. I don't know any of his family or friends. I don't know what his real life is away from here. Or what my life is going to be. I am always being told all sorts of odd things about him and yet I can't help it. I must go with him and live with him and watch him and listen to him and if I don't like the life, well it can't be helped.

The week after they became engaged she prayed that one of them might die a dramatic death before the wedding. 'I must say I rather hoped it would be him and not me because I really wanted to see more of the world but I thought I simply couldn't really get married.' Rachel added:

I have always had a perfect horror of all and any clergyman, and I always have thought I would have as little to do with them as possible. So I am not going to get all that dislike out of me in a few weeks. All the same if he wasn't a clergyman I should be so pleased. I have a ridiculous feeling of shame whenever I have to tell anyone that he is a clergyman. It's beastly of me and not honourable to him nor to God. I feel almost that I shall not be admitted into heaven for such an offence. I should feel like a spy going into his camp under false pretences. I must try not and I think God will have understood.

Meanwhile her first cousins, the Fowell Buxtons stormed at their brother Noel for ever having allowed Rachel to meet Rosslyn, whom they considered theatrical, a flirt and 'an odd type for a parson'. How dare Rosslyn marry *their* Rachel—or rather what Noel's brother, Harold privately regarded as *his* Rachel. And how dare Rachel marry *their* Rosslyn, or rather what Mabel, his sister, considered to be *her* Rosslyn, both admitted many years later.

Noel wrote begging Rosslyn to think carefully, and Rosslyn showed Rachel the letter. 'How *dare* Noel say that!' Rachel exclaimed,

Noel wrote next an amusing letter explaining that the only way he had of showing his affection was to rot. 'What a confession for a Buxton!' Rosslyn wrote: 'People's opinions are very delightful,' and he went on:

Mrs. Wodehouse had already told everyone Brucie makes no jokes and is quite shy in her presence. I wonder if there's anything in it. Another says 'I know Norfolk well and the only girl in it who knows how to put her clothes on is Rosslyn Bruce's fiancée.'

Nellie, of course writes: 'You don't know how much a lady will help me, especially now I am away so much.' The rest are rather too gushing or too conventional to quote. They'll keep.

Hilda reminded him that as children they always used to talk of their little sister, 'Rachel', as an imaginary character.

Madge Titheradge sent a telegram WE ARE FILLED WITH JOY UNSPEAKABLE FOR YOU AND YOUR DEAR ONE.

'The Bishop of Hull wants to know what relation you are to his dear old friend. I will tell him, thanks to the half-hour in which you concealed your confusion behind a screen of your aunt's dead baby and robbed me of quite 20 kisses.' Later he wrote: 'Everybody without any single exception says they're relations or connections of yours. The social caste in the village here turns on how much each can remember seeing you here. When do you think I may begin to enjoy myself with the banns?'

Rosslyn wrote on a postcard:

Do you know I've been thinking it over as to what to call your very very dear mother. Old-fashioned people say Mrs. Gurney always and I love old fashions. Nellie used always to call her father-in-law Sir Hervey, though he lived with them and she nursed him. Modern people have a sort of playful way of calling her *yer mothur* but that is not nice enough. The only other way besides Mrs. Gurney would be Mother like you do. That might jar on her as I am so very old. But again as I have never had a mother since I was eight, nor called anyone so, even in fun to them (Nellie, I mean) I should like to. Perhaps it will work right.

Rachel wrote excitedly that letters were coming in shoals and so were silver cream jugs. Christopher was determined to give them a pony and cart. 'We are all five at home today but perhaps for the last time as children. Though we have been playing baby games the whole afternoon in the rocking boat. I really didn't feel a bit shy in church although everyone kept staring. I have found out that all the servants think you are 28 or 29.' He was, in fact, 37.

'Can't you send me Christopher?' Rosslyn wrote. 'I do want to see him so much.' He suggested for his best man his sailor brother, Wilfrid, and, failing him, his cousin Benjie. 'Failing him I have a great mind to ask Henry Woodward, the actor, who is a perfect dear. But that would be shocking surely—the respectability?' Rosslyn teased.

Rachel replied that she intended to invite her Hanover Square dressmaker, Lily Levilion, who was making her wedding dress. She was amazed to find that Rosslyn knew her already. She was married to the brother of his actor friend, Leon M. Lion.

Walking round the rectory with the Kerle-Smiths, Rosslyn realised it was considerably larger than he had supposed. The kitchens, pantries and larders stretched away through a series of yards ('Though useful for keeping puppies in') to the rambling stables. The garden was as big as the whole of Soho Square. There were fourteen bedrooms. The Kerle-Smiths kept, he wrote to Rachel,

a cook, a little kitchen maid (to please the cook) a housemaid, another housemaid they call the parlour maid (but she doesn't parl), a lady's maid who sews and reads novels, and a butler. But *they* have £11,000 a year and I hear in the village that the maids are tumbling over each other to make jobs for each other. They also have three men in the garden and two in the stables. 'But the revolution of the bedding out would save a whole man's time and make the mowing easier by saving wriggily journeys round beds.'

Rosslyn had anyway never liked formal gardens, preferring the wild woodland effect of Binton Rectory.

Rachel wrote various suggestions for cutting down the domestic staff and Rosslyn replied that they should have '1. Head gardener, 2. Housekeeper, 3. Coachman, 4. Master of the horse—all done by Rachel, 5. Master of the Dog, 6. Gardener, 7. Vet for stables and canary cages, etc., 8. Master of the rabbits and pigeons, 9. Master of the pheasants and fowl—all done by Rosslyn.'

Rachel asked him to be serious and he replied: 'All right, one gardener, Mr. Mudd. One garden boy to grow during the winter and be a man soon. One groom, one housekeeper, one cook, one house-maid, one tweeny, quite weeny.' The wages would be £171. House-keeping £250, extras £75, garden seeds £25, two horses £50, Rachel's veils £98, Rosslyn's snuff £1, rates, taxes, insurance, dentists and doctors, £100. With a free house and the rent from the Glebe when it was let and Rosslyn's stipend and his earnings from writings and animals; with Rachel's inheritance from her father, her new life as a parson's wife would not, at any rate to start with, be one of skimping and overwork—'I never want pocket money much,' he said 'as I don't smoke or buy things except from the village people, eggs at 2d each, because the hen is pretty and speckled, or plums at 1d because I want the stones.' 'Nature made you just a perfect lamb,' he added, 'though God has made you an angel forever.'

He wrote while surrounded by twenty confirmation candidates strumming on the piano and looking at photographs till it was time for their class.

Next time he came Rachel asked him to look his best to meet some more relations.

'How can you imagine me looking my best unless I am quite alone with you?' he asked. Later he wrote:

'I am arranging a jumble sale of all the suits which you have re-jected. I *won't* sell my Alpaca coat, boo hoo.'

Rachel's letters were full of the amazing presents—the diamonds and pearl rings, the silver soup tureens and the arm chairs—that rela-tions were showering on her.

Rosslyn wrote:

Kathleen doesn't know where to be married and at last said, for once, I begin to wish I had a home. You see how all wild they are. And she won't let him give her any jewellery not even a ring nor will she submit to the usual veil and orange blossom. This particular moment it is a little difficult for Scott, who has to think a little of what the navy considers comme il faut. I have proposed that they be married here quite quietly and I believe they may, with hardly anyone here, and little uncle Admiral Sir Jimmie Bruce to give her away. Or again it may be at St. Margaret's, Westminster. But anyhow it will be quite at once, for they both hate the waiting period as being waste of good time. Poor Kathleen! After eight pages of wondering how it can be managed quickly and quietly for her, she ends up 'don't let your Rachel go to America if you can possibly help it. Americans are all so unsettling.'

Captain Scott wrote from H.M.S. *Bulwark*, Home Fleet:

Dear Bruce,

Your letter reminds me that, to say the least, I've been discourteous in not writing to you before—of course Kathleen has told me of her family and especially of you and your brother Wilfrid—I scarcely know why it did not occur to me to write, possibly it was the suggestion of the independence to which you refer—in any case I am sorry to have omitted such an obviously proper course—it's very pleasant to read your appreciation of your sister though no one knows better than I how much I'm to be congratulated. Probably Kathleen has told you that my very indefinite professional programme makes it impossible to fix the exact date of our wedding—it will not be later than September I hope—the announcement has been rather a trouble, we both want it to be appropriately simple. I have asked Kathleen to have it in on 20th or 21st and submitted my suggested form of words. The text, from memory was 'A marriage has been arranged between Captain R. F. Scott, R.N., and Kathleen, daughter of the late Rev. Lloyd Bruce, Canon of York.' I expect you will have acted but do write her if you wish it to be different.

I hope I shall very soon have the pleasure of meeting you— Kathleen will have told you we propose to inhabit 174 Buckingham Palace Road for the present. She is busy and happy with this preparation—we don't know where to be married but your aunt has suggested Hampton Court and it sounds delightful—no to be more honest—from male man's point of view it seems as pleasant a place as can be chosen for a trying ceremony.

I couldn't under many pages attempt an explanation of the why's and wherefore's of the step we propose—I suppose it can be summed up by saying that we agree to take a risk to get what we most value. I'm sorry that for the present I must be such a very shadowy person to you and others who take an interest in our dear lady.

Yours ever sincerely R. Scott.

Rosslyn wrote to Rachel:

Kathleen's wedding is on September 2nd from our aunt's apartment at Hampton Court. Would you care to go? I had hardly thought about it or even about going myself unless I have to give her away. You cannot imagine how catching her indifference to the ceremony part is. I suppose someone will wake her up to caring about it before the day, but I've heard nothing of invitations or anything. One way I admire her plan, very coldly, but I much prefer the other way, the usual way. You see although things are only forms in themselves, they generally represent what generations have found to be the most pleasant and kind and convenient all round. We won't be at all eccentric, which will be quite unusual enough now-a-days.

Rachel decided against going to Kathleen's wedding but asked Rosslyn, who was coming on to Northrepps not to change out of his wedding clothes as she wanted to see him in them. In that case he would have to leave his luggage 'accidently on purpose' at Bloomsbury, he said, 'Naughty Rachel! I never make mistakes like that as a rule.'

Kathleen's 'simple, quiet little wedding' made front page news in the *Daily Mirror* under FAMOUS EXPLORER MARRIED, and was reported in all the social columns.

The wedding took place by permission of the King in the Chapel Royal, Hampton Court Palace. The bride was married from the palace apartment of her aunt, Mrs. Thomson, widow of the late Archbishop of York. She was given away by her brother, Lieut. Wilfrid Bruce, R.N., of H.M.S. *Arrogant*. She wore a dress of white satin trimmed with Limerick lace and a bodice of chiffon with a wreath of natural myrtle and a tulle veil. Captain Henry Campbell, R.N., Assistant Director of Naval Intelligence, was best man. The bride's brother, the Rev. Dr. Rosslyn Bruce, assisted by Rev. Ponsonby and the Chaplain of the Chapel Royal took the service.

Choristers, in scarlet cassocks, sang.

Kathleen said afterwards she had not particularly enjoyed it. After walking through the cold dark cloisters, the haunted gallery and the armoury on a lovely day when she could have been outside, she hurried through the champagne reception for a hundred and fifty guests, as fast as she could, even though Rodin and his wife were among them.

'A telegram arrived with congratulations from the King.' The report continued 'Huge crowds gathered as Captain and Mrs. Scott left by motor car for London and then France. The bride was wearing a tailor-made costume of blue serge and wore a large brown hat with blue wings.'

Rachel read all about it. If all this had been whipped up in a few days why was she making such a fuss with still six weeks to go?

The schoolroom party left no stone unturned in adding to the confusion of that six weeks with their usual exasperating practical jokes. The invitations had been printed and envelopes were addressed into which they put the wrong invitations. Rachel wrote to Rosslyn:

Please don't ask any more clergymen to marry us as we have now got cousin Sidney Pelham and the Rector of Northrepps, Mr. Blyth, and your brother Lloydie and the Bishop if he comes. I was horrified when I got back from London to find this letter from the Rector of Roughton asking if he could marry us too. I really don't know the old man except when he comes here to garden parties and to meetings. We always call him the Corkscrew, if that conveys in your mind his character.

Only after much letter-writing and summonsing of Mr. Blyth, the Rector of Northrepps, was it revealed that the Corkscrew's self-invitation was another of 'Turveydrop's' and Taffy's hoaxes.

Rosslyn replied to them with an agonised letter that for a while they really believed came from the Rev. Corkscrew himself.

Meanwhile he assured Rachel that the Bishop would be unlikely to accept. To his surprise he did. 'No Bishops must ever override Rachel's plans!' he wrote. 'You have stirred him up. The poor puzzled Bishop! I notice his reply is dated four days wrong. Is that the way you always manage ecclesiastical dignitaries? You dear wee power!'

CHAPTER FIFTEEN

Married Bliss

Midway between Kathleen's and Rosslyn's weddings, Rachel and her mother were invited to stay at Clifton. There was some trepidation on both sides. Rachel feared her mother might be too holy for the Bruces and Nellie was worried that the new paint on the outside of the windows sashes might upset the Gurneys.

Rosslyn wrote warning Rachel: 'There will be rather a frumpy old lot here I fear, but Ronnie and his wife and Benjie will be coming later. We shall run away most of the time with an excellent excuse of looking about the Rectory, shan't we?'

The visit went well and Rosslyn was commended by his young cousins on his choice of beauty and charm. 'And we are to choose the best armchair we can find from Lady Byron. It *must* come from London, must be a very good one or she won't pay for it. She's the one who's ninety.' Presents cascaded into both houses. Rachel already had 212. Rosslyn had 120.

He gave her a Bechstein piano, she gave him a watch and a shooting stick and the bridesmaids paste buckles and the pages riding-crops.

But the greatest bounty of all came from Rachel's mother who showered them with linen and carpets and household goods.

'You really must stop the flowing tide of dear mother's generosity. It is getting quite *indecent*, isn't it?' Rosslyn wrote.

A notebook survives revealing that Rachel's trousseau alone cost her mother £404 2s. 2d., which a pearl necklace on a page by itself brought up to £500. At first glance it would seem that Rachel was about to marry a Governor General rather than a country parson. An abundance of formal dresses, flowery hats and fur and feather boas suggest frequent attendance at state functions and garden parties; three riding and hunting habits and six pairs of boots suggest regular hunting with the Quorn. But the point was the trousseau was bought to last. From Watson of Conduit Street, three identical tailored dresses in grey, blue and white serge were ordered that could be expected to stand up to half a century of Mothers' Unions and parish councils. From Liberty came an opera cloak intended, presumably, for warmth in the parish hall rather than the opera house. From Peter Yapp of Sloane Street came £27 6s. 7d. worth of boots and shoes. From Harrods, £12 8s. 2d. worth of gloves. From Woolland, twenty-two combinations and from Mrs Scoones of 82 Queens Gate, corsets and sundries costing £54 1s 3d. 'Sundries'—unmentionable in case the book was seen by the bridegroom—covered several dozen pairs of drawers, flounced at the knee and gathered into buttonholed waist bands. The Invalid Benevolent Association stitched £11 11s. od. worth of flannel nightgowns. Mrs. Carter, the coachman's wife, was paid a pound for marking ninety-six pairs of stockings 'plus bodices, linen, etc.' Tweed from Marshall and Snelgrove was made up into a cape in Cromer where nothing was actually bought except six pennyworth of boot laces.

Rachel refused an invitation to meet Rosslyn 'because of all my fittings, with so many people sticking pins into me'. 'I wish I were a pin,' Rosslyn wrote wistfully.

At Northrepps they became more and more involved in preparations, including presentations of a sugar basin from the Sunday School, a hot water jug from the tenants and her first public speech of thanks.

After church this morning Gerard Gurney and I counted seats. Three hundred and by the way 'Christ is our corner stone' is for dedicating a church.

This is from a *tippical (sic)* relation. I don't think she has a religious mania. Is it much wonder that I wish them all dead sometimes? Mother was very cross because I laughed when I read it.'

It was a tract headed *Are you a sinner or am I?*

Rosslyn, mindful of his profession, wrote saying that her mother was right. Serious things should not be laughed at and he too could learn much from mother's blessed piety.

Inevitably nerves became frayed.

I got three such grumpy letters from three such grumpy men this morning. Two did not matter a bit but your letter made me weep for a bit. You Bruces are quite *unordinary* in your *huge* amount of love. It's a wonderful gift which I wish I had but it makes it difficult for you to understand that I have got mine in *me* only I can't show it like you do. But as long as it's somewhere, it doesn't matter does it?

Rosslyn replied offering 'double thoughtfulness, in thoughtful devotion, in not being too outwardly devoted'.

You don't understand a bit, [she wrote back] I've suddenly begun to realise that I am going to leave my home and, say what you like when you are made to pack up your books and music and things and you know they will never come back even if I do—I hardly know what one feels. But you can't really understand, however much you want to, because you haven't always lived in the same house with the same mother *all* your life and you are not very young like me and you know all about the great world and I don't.

Rosslyn replied with soothing words by every post. He called her Charle, an anagram of Rachel; he pronounced it Charlie as in the Greek name, Zoe.

Kathleen says she's determined to have a jolly good time at our wedding and Wilfrid says 'Chins in the air and no nerves please'. Let's be jolly collected outwardly and not giggle and bow as most people do till we are out of the church. Quite a solemn little unhurried procession is so much more impressive and proper.

For the honeymoon Rachel's Aunt Maggie offered them Keswick Hall for the night after the wedding. Rosslyn thought they might be shy of the quantities of footmen that seemed necessary at Keswick. However, Rachel wrote:

> I have accepted Keswick for one night, taken a room at the Grosvenor House for the Wednesday night, a room at a small but nice inexpensive hotel in Paris, engaged a room at Lugano. Cook's tickets are £30 first-class for two. It seems a lot doesn't it? But I suppose two of us can't expect to be abroad for five weeks under £50 and we shall just have to be on the bust.

Two nights before the wedding Rachel said she could not sleep so she threw open the window looking out on to the woods and sang at the top of her voice. 'Rather mad and a bit noisy but nobody woke except one of the ducks on the pond.'

On the wedding morning she passed the time writing the lyric for another song.

> Oh happy morn so deeply pondered on
> Serene and bright may it be dawning, be dawning
> For I wed the man that I adore
> Yes I wed the man that I adore
> And I trust he'll not consider it a bore . . .

Christopher came in and added three rather more questionable verses ending up 'And do forgive me if I snore'.

Half the household helped her into her white satin dress, draped with exquisite point d'angleterre lace. Round her neck was the pearl necklace and diamond pendant from the American Buxtons. Her shoes were bead encrusted. A court train hung from her shoulders and over all was arranged a Honiton lace veil with a small wreath of myrtle from a bush planted from a sprig from her mother's bridal bouquet.

The carriage and a new pair of horses—called Bryant and May because they were such a good match—were at the door. Quintin, who was to give his sister away, hurried her in and told the old coachman to make haste. They moved at a sharp trot, down the drive, into the lane, and under the two railway bridges. Along the straight, the

Clifton cottages (*above*) and a revival of May Day rites. The May Queen was chosen for her biblical knowledge and good attendance at Sunday School.

Purity (*above left*) and (*right*) Rachel Gurney of Northrepps, on her engagement to Rosslyn in 1908. (*Left*) Lady Bruce with rabbit at Clifton, with Rosslyn and Kathleen Scott, before Peter was born.

horses broke into a canter. In the village hardly a cottage was without a display of bunting of some description.

Quintin leant out of the window and was bumped back on to the bride's train, ripping it from her shoulders.

'I suppose you know the facts of life?' he said as he tried to remedy the damage. 'Because I don't.'

The Gurney family had lived at Northrepps since 1790. This was the first Gurney to be married in Northrepps church since 1856. Triumphal arches of evergreens studded with flowers were erected with the initials of the bride and bridegroom on one side, and such mottoes as 'God Bless them Both' and 'Happiness to the Bride and Bridegroom' on the other. The gap between the carriage and an awning to the church porch was lined with schoolchildren, dressed by Rachel in scarlet capes for the girls, and scarlet ties and slouch hats for the boys.

'Never before,' observed the local paper, 'had the inhabitants seen so large a number of such beautifully appointed and powerful motor cars. Within, the communion rails' white lilies formed the principal decorations. The pulpit and reading desk were treated with chrysanthemums.'

There were seven bridesmaids in cream romany dresses trimmed with Valenciennes lace, wearing brown straw hats swathed with shaded tulle. Under the brims were quaint lace caps, a salute to the Quaker ancestry. Two pages in scarlet Peter Pan tunics—a salute to Rosslyn's friendship with James Barrie—carried Rachel's train. The bride's mother wore a dove-grey velvet dress covered with almost as much lace as were the bridesmaids'. *The Queen* reproduced drawings of them all with the Winston Churchill's wedding in the next issue.

The bridegroom walked with a romantic limp and once again Wilfrid Bruce was best man. The Bishop and the three parsons took the service collectively, Lloydie preaching inevitable love and sweetness because of cousin Pelham's sore throat.

Out came the bride and bridegroom in a shower of carefully chosen autumn leaves warmed in the hot hands of the school children. It was a brilliant sunny day. Rosslyn insisted on returning to the Hall at an amble round the outside of the Home Wood. Most of the guests had already arrived when the bridal couple entered the flagged marquee on the back lawn.

Gurneys, Buxtons and Barclays 'bellowed and thundered'. The Bruces made enigmatical observations in quieter voices while Rosslyn's stage friends dazzled both with their flower and bird laden hats and make-up. Among his Oxford friends present were Hugo Law, now a robust Member of Parliament, and Gabriel Gillet, now a staid parson.

The bride left in a Hussar-blue cloth going away dress, braided in black, the skirt bordered with a classic key pattern, a salute to Rosslyn's Greek grandmother. Rachel's huge hat was swathed with blue ostrich feathers.

According to the trousseau book, she took on her honeymoon £10 8s. 6d. worth of boxes from the Army and Navy Stores—huge reinforced trunks and hat boxes the size of tea chests—into which were packed her honeymoon dressing-gown, a pale pink crêpe-de-chine kimono, laden with costly Irish lace, a nightdress case from Liberty—London shops had not yet acquired the possessive 's'— and a dozen hand-embroidered white lawn night-gowns. Each voluminous garment was gathered into lace insertions threaded with ribbons and buttoned up to the neck and down to the wrists with inches of minute pearl lozenges.

The honeymoon in itself had its ups and downs. Hardly had Rosslyn seemed to have extracted Rachel from her greatly extended family than, in Paris, her cousin Hugh Gurney, in the diplomatic service, appeared at their hotel to lunch with them. In a mountain village in Italy Rachel asked for wild strawberries that cost more than their hotel bill for three nights. Rosslyn had never had a holiday in his adult life before, unbacked by a worthy cause. Delightful as his present cause was, he was glad to get back to the busy round at Clifton where he was immediately called out to doctor a sick pigeon on his way to comfort the bereaved and play in a cricket match in Nottingham.

Rachel introduced more than a touch of Northrepps Hall into her her first home. She brought some of her mother's maids as well as her furniture, both of which she arranged with the same puritanical simplicity. She ordered bland, schoolroom-type meals even for dinner parties. To parish gatherings she brought the spirit of the Northrepps missionary meetings with muslin tea bags and flat slabs of iced cake cut into cubes. Monday evening hymns round the piano with her brothers and sisters were reproduced in Clifton church. 'Last evening the village orchestra under Mr. Mudd rendered several sacred selections. A special anthem was given by the choir and Mrs. Rosslyn Bruce employed a sweet soprano voice attractively in her rendering of "Angels ever Bright and Fair."'

At Clifton Hall, Nellie treated her as a daughter-in-law, giving advice that at first Rachel took gratefully. Nellie told her it was correct to wear her wedding dress for the first six months for all the grand dinner parties to which the bridal couple were invited. This Rachel did, till the hooks and eyes no longer met. Kathleen came to stay in a similar condition, already wearing a loose draped tunic brought back from Paris by Isadora Duncan. Kathleen bathed unchaperoned in the river without a qualm. She was convinced that her baby would be a boy and already referred to him as Peter. Rachel guarded her 'secret' more modestly—particularly from her own eager family—and cancelled social engagements, only appearing discreetly at the Northrepps versions of parish garden parties, complete with bands, that were held at the rectory with Rosslyn's animals and birds on show, sack races, tugs of war and dancing on the lawn till ten o'clock.

On May Day, Rachel's birthday, the May Queen was chosen, as at Northrepps for her biblical knowledge and good behaviour in Sunday School. Her head was piled high with a pyramid of flowers and, dressed in white, she was followed through the village by girl attendants in white embroidered frocks, shoes and stockings and boys in straw hats with white ribbons.

When Gladys came to stay, with her hair still down, Rosslyn took her visiting with him and introduced her as 'my new wife'. Most people accepted it as Rosslyn's brand of fun but Martin Harvey, who was playing at the Theatre Royal, Nottingham, believed it to be quite in keeping with his old friend to marry a schoolgirl. While he was there, Martin Harvey, Rosslyn, Frank Grainger, Barry Jackson and the Duke of Portland together launched an appeal from the Shakespeare Memorial National Theatre, Angel Row, Nottingham, in the hopes of bringing sympathy 'to every thinking man and woman in the desire to raise a noble and lasting monument to that consummate genius and fellow countryman, Shakespeare.'

At one meeting for this particular cause, Rosslyn said he never missed a chance to see Sir Beerbohm Tree acting. As he was leaving the hall he was buttonholed by a lady who expressed herself shocked to hear a clergyman say he frequented the theatre. 'Madam,' he said, 'come with me. If we hurry we may yet get two seats for *The Taming of the Shrew* tonight.'

Rachel's son was born on August 3rd, 1909, small, red-headed and strong. Now Rachel was touchier than ever about her family's tender inquiries. Rosslyn toned down her reply with a covering letter:

My dear Mother,

Rachel wrote this and asked me to read and send it if I thought wise. I don't think it all very wise but I send it to show how very careful we have to be not to excite her. Of course she ought not to write at all for a week or two yet. Nurse was much disappointed that she had done so. But I send it and beg these two conditions. Any references to her bodily affairs always upset her. Secondly, that you will destroy and not say a word about it to anyone. Lying in bed must make us all sensitive, quite apart from other things, mustn't it?

Next he wrote:

She's very happy and wrapped up in Merlin. No, Tennyson's Merlin had no influence in the choice of name. As far as I remember he was a weird old man, not too nice and generally voted a fool. But who is Lord Tennyson that he should spoil a pretty name? My bird book said Merlin is a splendid dashing brave bird, who fears nothing except disgrace and defeat. The chief recommendation is that it is pretty, simple, clear and uncommon, without any family associations, and Rachel likes the final *lin* as a suggestion of his father's name. He will pull the name through, I hope, if he grows up as his darling mother means to bring about.

Martin Harvey came over to Clifton to view the new baby and then sent a congratulatory present—the daughter of a terrier Rosslyn had sold him in Soho—'a beautiful dog with a very fine pedigree and one of the sweetest dispositions I have ever come across. I want, if you will accept her, to give her to you as a remembrance for Dixie and all your kindness and care. With my love to the dearest baby and to Her and the sweetest remembrances of our last visit.'

Among the sheafs of letters of congratulations came one from Aunt Zoe who, having missed none of Rosslyn's mother's confinements, spoke with authority.

Warmest congratulations on the birth of your son. I do hope they are both going on well and that your wife will make a good recovery. Tell her with my love that if she will have patience and not put her foot to the ground, even to walk to her sofa, for twenty-one days she will be much stronger afterwards. What an added happiness this baby will be. I hope Kathleen will have a good time and will try to see her. Much love,

Your affectionate Aunt Zoe.

Kathleen continued to work, walk, swim and roam about abroad till just before Peter was born with no intention of heeding her great-aunt Zoe's advice afterwards.

The third cause for congratulation among the Bruces at Clifton was Percy's second marriage, to Evie Leith.

Rosslyn dear boy, Thank you ever so for your letter. I can't answer it because I've lost it somewhere but I know you wished me luck and sent me a message from Rachel which I am grateful for and please thank her. Well, there is little to be said. It is all very very good and I feel at peace again. I am absolutely content for all four of us. Evie loves the bairns and they love her and I love her and she loves me and that is the conclusion of the whole matter: it covers the whole situation.

Percy

Next time they came to Clifton, Gervase, Percy's jolly little boy of nine, sought Rosslyn out in his 'new' rectory for advice on breeding from his sheepdog.

Rachel was pushing Merlin in his pram in May 1910 when she and Rosslyn saw their first aeroplane. A few days later, on May 6th, came the news of Edward VII's sudden death from bronchitis. That Sunday evening Clifton church was packed. Nottingham people who had heard Rosslyn preach wanted to hear what he had to say about the King's spiritual future. Some sought comfort, others felt a little country church on a summer evening after a walk through the lovely Grove completed the mood of that historic week better than a slick city ceremony.

'The church is bracing herself today to bear an irreparable loss with courage and hope,' they heard. 'The country has lost its chief citizen, the Empire its controlling genius and Europe its first gentleman. But you and I are mourning a father or an elder brother.'

The choir sang 'God shall wipe away all Tears' with Rachel singing the soprano solo part.

National mourning inspired Rosslyn to break forth into more verse. Three of his poems appeared in the press, 'Blow blow ye winds, a sorrow stricken blast', one began and another was based on Lord Byron's little daughter hearing that her father was going to the King's funeral asking 'Will he smile at you?'

Rosslyn then went off to camp at Salisbury as chaplain to the Royal Horse Artillery. Transformed overnight from a reverent poet to racy army officer, he wrote to Rachel who was staying at Northrepps:

> They have made me mess president so I have to look after the tent affairs, wine, food, stationery, piano, newspapers, etc., but as the caterers are good men at their job it really only comes to jogging them about a bit. Archie Wright is one of the chief officers. We were kids together at Carlton, since when he became a county cricketer and a baronet. Then Joe Laycock, after a divorce case, is really a topper, filthily rich. There is a beautiful boy like Gladys with a dash of Benjie whom you would adore. Also Lord George Cholmondeley and Henry Bentinck. They lend me a horse whenever I can use it and a motor car always. Poor old Bishop Baines

shows some hair on the legs on these occasions. The language in the mess, as the Methody batman put it, is 'somethin h'awful'.

Rosslyn's luggage, with his robes and uniform in it, was lost on the way. Pictures show him riding with the Territorials in a half high hat, tweed jacket and clerical collar with borrowed army breeches.

Back at Clifton, as chaplain of the Royal Horse Artillery, Rosslyn took services of the Frontiersmen Legion who would ride over from camp and then lunch in one of the many 'Teas' cottages, before Rosslyn rode back with them anything up to twenty-five miles. Clifton was noted for its teas. Almost every thatched cottage provided new-laid eggs and homemade bread and fresh butter and cakes. It was a common treat for Nottingham people to walk beside the river and out through the Grove for tea at Clifton. Many of Rosslyn's followers who had heard him preach or speak came on to call at the rectory.

The young Cecil Roberts, as a schoolboy, after a cottage tea, first met Rosslyn walking down the broad village way. Emboldened by the fact that he was carrying a ring-tailed lemur, the boy went up and spoke to him. Soon he was taken 'through the magic door to see the menagerie'. Cecil Roberts confided in Rosslyn that he wanted to become a writer. Rosslyn advised him to start writing for the local papers, as he himself had done, beginning with letters and unpaid articles till his name was known. Cecil Roberts wrote in his autobiography:

Clifton had a fabulous rector, Dr. Rosslyn Bruce, a man of about forty, related to the squire. He lived in a large Georgian house behind a high brick wall. Inside the grounds he had a menagerie. His hobby was the care and breeding of animals. Horses, monkeys, mice, birds, rabbits, iguanos, snakes, ferrets, fox terriers of which he was a champion breeder, a bear and once an elephant. He hunted twice a week, and knew everybody, was loved by everybody, was cheery and robust and when one winter he gave a course of lectures on Dante, I attended, now a boy of eighteen. He was a racy, fluent lecturer, and he introduced me to the wonders of Dante's world. He always had a contagious zest.

Rosslyn's repeat in Nottingham of his Soho Dante lectures attracted a surprising following, many of whom returned for a series called 'Christ in the Modern Poets'. The lectures were billed as 'Tom Hood, Social Reformer'; 'Walt Whitman, the Prince of Optimists'; 'Longfellow, the Enthusiast'; 'Tennyson, the Moralist'; 'Browning, the Spiritual Seer'.

Kathleen and Con Scott, with baby Peter, stayed at Clifton and Rosslyn saw them several times at Binton, where they went so often that they kept their country boots there. The last time Scott went to church in England before his 1910 Antarctic expedition was at Binton. Rosslyn teased him because he liked sitting close to the fire. He admitted he hated being cold.

Rosslyn told Benjie later that Con had confided in him that he had an ambition to reach the moon. 'I am going to make a success of this, Ross, and when I have, you must not mind what I say next. I'm going to the moon, and I have three other men who are going with me. We are going to get there and I don't see why we cannot do it.' Standing with them was Kathleen. Rosslyn turned to her and asked, 'Kiddie, what do you think of that?' She smiled and said, 'If he wants to do it—he will do it.' This was in 1910.

Rosslyn said, 'Scott has an insight into inter-planetary travel. He seems to know the hazards of getting through the stratosphere. He also says he is confident of reaching the South Pole, though he is not stating publically that this is his prior aim. His second Antarctic expedition, starting this year comes first. Scott is very much in earnest.'

Wilfrid, Kathleen's brother, now a lieutenant in the Royal Navy, volunteered with eight thousand others for the expedition. He had already seen three years in a sailing ship in the Merchant Navy. Originally Scott had not wanted to impose the risk on Kathleen, if anything went wrong, of losing two of her dear ones. Rosslyn said it was the only time he heard Con being hesitant about the success of the expedition. When the selected navigator was unable to travel, Wilfrid was overjoyed to get a telephone call from Scott asking him to take the position.

He sailed with the *Terra Nova* from Cardiff on June 15th, 1910, under Lieutenant Evans. Scott was to join the ship in South Africa and sail with it to Australia. Kathleen longed to go too to see him off at the last possible moment. Rosslyn and Rachel offered to look after Peter so that she could do so. There were other loving offers, especially warm from the Binton twins and Podge at Scarborough. Eventually Kathleen settled to leave him with friends to avoid family competition over her 'nine months laughing tawny-haired baby Hercules'.

Meanwhile the Norwegian explorer, Amundsen, set out in the *Fram* on an expedition to the North Pole which he had announced at the Royal Geographical Society the year before. Scott joined the *Terra Nova* at Cape Town and six weeks later reached Melbourne, where Kathleen was waiting for him. Also waiting was a telegram: AM GOING SOUTH. AMUNDSEN.

This was interpreted by the British press as 'My expedition to the North was only a feint. I now challenge you to a race to the South Pole.' There was much feeling against Amundsen for his 'deceit'. In fact the news had only come to him, after he had set out for the North in the *Fram*, that elderly American-born Peary had already beaten him to the North Pole by sledge in April 1909.

Scott's expedition was essentially a scientific one, equipped for careful unhurried studies. Nevertheless Amundsen's telegram was disturbing. Britain would expect Scott to take a sporting chance and make a dash for it. Scott left the ship at Melbourne to be with Kathleen and rejoined it with her in New Zealand for the last few weeks of refitting, reloading and final celebrations ashore.

On November 22nd, 1910, the *Terra Nova* slipped from the wharf at Port Lyttleton with crowds—brought by special trains—waving, all ships dressed and a general hullabaloo. At Dunedin next day she took on extra coal and there was more dancing and gaiety. The wives stayed aboard till the ship reached the open sea.

Kathleen said good-bye to her husband and brother off Port Chalmers.

A postcard came for Rosslyn from Wilfrid posted in Dunedin: 'The last few days worry have been pretty bad, we're all glad to get off. Good-bye to you all and don't expect to hear from us for ages. We may be back soon but it may be four years.'

Kathleen wrote a week later: 'I leave Sydney on December 17th, a fortnight in Egypt and home February 11th [1911]. Hurrah for

Rachel no such luck for me.' Rachel was expecting another baby in March.

The night before the baby arrived the River Trent flooded and the bridge over to Beeston, where the doctor lived, was washed away. Early next morning Rosslyn rowed across to bring the doctor. Rhalou, named after Rosslyn's Greek grandmother, was born on the first day of spring.

CHAPTER SIXTEEN

The New Church

A week later a letter arrived from Wilfrid in New Zealand written on British Antarctic expedition paper, with its hallmark of a penguin standing on the globe.

Going strong old chap. We've done what we came to do, so far, except that we failed to land the party on Keiland. Too much ice. You've seen all about it in the papers. Our telegram is pretty voluminous and doubtless it will be largely increased by the paper people. We left Scott and all the party fit and well. Found Amundsen hiding in a corner and I think the beggar will arrive at the Pole before Scott unless his dogs go wrong, for he's got 120 of them and is travelling very light apparently. It's only a dash, there's nothing scientific about it, a low-down trick, for which he has no excuse and will get mighty little kudos, even if he gets there. If he doesn't, his name will be Mudd! Personally, they seemed decent sorts and how he has persuaded naval lieutenants to play this hole-and-corner game is hard to understand. We've just come through our second really heavy gale. The first with the ship deeply laden three days from New Zealand nearly finished us. This one, much heavier and lasting three days, hurt us very little but drove us 150 miles from a place we were trying to get to and had got to within 12 miles of. It's rotten luck. I hope you are all as happy as we are. We shall most of us be rather glad of the rest some day soon. We've done some work in the last two months. For the first Antarctic landing, for some days we were breakfasting at 5 a.m., starting work at 5.30, turning out stores and sledging for a mile and a half over the sea ice to the camp and going on with two half-hour breaks for meals till midnight. We were taking advantage of the fine weather, of course, but imagine asking a working man to do that even if you paid him for it! We're practically all volunteers. We've had a lot of exciting incidents, men, ponies, sledges and motor all going through the ice at times, the motor sledge sinking forever in deep water. Probably the most exciting was an attack on two of our dogs by whales. Sounds queer but it's true. Tell you all about it some day; I was a very close and interested spectator. Now if you haven't written to me at Lyttleton, you are a beast. I won't write any more. If you have I'll tell you all the rest later. See you in the Spring of 1913 I expect. So long. Be good. You won't worry to come out to my wedding will you? The date's not fixed yet and there are three brides at least but perhaps they'll sort themselves out in time. I can't be expected to do it can I?

Wilf.

Whenever he was in London, Rosslyn stayed with Kathleen in Buckingham Palace Road. She had a studio in the garden and worked hard at her sculpting with cheerful, sturdy Peter waddling about her. As a believer in the benefits of the sun's rays, she dressed Peter scantily, or not at all, in contrast to Merlin, among the flowerbeds at Clifton, who still wore white tucked dresses over two layers of petticoats. Kathleen was very much involved in the Home End of the Antarctic expedition, doing her best to moderate the controversy excited by Amundsen's dash to anticipate Scott.

The next letter from Wilfrid thanked for Rosslyn's, telling of the conflicting reports in the press about 'Scott's dash South'.

Good letter old chap. Yes, Shackleton's tongue is a trifle too long and I fancy he forgets that every word he utters re Antarctic is printed and kept and that Scott will eventually see them all, if he troubles to which he probably won't for many moons. Congratters on Rhalou, I bet she's a whale among babies.

I am not engaged yet and shan't be for a few months but I think the dearest girl in the world is at last discovered. We leave here tomorrow morning for three months sounding continuously off the Three Kings Islands just North of New Zealand. I said good-bye to her and everyone and am alone on board keeping ship on the last night. For a volunteer, desperately in love, of course, how's that for self-sacrifice? As a matter of fact I'm just dead tired. Our farewells have been many and chiefly dances and every one lasted until 2 or 3 every morning and I've always caught the 7.30 train to the ship and worked all day. We intended to slink away to sea early tomorrow morning but the harbour master has been bribed to prevent us leaving before 8 and the town band is ordered to play us out of port and we're going surveying. How small our caps are getting! So young Gladys is out, as pretty as ever I suppose? When did she break up at last? We've got some wild young pals here. I've seen some mad things done with the horses by girls on the stations here. I would never have believed them unless I'd seen them. Our little ship looks smart and neat and we hope she'll be somewhat less of a sieve than she once was. We spend a lot of time and trouble on her. She really ought to be decent now. Had *The Whip* and the Sheffield choir here last week both interesting in their way. Both considerably over-rated in my opinion. Drove a horse and trap ten miles on a back block track in the dark last week one candle lamp and a road I've never seen and through three creeks. I missed the ford in one, had to swim and climb the eight-foot shingle bank to get out, scared for both of us but we arrived. My host was in bed having given me up as I had missed the trap he'd sent for me so I found the stables, put my gee up and then woke him up. Haven't handled a horse for years and never drove in the dark in my life and you should have seen that road.

Rosslyn replied with homely pictures of King George V's coronation junketings, Clifton-style, with village feasting and take-your-mug-home afterwards. He wrote a coronation play which the school children acted. There was a cricket match and dancing in the rectory garden. The closest touch with His Majesty that week was having his favourite smooth fox terrier bitch, Sandringham Peg, in the rectory kennels while she visited Rosslyn's famous stud terrier, Force.

Next time they stayed at Northrepps, Rosslyn and Rachel met Sir Edgar Speyer, financier, who had a house at near-by fashionable

Overstrand. They discussed Scott's expedition and he promised Rosslyn to look into the money side of it. The bad weather had added enormously to the expense. Rosslyn's Nottingham friends, Sir Jesse and Lady Boot, as they had lately become, were also among the 'nine millionaires', with holiday houses on this crumbling North Norfolk cliff. They also took a useful interest in Scott's expedition.

Rosslyn left Rachel, the two babies and their nurses at Northrepps and went to Germany for three weeks as chaplain of the English church at Bad Nauheim. With a territorial camp in the park at Northrepps Hall, he was satisfied that Rachel and her sisters would not be dull in his absence. 'I can see you flirting with the majors,' he wrote, 'while the subalterns are making up to Turveydrop. I do hope she won't rush into terms with one of the war boys before she has ever known a man but I suppose she will. She must be a dazzling glory of fascination to them and with you and Rhalou I think the Norfolk Yeomanry are getting more than their share.' He said it had been a long lonely journey down the Rhine valley.

Twelve miles from Nauheim the engine lost all interest in the game and got out of breath and attached itself to a luggage train, then left go and went to several watering places just to show them to me, but always coming back like a good train for meals. We tried Homburg and Freiburg and Baden Baden and at last we came back to Nauheim and I nipped out quick before it could get off again, just in time to see it wambling home to tea for the third or fourth time.

In between taking services Rosslyn gave over twenty lectures. Everyone made a great fuss of him, particularly the Americans. He played tennis every morning and once nearly became involved in a duel with a Prussian count whom he had inadvertently offended by serving a lemon instead of a tennis ball, by way of a practical pun on the constant cry of '*Bitte*'.

Part of Rosslyn's job was to raise money for rebuilding the English church. The second Sunday he was there the organist was away and he was advised in German to go to a house where a famous musician was staying. He met the lady with her brother and instantly recognised why she was famous. The brother was the Kaiser. He was wearing a strange kind of Robin Hood outfit, more suitable to a shooting party than taking the waters. He had just finished eating an apple and was about to throw the core away when Rosslyn was reminded of his fund-raising and quickly held out his hand to relieve him of the core, whose pips (except for one which he kept) he afterwards auctioned for the English church and raised five pounds each. The Kaiser's sister came to the little church on Sunday and played the organ.

Rosslyn brought his pip home and planted it and, after a weedy start, in three succeeding parishes and two wars against Germany, it eventually bore a crop of green apples.

By the following February Kathleen was beginning to worry and expect news. Rosslyn prayed for Scott's expedition in church. Kathleen said one night that the clocks went wrong. Afterwards she learnt this was when Scott started his last dreadful journey. Expecting news, she gave a party. Rosslyn attended it and saw many old friends but he felt the strain she was under, although she looked as lovely and exciting as ever. 'A new beam of courage has grown into her face,' he said.

Next day the news came by cable that Amundsen had reached the South Pole. A rumour started that Scott had reached it simultaneously, which Kathleen spent the next day denying to the press. It was a year before news of him reached her.

Rosslyn had been at Clifton eight years, four of them with Rachel. In many ways it was a halcyon life. He had a beautiful wife, two healthy children, animals and birds as never before, with the peace of an old-fashioned country parish for writing and meditation. He had a charming rectory, conducted like something between a grand country house and a public zoo. Nottingham was only three miles away for pulpit, platform and committee appearances. There were fast trains to take him to London and the more influential scene and to bring back exciting guests to stay.

All, however, was not entirely easy. The 'new' Sir Hervey and Lady Bruce—Nellie, once Rosslyn's 'sort of mother'—still spent six months of the year at Downhill. In their absence Rachel, who had seemed so shy and young for her years when she first stayed at Clifton, revealed surprising skill in organising parochial matters In fact for nearly a decade before she married, since her father's death (when she was thirteen) she had been a key figure on her family estate in Norfolk, taking a large share in family decisions concerning the gardens, the stables and entertaining. In the village she had run the Sunday School, the almshouses, the church flower arrangement and most of the parish feasts. Now, at Clifton, she had crept into the hearts of the villagers, whom she visited assiduously, more dearly than seemed proper for a cousin-in-law of the hall.

With Rachel's friendliness in the village and Rosslyn's siding with the working man in Nottingham, it began to be suggested at the Hall that the rectory was 'rather red'. Their constant guest, Noel Buxton, they had hardly taken seriously as a Liberal M.P. Now he had been elected Labour M.P. for North Norfolk and enticed the Secretary of the local Conservative Association, Lucy Pelham-Burn, to his party with a proposal of marriage. And then there were all Rosslyn's other extraordinary friends who stayed at the rectory, 'most of whom were quite unfit to dine at the Hall'. There was the mad artist, Louis Wayne, who drew cats all over the walls and even the table napkins; and Isadora Duncan who took her illegitimate children sailing in an open boat without life jackets, 'trying to drown them', Hervey supposed. 'And all those bacchanal actors and meretricious actresses Rosslyn has picked up in the cafés of Soho.' They were certainly no company for Hervey's own youngest son and a ban was put on Benjie's visiting the rectory when he was on leave at Clifton. As most of Rosslyn's friends were Benjie's too, Benjie put his diplomatic training to work and returned from visits to the rectory via a ploughed field, so that the mud on his boots would suggest he had been for an agricultural walk, rather having enjoyed an hour or so of the lighter and less restricted atmosphere than the Hall's.

Fortunately Percy's children, Gervase and Sheila were considered impervious to the influences of the rectory and continued to skip in and out as before. Meanwhile Rosslyn remained faithful to old friends.

Madge Titheradge wrote to Rosslyn from the Globe Theatre:

Just a little letter to tell you that I am engaged to be married. His name is Charles Quartermain and he's a dear. I should simply

love you to marry us but I'm afraid it is too much to hope for. It
makes so much difference if it's someone you know and love.
Marie Löhr is to be my chief bridesmaid and Stella Patrick Camp-
bell and Beatrice Terry and Angela du Maurier and Rosalie Tollee.
Do you know where Wilfrid is? Will you write me a little letter?
With best love, dear Rosslyn,
Your friend

Rosslyn agreed and she wrote again: 'You can imagine how frightfully pleased Charlie and I are that you say you will be a dear and
marry us. Thank you awfully much. Cyril Maude will give us away.'
Madge's mother was in Australia and afterwards wrote thanking Rosslyn for 'marrying my little Madge to her chosen partner'. She had been
very upset by being so far off but was comforted by the thought that a
dear friend was with her. Everyone who knew her little genuine
Madge would wish her joy. Her sister had described 'how Madge's
nervousness and anxiety subsided at the first tones of Rosslyn's big
sympathetic voice, with his exquisite little address and the reverent
feeling he instilled'.

It all seemed on a simple and Christian plane, but when Hervey
saw the photographs in the press of the crowds who had turned up to
watch the glamorous spectacle of the Edwardian star's wedding, with
Rosslyn among the leading lovelies of the London theatres, he practically exploded. The stage, to Hervey, was iniquity at its lowest ebb.
Actors and actresses were all scallywags and vagabonds. The rector
of Clifton—*his* living—had no right to go pettifogging among them.

'The fellow's an eccentric!' he exclaimed, by way of a total write-
off. Coming from Hervey—who stamped about his country estate
with, Benjie said affectionately of him, 'his legs festooned in leather
gaiters-cum-spats on the model of those worn by Napoleon's old
guard, an underkeeper's suit crowned with an enormous jewelled
tie-pin, a reproduction of the Bruce crest—a lion passant in rubies
and diamonds—and a buttonhole the nearer the size of a prima
donna's last night's bouquet the better, with a monkey glaring from
under his coat'—Rosslyn's eccentricity at that time must have been
outstanding. Although the current Sir Hervey Bruce had a fine respect
for order and hereditary decoration and kept the house and gardens

and hothouses immaculately, he saw nothing amiss in installing a billiard table in the particularly delicate Chinese drawing room. Scoring boards, cue racks and raised platforms were all fastened to its Georgian walls, only just missing the rare panels of Chinese wall paper. The gas lamps lighting the table branched from a bare iron pipe hung from the exquisitely carved ceiling centre. Yet when Rosslyn dared to let more sunshine into the rectory garden, by cutting back some old pear trees it seemed to Hervey vandalism of the worst order.

'My dear Rosslyn,' he wrote from Downhill, 'Haynes told me you have been cutting down some pear trees in my part of the garden and that he has taken them away for my use. I don't suppose it is a matter of any consequence and what you have put in may be better than you cut down —' But it was a warning. Rosslyn replied in a warm and playful letter, for which he was reprimanded by Nellie in person. Nellie backed her husband in everything, no doubt moaning a little the loss of an entertaining bachelor 'sort of son' for dinner parties who, as the protegé of the old Sir Hervey had heeded his word rather more than his own grandsons had.

The last straw, as far as Hervey was concerned, was the Church Army. 'I love the Army, the whole thing,' a local paper reported Rosslyn's address at a huge open-air service at Nottingham. 'I love the uniform which the captains wear with the little C.A. badge. I love the captains inside that uniform. I love the sisters' uniform. And I love the sisters inside.' (loud applause and laughter). 'I love the Church Army right from the uniform to that splendid creation of Almighty God, their chief, Prebendary Carlile, whom I look upon as a model of what a parson should be.' The people cheered, but Clifton Hall showed disapproval.

'You might have got by if you hadn't undressed them,' Benjie observed.

Prebendary Carlile, however, who was searching for an exceptional padre who could eventually take over the Church Army from him did no more than issue a light warning when next he asked Rosslyn to preach for him.

'Dear brother,
So glad you can come to St. Jude's. Do forgive a caution, they are

210

low, old fashioned and afraid of a laugh (God save them). Their vicar is deep and good. I feared less they might think you did not deeply feel for and rejoice in the Lord. I know you don't mind if we style you Honourable Midland Secretary.

Affectionately, Yours in Christ

P.S. Will you come and lunch on Monday and sleep?

Rosslyn accepted and Prebendary Carlile begged him to return to London to throw himself completely into the work of the Church Army. But Rosslyn had already been asked to succeed Archdeacon Burrows, who had been Principal of the Leeds Clergy School in his day and was now to become Bishop of Truro. St. Augustine's, Edgbaston was the largest parish in Birmingham with a rising population of eleven thousand and tremendous scope for Rosslyn's ability and energy. With Easter offerings and funeral and wedding fees, the stipend was high enough to cover the cost of four curates to whom work could be delegated.

Prebendary Carlile wrote: 'I know a big parish is more inviting, but with us, the outcast is so great that I pray you may not be tempted to desert the poorest of the gutter. I am getting old. The Church Army needs you. You could strengthen my hand possibly. Mrs. Bruce might be able to help with the women's work.'

When Rosslyn wrote back that he had already accepted Edgbaston, Prebendary Carlile wrote again saying: 'I think we can give you: *One*, personal touch with the souls of the worst homes; *two*, an open door for evangelist teaching; *three*, a chance of moving the upper classes for God and the bottom dog.'

Rosslyn wrote recommending a successor to Hervey at Downhill who replied: 'Dear Rosslyn, I know nothing about Mr. Vaughan. I have not taken any steps, have I, about the date of your resignation?'

Aunt Zoe wrote from an hotel in Harrogate: 'My dear Rosslyn, I am delighted to hear of your appointment. I hope it suits you all in every way and that Rachel will not miss the garden and country air for the children.'

Rosslyn replied that it was a wrench to leave the thatched cottages and music of the thrushes and the warm-hearted people who had known him from his cradle, and his parents before his cradle was made, but Divine guidance led him now from the feudal conditions of Clifton to the most democratic city in the kingdom, to the centre of England's industrial life. Rosslyn added that he was a liberal in religious and social thought but *not* a politician—and a convinced believer in woman's power.

The only member of the household loath to move was Ada, who as a Northrepps schoolchild had thrown autumn leaves in a red cloak at Rachel's wedding, and had joined her later as nursery maid. She was now thirteen and walking out with the youngest garden boy at Clifton Hall.

The vicarage of No. 4 Manor Road, Edgbaston, was as different from Clifton Rectory as a bed of roses from a potted aspidistra. White plaster and Georgian windows were now replaced by maroon bricks and gables, stained glass and a salami paved hall. The only trees were a row of a dowdy pink mays between the in-and-out gates set back from the pavement. The garden at the back was just big enough to contain a tennis court. Rachel planted apple trees instead and Rosslyn lined the fences with aviaries and animal cages and turned the neo-Gothic stables into kennels. Nurse and nursery maids now had to hump babies, meals and coal up the two flights of stairs to the top-floor nurseries, leaving room for guests beside the marital chambers on the first floor. Compared with Clifton Rectory, the kitchens were poky, the drawing room, dining room, study and conservatory were heavy, and the hall was dark. At the end of Manor Road, electric trams, with characteristic Birmingham open-ended upper decks, swished and clanged along busy Hagley Road. Hansom cabs augmented the early taxis that brought guests and their luggage from Snow Hill or New Street stations, and took Rosslyn and Rachel out in the evenings. Rosslyn mounted his stately Sunbeam bicycle for visiting and near-by assignations. But trams and trains were ever his favourite form of transport for the friends he made, and the audiences they provided for his latest stories.

Rachel sold her riding habits and hunting boots and prepared herself for town life. She found a Court dressmaker and a tailor who specialised in miniature hand-stitched children's clothes. Early memories of the young vicar's wife in Birmingham were mostly of a willowy beauty within a mist of floating panels. Rosslyn dissuaded her from taking more than a nominal part in parish life and encouraged her preoccupation with the nurseries.

For eighty pounds a year and maintenance they were able to keep a cook, a house parlour maid, a nurse, Ada, and Fox, who combined the duties of church verger, gardener, kennelman and chauffeur for their first T Model Ford. Fox changed into cassock, breeches, white coat or maroon livery according to needs.

The household ate well, if plainly, and there was a constant stream of visitors. In spite of the curates attending a good many meals Rachel's housekeeping books rarely totted up to more than ten pounds a month. Many of the parishioners were enormously rich and their dinner parties more ostentatious than anything Rachel had ever seen in the country. Even the ladies talked about cars. 'Yes, we've got three of them,' Rachel was astonished to hear. 'You see it's me 'usband's 'obby.'

Rosslyn threw himself into a diversity of activities as soon as he arrived. A new church was needed in another part of the parish and it was his task to collect the money for it and see it rise. The only part of the project waiting for him was the name, St. Germain's. He appealed for advice to an old London friend, Cecil Harris, who came as their first visitor to view the site.

He interested Rosslyn in the appropriate architectural books and together they visited other churches 'for ideas'. Cecil Harris wrote thanking him for introductions made in Birmingham, commenting on the 'big sphere' of Rosslyn's work and promising further advice.

Building was something entirely new to Rosslyn.

'Every man should be involved in the building of at least one house in his life,' he said. 'If he can't build a house, then make it a church.'

He started holding services on the proposed site of St. Germain's before it had even been bought. The unusual design by Edwin F. Reynalds, R.I.B.A. was chosen in competition from twenty-one Birmingham architects. It had a semi-circular apse and semi-dome; the columns supporting the arches on each side of the chancel were to have Swedish green marble shafts. The roof showed massive timbers with coloured patterns.

Rosslyn raised money in all kinds of unorthodox ways. He persuaded a circus to come to Bingley Hall and give a performance in aid of the church. He, himself, went round the city advertising the show on the back of a motor bicycle with a sea lion in the side-car. He accepted bets involving riding certain distances in strange attire, and won them.

Two very wealthy parishioners, knowing he would call on them to ask for donations, got together and planned to tease him. The first said he would give a thousand pounds on condition Amen was not pronounced in the church with a short A. The second said he would do likewise on condition Amen was not pronounced with a long A. Rosslyn asked them both to tea and announced that it had been decided that 'so be it', at St. Germain's would be pronounced as in the Hebrew, 'Ermeen'. Both paid up.

CHAPTER SEVENTEEN

Very Brave and English Gentlemen

St. Augustine's church—a large well-endowed example of opulent mid-Victorian architecture—continued to be filled. The new vicar's preaching, observed the *Birmingham Post* 'had the rare quality and finesse which are a joy and a possession to all who have the privilege of hearing it. His saving sense of humour enables him to see the component parts of life in their proportions. He truly belongs to the intelligentsia.' Yet most immediately popular was his Young People's Service, known as 'Y.P.S.' which promised to be no longer than three quarters of an hour. A series of ten-minute talks under the title of *What Jesus Did* 'for those of any age who still retained a child-like teachableness' were advertised with each Sunday's subtitle:

> He grew
> He lost Himself
> He camped out
> He won a fight
> He climbed a mountain
> He went fishing
> He made water blush
> He cured invalids
> He expected gratitude
> He went for a country walk
> He came eating and drinking
> He told lovely stories
> He raised a dead boy
> He let goblins make pigs of themselves
> He chose some friends

He raised a dead girl
He provided a huge picnic
He cured a mad baby boy
He started a society
He disliked humbugs
He blessed child-like people
He studied natural history
He cried
He scolded the greedy rich
He suffered frightfully
He rode a donkey, and then died
He awoke to life again
He started a love-feast
He made others happy
He was greatly changed
He enjoyed music
He loved tame animals
He promised peace
He promised to be here always
He passed from sight
He spoke to St. Paul
He spoke to you

One Sunday at Matins Rosslyn began: 'In divine worship there is no room for what is undignified, trivial or commonplace, cheap or slovenly in style. Nothing but the highest and best is worthy.' He then preached a sermon that caused a considerable stir based, no doubt, on Rachel's influence.

The *Daily News* ran headlines 'Consider the Lilies. Why an English woman should dress well.' In the *Observer* 'Sayings of the Week' he was quoted 'Every woman should look as nice as she is able. It is her duty as a Christian woman.' The *Sunday Pictorial* devoted a whole page with suitable illustrations to Rosslyn's sermon and *Punch* broke into verse:

Determined to be orthodox
She's ordered half a dozen frocks

And tried on half a dozen toques
To see which suits her beauty
For she had heard a parson state —
And parson's least words carry weight—
A woman ought to titivate.
It is her Christian duty.
That duty she will never shirk
But in silk stockings open work,
She'll go and decorate the kirk
With Bond Street's latest creations
And all because she's not obtuse
But knows that Dr. Rosslyn Bruce
Though most devout, has got no use
For dowdy congregations.

Rosslyn sometimes invited adult questions after a sermon. Encouraged by the results he livened up the parish magazine by introducing an Agony Column which, to begin with, he wrote almost entirely himself under such pseudonyms as Anxious, Disappointed and Deafened. There was a touch of the Oxford Union about some of the answers. Presently parishioners' own questions came along and Rosslyn answered them seriously or playfully according to their lights. The circulation of the parish magazine rose and his answers were often quoted in the secular press.

The Master of Music, Alfred Gaul, with Victorian sideboards and a delicate expression, had been at St. Augustine's since its foundation in 1868. He 'joined the choir invisible' as the tablet erected a few feet from his old seat put it, during Rosslyn's first year. He was succeeded by young William Harris, (always known, after he became a Doctor of Music, as Doc H, even after he became Sir William Harris) as organist and choirmaster of St. George's Chapel, Windsor. His setting of 'The Hound of Heaven' won him a Carnegie award and many of his earlier choral works were composed specially for the choir of St. Augustine's.

Rosslyn became vice-chairman of the council of the Edgbaston High School for Girls and, in the Birmingham Botanical Society, he became chairman of a sub-committee formed to introduce a zoological collection in the gardens. He gave or lent many of the animals and birds personally. An attractive white kid that romped with the children had engraved on its collar 'I'm Dr. Bruce's kid. Whose kid are you?' He put seals into the fountain and tropical birds and fishes into the greenhouses. He gave a llama that delighted visitors by spitting at them. His largest animal, for whom a special house had to be made, was Gladly, named after the hymn 'Gladly my Cross I'd Bear'.

Rosslyn was also on two hospital committees and chaplain to three others. He continued as chaplain in the Territorial Army, was chaplain to the existing Masonic Lodge and was a founder member of Birmingham Rotary, whose fellow members kept mementos of many of the 'unforgettable occasions of Rosslyn Bruce'.

He defined Rotary as 'a sort of mutual admiration society, not a political organisation. They were not even allowed to sing 'God Save the King'; not a religious body, but a useful forum through which any distinguished visitor could address the industries of the city.'

On their first Ladies' Night the 'Georgian Quartette' was billed for entertainment, but failed to turn up owing to missed train connections. Rosslyn and three other Rotarians got together to replace them and concocted suitable lyrics on the backs of their programmes. They introduced themselves as 'J. Parker Garner, Uncertain Baritone, J. Percy Plant, Chapel Bass or Vacillating Baritone; Andrew J. Harrison, Bona Fide Baritone and Dr. Rosslyn Bruce, Cross-bred Nine to Tenor.' As they wandered about in various keys, apologies were made for the faults of rendition. 'At times their theme distinctly suggested an air,' said one Rotarian, and another, 'that it ought to be set to music.'

'We are four Rotarians who are singing this glee,' they sang merrily:

> 'There's Percy and Rosslyn Bruce and Parker and me
> On Mondays you'll see us all sit in a bunch
> We all pay four shillings for a half a crown lunch
> Those who are here with us will say with regret
> Oh how we wish we had heard that real Georgian quartette.'

The Repertory Theatre was another great delight. Rosslyn never missed a new show and was often called upon to appear before the curtain. Thus he kept in touch with many of his old theatrical friends nearly all of whom stayed at the vicarage during engagements.

His old friend, Mabel Dearmer, whose little boys had been his first guests at Clifton, wrote a Christmas play *The Cocky olly Bird* which was put on annually at the Birmingham Rep.

Dog shows, bird shows and lectures filled any time left over from family life at 4 Manor Road.

In November 1912 Rosslyn asked Kathleen if she would bring Scott to stay and speak at the British Association in Birmingham when he got back.

She answered on a postcard 'Off to New Zealand January 4th. The White Star Line has given me a free pass to New York, which is civil of them, isn't it? Love to do the Birmingham thing. I sail from Liverpool. Where is it? Love to Charle.'

She left Peter in charge of Viscount Knutsford, who kept tame bullfinches and labradors trained to land trout.

She crossed the United States by train and was seen off from San Francisco by reporters and the Mayor, at the same time as the *Terra Nova* was approaching Lyttleton, New Zealand, on her third and last journey from the Antarctic.

On February 12th, 1913, a cable to Aunt Zoe was forwarded to Rosslyn. CAPTAIN SCOTT AND THREE OTHERS PERISHED IN BLIZZARD AFTER REACHING SOUTH POLE JANUARY 18TH LAST YEAR—six weeks after Amundsen reached the Pole.

Rosslyn immediately started to arrange a memorial service to coincide with one at St. Paul's Cathedral. He left a note for the assistant organist, after hearing that efforts to communicate with Kathleen's ship had failed as wireless was not strong enough to reach it until it was nearer land.

I am afraid that my brother will have the terrible duty of breaking the news to my sister on her way to New Zealand. I can't picture any more pathetic figure than that poor little lady going out there expecting all the triumph and the delight of getting her husband back and knowing as she does how keenly interested the whole world is in the expedition.

'Thank you for letting me know about the memorial service,' wrote Oliver Lodge, Vice-Chancellor of Birmingham University. 'Can you spare me a few tickets? I shall certainly try to attend. I knew Captain Scott slightly before he was married and he afterwards brought his wife to our house before he started on his second expedition. They were both very charming people. Our heart goes out to your sister in her terrible bereavement.'

Sir Fowell Buxton, Noel's father, wrote the same day 'Dear Rosslyn, We are feeling much the tragedy of a year ago. Victoria and I cannot but remember your connection with it. The grievous shock that it must be upon your sister, Mrs. Scott. We shall be anxious to hear about it in the course of time. You brought her here but we have not seen her since.'

His old friend, the Rev. C. H. Daniels, Provost of Worcester College wrote:

My dear Bruce,

With all England I may say all the world, we in this house, are lamenting the terrible catastrophe which is in all our thoughts—the heroism and the man, and the terrible sorrow of his wife. You may imagine with what sympathy we are praying for her and her child, and for you too. There is some consolation in the world's admiration and sympathy as well as in the more personal, and therefore more vivid, feelings of friends among whom we claim to be. In sorrow, as in well being,

Yours sincerely, G. H. Daniels.

P.S. The Oxford Corporation will have a memorial service tomorrow and I have ordered the funeral march for evensong in chapel. This is of course my wife's message and my daughter's as well as from myself.

The family exchanged condolences.

Dear old boy, [wrote Percy Bruce]

One line to tell you how sorry I am for Kathleen's sake. Some day I may be able to talk or write to her about it. The tragedy of it all is patent but my goodness what a lesson. It just shows how one can face death. You and I have been pretty close to it together. I often think of it. The little things, political arguments and such like don't seem of much moment now do they? How splendid it all is. I can't help feeling even a little proud myself of being of the same flesh and blood even. This is indeed a case of death where is thy sting. When I think of Con facing death as he did it almost makes me feel inclined to say hurrah! not quite though. The other side of it all pokes its head up and one has to think of the other side. Well, he died a hero's death and that is something. You are nearer to him in many ways maybe than I am and I'd like you to know I am sorry for the sad part of it.

Wilfrid had already written on January 31st from the *Terra Nova* headed 'At Sea', and now his letter arrived.

Sad story, old chap, isn't it? They died bravely after achieving their object and no human power availed to save them. We are not a lot of whimpering school girls and after the first shock, have become reconciled to the fact that the risks of these expeditions are enormous and no one can complain that the higher powers are unkind. They were extraordinary lenient to the Norwegians, that's all. The women folk have to suffer though. I am dreading the effect of the news on Kathleen, Mrs. Wilson and Con's mother. They too of course knew the risks (Kiddie before she married him) but it's rough. I am bringing her home at once, if she doesn't crock up, and I think she won't. She's strong and proud. There are big lessons to be learned from this story. I can't write more. Have an awful lot to tell you when we meet. Kiddie and I home in April, I hope. My love to Rachel and the kiddies. We're simply romping home just now, but it will be a dreary arrival. And there's Kiddie to meet! Ugh!

> Love from your brother Wilfrid.

Then came an unbearably cheerful letter from Kathleen dated February 20th written before the news had reached her. Rachel had sent her a pair of long white gloves to wear at the Government receptions that were expected to fête Scott on his return. Rosslyn had sent her a form of the Thanksgiving Service he had planned. Kathleen wrote on her way to Lyttleton on Union Line paper with a coloured picture of a tall funnelled liner on a tossing sea, against a hopeful sunset.

> Dearest Rachel,
>
> I don't believe I ever thanked you for the gloves. How hideous of me if I didn't for I like them enormously and I liked Rosslyn's 'Service'. I've had a wonderful time camping with ten cowboys on a cattle ranch in Arizona, rounding up the cattle, on horse-back all day and sleeping round a cedar wood camp-fire at night. Very lovely — [The letter broke off and continued on the back page in pencil.] February 20th. I've just had my news by the wireless. Just the barest fact. No details. I shall probably come straight home and thus will be back about the middle of April. I shall probably come on a Liberia but I'm not sure, much love,
>
> Yours, Kathleen.

She said afterwards that she was sitting on deck after breakfast, not feeling very well, when she got the message. The Captain asked her to speak to him in his cabin. His hands were trembling when he said, 'I've got some news for you but I don't see how I can tell you' and then showed her the message. She remembered saying without the least truth, 'Oh well never mind. I expected that. Thanks very much. I will go and think about it.' And she went downstairs and finished her letter. She had a Spanish lesson, lunch, and discussed American politics. As the ship neared New Zealand wireless messages of sympathy kept coming in and blocking the line for the news of details that she wanted to hear.

Two days later, and five days before schedule, they arrived at Wellington. Wilfrid went on board via the medical officer's boat. Mrs. Wilson stood on the wharf. Wilfrid had never needed such courage as then.

Kathleen spent the whole night reading Con's last journal, in which he wrote:

> The causes of this disaster are not due to faulty organisation but to misfortune.

1. The loss of pony transport in March 1911 obliged me to start later than I had intended and obliged the limits of stuff transported to be narrowed.

2. The weather throughout the outward journey and especially the long gale in 83° South, stopped us.

3. The soft snow in the low reaches of the glacier again reduced the pace. We fought these untoward events with a will and conquered. But it ate into our provisions reserve. Every detail of our food supplies, clothing and depots made on the interior ice sheet and the long stretch of seven hundred miles to the Pole and back, worked out to perfection.

The advance party would have returned to the glacier in fine form and with a surplus of food but for the astonishing failure of the man whom we least expected to fail. We'd got in frightfully rough ice, and Seaman Edgar Evans received a concussion of the brain. He died a natural death, but left us a shaken party, with the season unduly advanced.

Then came the terrible weather and the sickening of a second companion, Captain Oates, who was quite unable to travel and the others would not leave him.

He slept through the night hoping not to wake, but he woke in the morning. It was blowing a blizzard. Oates said 'I'm just going outside and I may be some time'. He went out into the blizzard and we have not seen him since. We knew that Oates was walking to his death but though we tried to dissuade him, we knew it was the act of a brave man and an English gentleman.

'I do not think human beings ever came through such a month as we have come through'.

'For *four* days we have been unable to leave the tent, a gale blowing about us,' he wrote, only eleven miles from their old depot.

'We took risks—we know we took them . . .'

'Had we lived I should have had a tale to tell of the hardihood, endurance, and courage of my companions, which would have stirred the heart of every Englishman.'

In a letter to Kathleen after eight days without food and the temperature minus forty degrees he wrote: 'You urged me to be leader of this party and I know you felt it would be dangerous. I have taken my place throughout haven't I? Oh my dear, my dear, what dreams I have had of the future. Yet, oh my dear I know you will face it sturdily.'

His last message was: 'These rough notes and our dead bodies must tell the tale; BUT SURELY, SURELY, A GREAT, RICH COUNTRY LIKE OURS WILL SEE THAT THOSE WHO ARE DEPENDANT UPON US ARE PROPERLY PROVIDED FOR. (Signed) R. Scott.

This, the great rich country did through a Mansion House Fund that was set up and there were government pensions for the widows of the expedition and their children.

On February 24th it was officially announced from 10 Downing Street that His Majesty the King had been pleased to grant Mrs. Kathleen Scott the same rank, style and precedence as if her husband Captain Robert Falcon Scott, R.N., C.V.O., had been nominated a Knight Commander of the Bath as he would have been had he survived. 'Lady Scott is due to arrive at Wellington, New Zealand, and will probably hear the news by wireless on her way in.'

Because the news of all this came through so slowly, leaving months between reports to think about it; because Scott had such a fine sense of honour and magnificent command of the English language; because failure is sometimes more endearing than success, Scott's appeal for those left behind continued to be answered, not only with money but adulation. Peter Scott at three years old was already world famous. Born an attractive, robust, intelligent, cheerful and pink-cheeked baby, full of warmth and affection, he responded well to the many great men who were prepared to give time to him because of the words his father wrote to Kathleen a few days before he died: 'Make the boy interested in natural history. It is better than games. They encourage it at some schools.' He had already been made a Life Fellow of the Zoological Society as a christening present. His godfather, Admiral Sir Clements Markham, President of the Royal Geographical Society, took him to the South Kensington Museums. Lord Baden-Powell taught him the usefulness of being ambidextrous. Rosslyn gave him a bantam hen with a clutch of eggs and received one of his first letters in pencil:

'Dear Rosslyn, Twa hatched on the way Love Peter (Scott).'

Kathleen spurned the velvet tunics that followed the white lace frocks worn by Merlin and other four-year-olds and continued to dress him in short sleeveless shifts or nothing at all. She was years ahead of other young mothers and eyebrows were raised and stories circulated. But Kathleen had won her licence to do as she liked.

Rosslyn helped her to sort letters. There was one from von Tirpitz, Admiral of the German Fleet, expressing his admiration for the great work performed by Scott. 'I had thought the British Navy was living on its historic prestige and had lost its pluck; the exploits of Scott have dispelled that impression.'

To help to raise the Fund, Rosslyn lectured on the expedition with lantern slides from Ponting's photographs.

Kathleen's larger-than-life-sized statues of Scott were placed in London, Portsmouth and Christchurch, New Zealand. A smaller, more intimate memorial of hers was dedicated in Binton church and a day was set aside annually to commemorate Scott. Many top people came to Kathleen's studio to be sculpted. But it was a sad year. Isadora Duncan's two children, whom she and Rosslyn had known since they were born, were drowned when the chauffeur-driven car they were in, crashed into the Seine.

On June 14th Wilfrid reached Cardiff with the *Terra Nova* where it paid off. He had brought back Scott's possessions and took the pianola that had lightened many a long dark evening at Hutt Point in the Antarctic to Kathleen at Buckingham Palace Road. Some of his uniform, instruments and notebooks went to exhibitions and later were distributed about the family. Merlin was given, and used, his greatcoat and his sextant.

Within weeks of his return Wilfrid had announced his engagement to Dorothy Boot, daughter of Sir Jesse Boot and whose brother Rosslyn had coached at Clifton. Rosslyn married the 'family best man' later in the summer.

At the end of October Rosslyn was lunching with his Oxford Union friend, now Sir John Simon who had just become Chancellor of the Exchequer, when he was called home as 'Rachel was busy suggesting that the new baby was at hand.' In fact the outcome of the suggestion was measles from which she was desperately ill and delirious for two days. The baby, Erroll, was born a week later and, unseen by his mother, rushed by hansom cab into a nursing home to avoid infection.

Just before Christmas, Aunt Zoe died. Rosslyn went to Bishopthorpe to take part in the funeral. The procession went, not by the road, but through the palace grounds by the winding garden path and avenue of trees along which she had passed for twenty-six years on her way to services. To Rosslyn she left her beloved Archbishop's prayer desk and his Bible.

Rosslyn stayed with Noel Buxton at his 'final bachelor establishment' in London before he married him in April 1914 to Lucy Pelham-Burn who was now totally committed to the Labour Party.

Rosslyn and Rachel went on to Wales where they stayed for a short holiday in a house in Caernarvonshire belonging to Lloyd George, then Chancellor of the Exchequer. Rosslyn had met him with Noel. Rachel sent a box of wild flowers in gratitude and Margaret Lloyd George wrote from 11 Downing Street.

> Thank you so much for your kind letter. We appreciate it very much. Am glad you liked the view from our house. We think it delightful. I was surprised you had picked so many different kinds of wild flowers. I had no idea there was such a choice. My husband was pleased with your pleasant story, with kind regards,
> Yours sincerely, M. Lloyd George

At some moment when those wild flowers were still blooming in Wales I must have been conceived in that house. It is intriguing to fancy what influences this may have had over the Bruces' fourth child.

CHAPTER EIGHTEEN

Rosslyn in America

The news of Scott and his companions' heroic deaths after reaching the South Pole was only known eighteen months before the Great War began. After that, death and heroism were commonplace. But Scott's last messages had a great effect on the attitude to both. 'I do not regret this journey, which has shown us that Englishmen can endure hardship, help one another and meet death with as great a fortitude as ever in the past.'

Rosslyn and Rachel were at Northrepps with the three children when war was declared. It was Merlin's fifth birthday. Missing from his birthday party were the children of Sir Edgar Speyer, from Overstrand, whose German origin caused so much ill-feeling in the neighbourhood that they had returned to London. The Speyers' children's party, three days before, had been made memorable by a birthday cake shaped like a Bavarian cottage with a pond full of treacle.

Rosslyn went straight back to Edgbaston where he found he had been gazetted in the army list as a chaplain of the Royal Artillery.

However, his Bishop wrote: 'although you have been asked for by the Royal Horse Artillery, I am not pressing for the appointment, as I feel a younger parson would be more useful at the front and much less use in Birmingham, where the population will increase due to munition factories.' The Voluntary Training Corps of Warwickshire had just been brigaded and Rosslyn was asked to be chaplain to the 4th Brigade. As such, he merely had to take church parade regularly and give certain addresses. He was also able to continue as padre to the Legion of Frontiersmen without leaving Birmingham.

A young soldier on five days leave asked Rosslyn to marry him by special licence. When he heard that the bridegroom was in the artillery, Rosslyn promptly gave back the licence fee of seven and sixpence saying there was 'a special rule in the artillery about the first wedding present coming from another artilleryman'.

Fox was called up and the car remained undriven in the coach house. When two of the curates went too, Rosslyn installed a telephone to replace them. From the very beginning so many husbands, sons and brothers of his parishioners were killed or wounded, that there was no time to go at once to each one of them with comfort and prayers.

Both Rachel's brothers were serving abroad and several of Rosslyn's nephews and cousins. Noel went straight off to try to secure adhesion among the Balkan States in Turkey, where in October, he was wounded by a political assassin, who shot him through the jaw. Within three months of the outbreak of war came news from Clifton that Gervase, Percy's fifteen-year-old boy, serving as a midshipman in H.M.S. *Monmouth* had gone down with his ship.

Early in the war Rosslyn introduced a two-minute silence for remembering the dead at Matins.

In January Chloe, who had nursed him through his hunting accident, arrived from Scarborough, badly shaken after a Zeppelin raid in which the postman had been killed delivering a letter at her door. But after a night's sleep she donned her uniform, with its red cross emblazoned on her apron, and prepared for Rachel's impending confinement.

On January 12th Ada took up early morning tea as usual at 7.30 and not until she was directed to the cot did she know there had been any disturbance in the night. I had been born almost soundlessly at 4.15 a.m.

Business went on as usual. Rosslyn attended a meeting of the Botanical Gardens, arranged for the organ to be mended and registered the adverb, *Verily*, as my name. By now the names were being fitted into a kind of crossword puzzle system. Each was to have six letters and an R and an L, as in Rosslyn and Rachel and each was to have 'something the others hadn't got'. Merlin had M; Rhalou had H; Erroll had doubles and I now had V.

The 'Verily, I say unto you' jokes began at once, and Doc H

explained away my natural rotundity to 'Verily, thou shalt be fed' being sung in the psalm on the morning of my christening. It was a communal christening. The font was lined with primroses and wild violets brought from Binton, by one of the godfathers, the saintly Uncle Lloydie, and his twin. The godmothers were Mabel Dearmer, playwright; Una Burrows, wife of Rosslyn's old friend and clergy school principal, now Bishop of Truro; Jessica Tredwell, the brides-maid who was sent over from Boston in lieu of Rachel's visit to the United States; and Dorothy Gurney, wife of Rachel's brother, Chris-topher later of Northrepps.

The next ceremony was the cutting of the turf of St. Germain's church. In July the foundation stone was laid with Masonic honours. Since war broke out, building had almost come to a standstill. St. Germain's was probably the only church in the country begun and completed during the war. The site was given on condition that the church was dedicated by June 1917.

Building proceeded but there was trouble over the name. Anything remotely related to the word German produced antagonism.

Rosslyn consulted Oliver Lodge.

> It appears, [he replied] that St. Germain is a messenger or angel of St. Augustine and he may be regarded as a faint shadow of two really great men, Augustus and Gregory. May I suggest considera-tion of the last name as a contemporary, clearly associated with St. Augustine? Hereby avoiding the unfortunate association appar-ently thought to be with Germany?

He went on to say that Hilaire Belloc was coming to the university to lecture and no doubt would be staying at 4 Manor Road.

Bishop Burrows weighed in on the St. Germain's Germanic theme:

> It would be a good thing if some of you would give a short bio-graphical sketch of St. Germain so that the truly absurd objection to the name for a church should be given up. It seems to me Daily Mailism gone mad. Considering the whole working up of the new parish has been carried on under the auspices of this particular Saint I think it is rather hard to turn him down at this moment. I'm glad you are being called names though they are weak ones.

When you're a Bishop you'll be thankful for any rising of the sun upon a day when you are not compared unfavourably with his Satanic Majesty.

Later there was some dissent over the decoration of one of the seven stone panels on the outside of St. Germain's. Some backed the architect who wanted figures carved in low relief; others wanted it left plain. Rosslyn suggested, since funds were not yet all gatherd, leaving the matter in the hands of the Lord.

A year later he proclaimed that a miracle had taken place, for in the panel, ivy had crept up in the shape of a glorious angel blowing a trumpet. Thus the Lord had decided to decorate the church Himself.

Kathleen, returning from Italy where she had been sculpting during a holiday from munition work, said she too had been involved in that kind of a miracle. She had stayed at Massa and gone daily to Carrara to work on a statue, walking back over the mountains in the evenings. On one such walk she passed the stoneyard of a country mason. The men had gone for the day leaving their tools by the tomb-stone of an Italian soldier killed in action on which they had begun a rude overturned figure of an angel. Kathleen took the tools and, doing the best work she had ever done, finished the figure leaving them to find it in the morning and start a legend of a village miracle. She later worked in hospitals, modelling noses and chins to help surgeons to repair shattered faces.

In Birmingham, as in all the cities, food was short and morale was low. Rachel went more often with the children to Northrepps, where there was fresh garden and farm produce and fish from the sea. The cook had gone into munitions and Ada, still in her early teens, did the cooking with another Northrepps ex-schoolgirl, Rosa Bane, trained at Northrepps Hall, as house parlourmaid.

With Fox at the front, a sixteen-year-old schoolboy was combining the jobs of verger and assistant organist at St. Augustine's. 'Dear Vicar,' Rosslyn found a sealed letter from him on his desk, 'I have just got engaged to a divorced woman so I suppose I must resign my job at St. Augustine's? Please tell nobody except Mrs. Bruce till you have seen me. Nobody knows a word about it except my good friend Dr. Harris.'

He was not the only one of his age to cause anxiety.

Madge Titheradge was worried about a boy actor who had been in a show with her at Royal Drury Lane. He had been brought up by a churchy family, and had been to the Chapel Royal school, but had defected at an early age when he joined the theatre. Really he had given a great deal of trouble. She hardly knew how to put it. Now he had just come out of a sanatorium where he had been with a tubercular gland in his chest The vicar of Clapham had persuaded him to be confirmed and for a while he had shown almost fanatical enthusiasm for religion. But now, Madge said, he was often extremely flippant about religion. Would Rosslyn please look out for him when he came to the Birmingham Rep in *Charlie's Aunt*.

There was no need for Rosslyn to look out for the young Noël Coward. Hands went up to faces and aprons practically went over heads at the mention of the little terror. They called him the Bumptious Child. He giggled and undermined others on the stage and sang rude songs of his own invention when he was barely off it. He went about with one girl, wearing her clothes and followed her into the lavatory to finish telling her some long story. Moreover, as he himself admitted later, he was also not above a little light shoplifting. Rosslyn talked to this self-assured pale-cheeked schoolboy and was instantly reminded of his own questionable behaviour at the same age. They compared notes and Rosslyn had to admit that he had not had the same chances of creating hell as Noël had in the theatre. Rosslyn told him about Dante, but as far as religion went Noël had changed sides, he said. However, they got on well and Rosslyn asked Noël to stay at 4 Manor Road.

Later, while Rachel was at Northrepps, first Nigel Playfair stayed during the run of a play he was in, and then Betty Chester with Noël Coward. Noël was still growing and was perpetually hungry. He ate the remains of any stage food that was left over, and when they came in at midnight he and Betty cooked themselves meals from whatever they could find in the larder and store cupboard. Poor Ada, who always went to bed at ten o'clock, came down in the morning appalled, but she said nothing till the end of the rations were in sight. Then she went to Rosslyn.

But this was only one of the complaints made against his young guest. He had shocked the neighbours by coming home in girl's clothes, wearing lipstick, and disturbed the dentist's wife at two o'clock in the morning playing the vicarage Bechstein. Rosslyn took him into his study and gave him a good talking to.

'You know, Noël,' he said, 'behaving the way you do—wearing stage make-up in the street—everybody's talking about you.'

Noël slapped his knee with delight, and exclaimed crisply, 'They're not! How ripping! That's why I do it!'

Next morning Rosslyn found a note from Betty on his desk.

Dear Dr. Bruce,

I've been thinking over what to do. It really has been ripping of you to have us all this time and I really think you must turn me out (and the wretched boy too) neck and crop on Monday. But the hotels really seem impossible. I wonder if in the course of your district visiting, by asking a few pointed questions you couldn't find somebody who would let rooms. By the way Nigel told me that he had made it a condition that he should be looked upon as a polite P.G. and the same rule applies here and you must tell about it in the first, but I hope not the last, epistle of Dr. St. Bruce to the young heathens. It would do Noël good to be told he has reached years of independence but there is this excuse for both of us that househunting and the learning of long parts are incompatible, that is why we are so grateful to you.

Yours ever, Betty.

Meanwhile Noël, in a fit of patriotism had started to dig up the lawn to plant potatoes.

Rosslyn brought out *A Small Pocket Book of Prayers* chiefly designed for the use of servicemen, with a reproduction of Rossetti's 'Knight in Armour' in it above 'My soul is in armour and eager for the fray'. There were spaces for the owner's name, date of birth and baptism, which is perhaps one reason why so many of these little books are reported to be still kept by one-time members of his congregation, who still, when entering a church kneel down and say, as suggested in the book, 'Oh Lord I am now in thy house, accept me for thy service; make me attentive to what I hear, and obedient to what I understand, for Jesus Christ's sake Amen.'

One of the prayers was inspired by the fear that a lump that appeared over my eye might be malignant. During the operation to remove it the Mothers' Union was set to pray for my sight, or at any rate my life, both of which petitions were answered with the bonus of a lasting friendship between the family of the eye surgeon, Mr. Jack Jameson-Evans, who performed the operation, and myself.

In 1916, in the uniform of the Royal Artillery, clerical collar and wearing his cap straight as a bishop's biretta, Rosslyn left for France to relieve another chaplain doing hosptial work. He had been begged by friends, relations and parishioners to try to trace their wounded.

At Wimereux a car and a young officer were put at his disposal. But he soon learnt that the chances of finding anyone, however well their letters had been getting through, who was not hale enough to meet him by arrangement, were slight. 'You can't expect to find Jim's sister's maid's nephew just by visiting a dozen hospitals,' his colonel said. In fact he did see a number of his parishioners' menfolk though mostly by chance. Many were in a hopeless condition. Two brothers had virtually to choose between amputation of both legs or death. One chose the first, the other the second. Another lad whose parents he knew, came over to a table where he was lunching with the colonel and asked if he could verify the casualties as his younger brother, aged seventeen and a half was reported missing. The boy had arrived the day before and was going to the trenches that night. He was only nineteen himself. The brother had been killed. Rosslyn went out and comforted him.

Rosslyn took services and funerals but his chief job was ministering to the dying who were often unconscious or more tragic still, if their identification had gone, unable to speak to say who they were and to send messages home. The jaws of so many were frightfully damaged. An orderly pointed out that if they had been hit higher they would have been killed.

Rosslyn returned home via Kathleen's at Buckingham Palace Road. Geoffrey Dearmer, now just old enough to serve, was there on leave. Rosslyn talked to Peter in bed.

Peter came down to ask Rosslyn to tell him more about France and Kathleen reprimanded Rosslyn for frightening the boy. Rosslyn laughed and asked Peter to repeat what he'd said.

'Well, Uncle Rosslyn was wandering about at night and the sentry said, "Who goes there?"' Peter repeated with tremendous chuckles. 'And he said, "Army Chaplain." And the sentry said, "Pass Charlie Chaplin".' Peter went rolling merrily back to bed.

Here Rosslyn met Colonel House whom Kathleen had first met in New York on her way to New Zealand. He questioned Rosslyn on his time in the lines and Rosslyn told him how he had asked at a front line service if there was any message he should take back. 'For God's sake tell them to care more' was the answer.

Rosslyn was with Kathleen when news came that their brother Douglas's eldest boy, Robert, a lieutenant in the Cameronian Rifles, had been killed. Kathleen involuntarily snatched up her own seven-year-old son as though he were already in danger.

The meeting with Colonel House led to Rosslyn and Noel setting off at very short notice for the United States. Noel wired to Rachel from Paddington:

LET ME BEG YOU TO APPROVE PLAN PROPOSED TO ROSSLYN HE COULD DO IMMENSE SERVICE TO HUMAN-ITY WHICH WILL OTHERWISE NOT BE RENDERED AND WOULD ALSO GET REST AND PERSONALLY I SHALL BE OVERGRATEFUL TO YOU BOTH.

Their mission was to communicate personally with those who controlled the Armenian interests in America, to offer help, and to assure them of Britain's equal zeal and anxiety. They took a sheaf of introductions and an invitation to the President's Dinner in New York for the United Press.

'He's gone off with almost no luggage except his toothbrush,' Rachel said. 'But every now and again a parcel of shirts to be washed arrives to give me an idea where he is. I suppose he buys new ones as he goes along.'

The crossing took a week and Rosslyn took church services and organised games till he was too seasick to go on. In New York, Noel, who had now grown a red beard over his bullet-shattered chin, insisted on staying at the Waldorf Astoria.

On their first day in New York they were to address a meeting of forty ministers and a lunch party of the same number. Rosslyn rewrote Noel's notes till he failed to recognise them. At the lunch they met a man who claimed to be an electric flame inventor who wanted air railways, perpetual motion and Fletcherism which, Rosslyn said 'was one meal a day but chewed three times more than usual'.

Both spoke at meetings almost every day for a fortnight about their experiences in the Balkans and Rosslyn's more lately in France. In a letter to Rachel from New York Rosslyn said: 'Yesterday we slept in the woods, twenty miles out, at an American Ambassador's country house at Osining, one Morganthau, German Jewish, very pro-ally and very nice.'

They failed to contact the American Buxtons who had invited Rachel to stay before her marriage.

They motored to Oyster Bay to lunch with ex-president Theodore Roosevelt at his country house 'an amiable sporting Socialistic talkative egotist Dutchman who shoots big game and curses millionaires', Rosslyn told Rachel in a letter in which he drew the oval table and six places in which Roosevelt's married daughters sat each side of him and Rosslyn and Noel each side of Mrs. Roosevelt. 'We were there from 12 till 3.30 and had a very friendly and interesting time.'

They talked about the Armenian horrors and Roosevelt said that President Wilson, cold and classical, would make a doctrinal speech about it in excellent English and have done with it. Roosevelt said 'But we all agree with your Mr. Gladstone—the Turk must go!'

He said that Mormons sent out missionaries but only found converts in Protestant countries. He gave an account of how he nearly sent Admiral Dewey against Germany and gave ten days warning. At the end of seven days they thought he was bluffing and he reduced it to forty-eight hours. At thirty-six hours they agreed to his plans.

After lunch Roosevelt showed Rosslyn a candlestick used to melt wax for seals of the Russo-Jap Treaty signed at Portsmouth. He told him the Kaiser liked him very much and gave him a bust of himself and a vase with his portrait which he sent to the National Museum, 'because this house is wooden'.

Rosslyn noticed that Roosevelt's mangy mongrel was covered with sulphur wash. He told him a story of his little grandson saying, 'Did God make everything?' 'Yes, everything.' 'My leggings?' 'Yes.' 'Well! to tell the truth they are not very well made but I suppose he did his best so I won't complain.'

Rosslyn asked Roosevelt if he had ever been fox-hunting and he said 'Yes once' but wondered what he was meant to do when he saw a 'bullfinch'. He never thought of going through it. Afterwards Rosslyn wrote in his diary that Roosevelt was 'a real fraud as a statesman. He's only a simple old man with a taste for literature and a deep love of his grandchildren.'

However, within weeks Roosevelt was saying in a speech: 'One outspoken and straightforward declaration by this Government against the dreadful iniquities perpetrated in Belgium, Armenia and Serbia would be to humanity a thousand times as much as all that the professional pacifists have done in the past fifty years.'

It is frantically hot and we are busy every day. [Rosslyn wrote to Rachel from New York again] Interviews with 'Lay missionaries' (great folk here) politicians, journalists, Ambassadors, barristers etc. but manage to enjoy it. There are plenty of baths, etc.! Except for the Roosevelt ladies we have not seen or spoken to a female person since we left the boat. Poor spirits, aren't we? But there is no time. Fancy no news of you for 13 days! It is 8 p.m. and Noel has a tummy ache so we are not going to dine yet. At 11 p.m. we start by night train to Boston, arriving about 6.30 a.m.

In Boston they lunched on the lake with Colonel House who spoke of Kathleen as one of the very few English whom he really understood. 'She speaks our language and is a really great person.' Rosslyn could not help recalling Nancy Astor saying that Colonel House's voice was like an anaesthetic to her. She woke up after an hour and said instinctively 'Tell me, doctor, is it a girl or a boy?'

Oliver Lodge was there and, in a discussion on After Life, Colonel House thought: 'You may go on consciously or be returned to the great whole.' To which Oliver Lodge said: 'The brain is merely an instrument of the soul.'

House believed in the League to enforce peace which he said was well backed in America but must collapse if a disaster—Wilson's defeat—occurred.

Rosslyn and Noel stayed two days with Colonel House and

found him very patient and sweet with his verbose lady who obviously bored him. Once he rushed for a horn which he blew with a new light in his eye, describing the music and the voice of the hounds and the glorious joy of the chase! We went for a wonderful walk in the rain. Colonel House is quite won over to Noel and very cordial. We met a charming young mother with a baby whom she promised to bring to England to see Verily of the same age.

In Washington next day Rosslyn received the first letter from home with enormous relief and joy. He went to Congress with Noel and they sat in the Speaker's gallery and had many lengthy meals with excited politicians, in between which Rosslyn took 'patient Noel' to the zoo. 'Noel is a perfect dear as ever and so amusing.'

The *Washington Times* said of Chaplain Major R. Bruce, D.D., 'What is most admirable about him is his breadth of mind and sportsmanlike nature. There never was or could be anything petty or hypocritical about him. His very presence whether in church or elsewhere gives a breezy atmosphere to the surroundings.'

They returned to New York for the President's dinner with the United Press. Rosslyn sat with General Hamilton, Chairman of the dinner committee, and Flynn, Chief of the Secret Service, who explained how he 'arrests' a newly-elected president and guards him with twelve police night and day. When Wilson walked across the room to speak to his wife—the ladies were apart in the gallery—five men followed and preceded him. 'Every one made pro-Wilson election speeches and the President himself said "Power comes from below" but did not explain how.'

In fact Wilson was referring to the all-powerful public opinion, in advance of which he knew no U.S.A. President could afford to take action.

Rosslyn and Noel retired to the Waldorf Astoria writing room where they wrote a letter to Colonel House which, Noel said, would probably mark an epic in the history of the world's peace. 'Wait and see!' said Rosslyn.

They had seen the wonders of New York and the beauties of Washington and Boston. They had visited Harvard had Columbia University, spent time in the presence of Wilson, Hughes, Roosevelt, Lowell, Lodge, Strauss, Morganthau, Peabody and Barton and heard their views on affairs. Noel's appeals for help for the oppressed Armenians produced considerable sums of money.

The return journey across the Atlantic was less rough but still alarming with continual fear of possible enemy attack. Rosslyn said he was 'full of much wondering'.

They were back in England by the end of July. While he was away, Ronnie, whose wife Ruth had died in the autumn, and been married again to Margaret Jackson. Noel was on top of the world but Rosslyn was only able to pray that their trip had been of value, he returned to so much bereavement, suffering and anxiety in the parish.

After the sinking of *Lusitania*, Germany had announced that from March 1st, 1916, she would treat all armed merchantmen as belligerents and attack them on sight, as no submarine could tell whether a vessel was armed until she had been searched.

On February 3rd, 1917, the German Ambassador in Washington was handed his passport and the American Ambassador in Berlin was recalled. On March 12th the U.S. Government issued an order for the arming of American merchant vessels and quickly following this, German submarines sank five American ships.

Now American feeling was roused to the realisation that war was the only course open to the U.S. Government and on April 2nd President Wilson asked for a declaration 'The world must be made safe for democracy' was the phrase he used. America declared war on Germany on April 6th and by June 25th the first contingent of American troops landed in France.

Rosslyn's book *God and the Allies* had now been published. The object was to show that the Grande Entente was not a fortuitous alliance of nations but a practical link in the chain of a divine purpose working through the human means of friendly nations. In it he progressed chapter by chapter through the relationship between God and each of the Allies. 'The little book is a treasure in itself,' said *The*

Times, 'written with love and a simplicity that reveals real understanding'.

Following this, Rosslyn's 'Every Man's Daily Duty' was published on cards with a circulation of about twenty thousand.

At the hour of noon every day, wherever you may be, indoors or out of doors, make a rule of silently offering up one or more of the following petitions:

> Oh God save our country.
> Strengthen our defences.
> Fight with our forces and with our allies.
> Help the sick and wounded.
> Console the prisoners of war.
> Mercifully receive the fallen and the dying.
> Comfort the widows and orphans.
> Protect our loved ones in the hour of danger.
> Make us thankful for all thy mercies.
> For Jesus Christ's sake. Amen.

'We have a rota,' Rachel wrote to her mother, 'with somebody coming into St. Augustine's to pray every quarter of an hour so that the church is never empty by day.'

CHAPTER NINETEEN

Aftermath

So many friends and relations had been killed that the joy of seeing survivors again, even if badly wounded, was overwhelming. In July 1918 Rosslyn saw Benjie after his final escape from Petrograd, which he left as First Secretary of the British Embassy. With him at Clifton was his lovely Russian wife, Tamara Karsavina, whom he had first seen dancing in music hall at the Coliseum in 1909 not long before she danced as prima ballerina with Nijinsky in *Le Spectre de la Rose*. With their little son Nikita they had defied Trotsky's decree forbidding Englishmen to travel, and made a nightmare journey by peasant cart and boat, never far from the Red troops. Finally it was thanks to a Bolshevik Commissar recognising Karsavina's maiden name on her passport that they were able to hurry, on the worst and most alarming part of their journey, to the comparative safety of an English collier which, just off Aberdeen, was only missed by a torpedo by feet.

Rosslyn's godson Francis d'Assisi Law, a captain in the Irish Guards, returned wounded from France with the M.C.

Rosslyn's eldest sister Elma's boy, Maurice Keating, turned up at 4 Manor Road on leave from France and played the piano cheerfully despite the tantrum at his feet of the vicar's youngest—myself. Two months before the end of the war his eldest brother George was killed in action and his brother John, both in the Cambridgeshire Regiment, was severely wounded. Rosslyn's brother Douglas wrote from Dunbar just before the war ended:

Dear Rosslyn,

    I have been wanting to write to you for some time now. Why I cannot quite tell, as I have nothing particular to say and *never* write merely complimentary letters but I can resist the impulse no longer tonight. Perhaps what I really want to put on paper to you personally, and not only to Rachel, is my gratitude to you for giving me a holiday and a sight of your children. I love them much. I suppose it will be stale news to you that you made a great impression here. Somebody said how nice it would be if they had you here every Sunday which was rude to me but probably quite genuinely complimentary to you and true, you must come again when I am at home and preferably in spring. I am very very sorry for Elma. She was so devoted to George and now I hear John is wounded in both legs but perhaps that is a mercy keeping him out of any further danger. I had one of Robert's battalion, a Dunbar boy, in here today to tell me all he could about him. I liked him to say 'your son had his own way of managing his platoon, they would do anything for him' and that he was the most popular officer in the battalion. There seemed to be a good many like that but I believe every man that says it, means to be, and is, perfectly truthful. They are all the most popular in their own way. Surely not even death itself can burst the bonds of love forged in those strenuous years of war.

Your brother R. Douglas Bruce.

As the news broke on November 11th, 1918, that Armistice had been signed at 5 a.m. and fighting would cease at 11 a.m., Rosslyn hurried to the church and set Rachel ringing the bell to bring the people together. Some of them came actually running. Holding the many-coloured woollen tail of the bell rope was my earliest memory of a great historical event, with the boom of the guns and Merlin, who had been left unfetched at school, being taken from the sidecar of a stranger's motorbike by his father, fully robed ready for the first Armistice service.

When the time came to put up a war memorial Rosslyn went round to every house for a contribution, including the houses of the many Jewish families living in the parish. There were no refusals. The war memorial, he said, would bear no Christian symbol, as it was to be for everyone. Mr. Mendelssohn, who lived in the next house in Manor Road said, 'Go on vicar, have a cross if you'd like. We don't mind.' Kathleen was one of the artists asked to submit designs. In the dining room of the vicarage she produced in plaster a naked youth, with one hand raised, dressed in a handkerchief which she dipped in plaster, and swathed about the statue's loins.

Rhalou was a particular delight to Kathleen. She had taken an interest in Rosslyn's animals and birds since she could walk but it was quite unlike Peter's scientific approach. She liked to fuss round them in the study and Rosslyn would find little pencilled notes about them on his desk, decorated with kisses. 'Please look at Clarenz (Mrs. Rat). Don't you think she looks warm for tonight.' Her delight knew no bounds when she found two bantam's eggs in the garden. She carried them in and laid them on his blotter with a message 'For you. With the very best love and kisses and all the other nice things from the two Mrs. Bantams. We laid them for you.'

She started going to dog shows when she was seven and startled the Mothers' Union by bursting into their meeting in the dining room and asking 'Where's that bitch gone?' She showed considerable talent in drawing the dogs she saw and handled, and decorated a letter Rosslyn had written asking Kathleen to speak at a meeting.

Pete thinks Rhalou's drawings very good and has borne them off to a place apart [Kathleen answered]. I am inclined to agree with him. How old is she? Great thing to be born into an artistic family! All right. I will cope but try not to yawn, but could anybody demand to discuss anything more tedious than woodwork and sculpture? Women ought only to talk about babies. You will observe that I am in a thoroughly unreasonable mood but I am so *furious* with Curzon for letting down the Suffragette movement of which I am, if not a pillar, at any rate a gargoyle from the pillar. I'm sculpting Bernard Shaw by electric light and I've just done Stephen Gwynne, the first bad, the second excellent.

But her naked boy was not chosen as a war memorial for Edgbaston and remained in the corner of Rosslyn's study with its message scratched beneath it, 'Here am I. Send me.'

A simple pillar, topped by a rosebud-like flame stands in the

242

churchyard, 'a testimony both to the dead and to the human charity of the living'.

Soon after the war many thousands died of a particularly virulent 'flu virus. Weakened, physically by rationing, and mentally by anxiety and bereavement, people, particularly those like Rosslyn who had done several jobs at once, were open to infection. Rosslyn developed pleurisy after 'flu and was seriously ill and unable to take services for six weeks. So many were the inquiries that Rachel took the telephone off its hook on the wall in the hall and twice daily pinned a bulletin, dictated by Rosslyn, to one of the front gates.

Among the parsons who stood in for him was his old friend the Rev. Lord Byron who wrote warmly from Thrumpton Hall agreeing to help.

Rosslyn recovered and was soon helping to revive pre-war activities and to start others.

He formed a club at the university that made a special point of entertaining with smoking concerts and dances, the many American students who came to Birmingham after the war. 'I have seen something of them,' Oliver Lodge wrote to Rosslyn, 'and they are a fine lot of fellows.'

The Cadbury family also took an active interest in Rosslyn's social work and invited his Y.P.S. to their home for a picnic in their bluebell woods. Christopher Cadbury was in my form in the pre-preparatory part of the Edgbaston High School for Girls and one day went home in my shoes, to my delight, as he left me to wear his impressively manly brogues. We were both four.

Frank Chamberlain, son of Neville Chamberlain, M.P. for Ladywood, was also my age and his sister Dorothy a friend of Rhalou's. Rosslyn had made friends with Neville Chamberlain, over St. Germain's when he was chairman of the Birmingham town planning committee. Once, when they came to tea Frank heaved me on to his knee as he sat on the little gilt musical chair in the drawing room, for fear that his own modest weight would not be sufficient to set it in motion. But he soon had to relinquish me with a sigh as being 'heavier than he'd thought'.

However the chair played through its repertoire of two lively little Swiss tunes. Doc H tried, without success, to find their origin and would play them on the piano with improvised variations. One day he incorporated them into the church voluntary on the organ. Once a parishioner asked Doc H: 'Is the vicar *really* musical?'

This was after one of Rosslyn's spectacular renderings of what he called Scriabin. It was a tremendous performance with much pounding and crashing of discords, ending on a complete revolution on the piano stool to gather momentum for the final thunderous impact. So unfamiliar was Scriabin's music then, that listeners were never quite sure whether Rosslyn was serious.

One of the parishioners insisted that he was very musical. When he came to pay his first call after her marriage she found him in the hall playing on the tubular gong the notes of the wedding march.

In church he sang rather than intoned the responses. At Y.P.S. he introduced each hymn by singing the first line.

From the age of four I used to sit in the choir stall beside him at Y.P.S. and was once gratified to hear him quoting in his address, a dream I had told him about. I offered more dreams without the same success.

Nonconformist children were often sent to Y.P.S. at St. Augustine's, where there was always a chance that he might produce a kitten out of the pocket of his cassock that would walk round the flat top of the pulpit. At a baptism of a new baby, a toddler was also christened. Rosslyn advised the parents to let the child roam around and this it did, careering up and down the church with joy. By the time it was due to be named it was nowhere to be found and after much searching was discovered fast asleep on the pulpit steps.

He wrote several children's books specially for Y.P.S. and read them out from the aisle. He conducted Y.P.S. sports in a bumpy field at the back of St. Augustine's parish hall in Gillet Road. He was both handicapper and judge and everyone had a chance, however small.

If a child were sick he would lend a mouse or rabbit, or even a dog for a few days.

At St. Germain's he instigated the custom for probation choirboys to be admitted into the choir, in a ceremony in the garden of 4 Manor Road. It was witnessed by the rest of the choirboys assembled near the raven's pen. 'Dr. Bruce then placed on your head a piece of bun,' a choirboy remembered years later. 'You were then led into the pen. If the raven pecked the bun off your head you were then accepted into the choir. If it refused it you were rejected. But it always took the bun, to the loud cheers of the boys. Afterwards buns and lemonade were enjoyed by all at a great feast.'

Many of his schoolgirl confirmation candidates fell in love with him. He always kissed them all good night in turn when they left. One of the girls loved him so much that she and a friend deliberately walked past the vicarage in the hope of seeing him. She felt she had preferential treatment because she was lame, like him. Whereas he wore a slightly raised black shoe and bicycled nimbly about, she was made to wear a long black boot four inches higher than the other. 'He made me feel my lameness did not matter particularly. When he found how far I had to walk, he sent me from time to time postal orders with little notes in them saying "To give your satchel a ride", "More penny rides". They were signed A. Dneirf.' The little girl and her mother were quite sure that the friend was Dr. Bruce.

In 1919 Rosslyn's first cousin Sir Hervey Bruce died while he and Nellie were staying with Benjie and Tamara in Tangiers. He left Downhill and his Ireland estates to his eldest son, Ronnie, now Sir Hervey Bruce, 5th Bart, and Clifton Hall to Ronnie's twin brother, Colonel Percy Bruce, who, under his father's will assumed his grandmother's surname of Clifton. Rosslyn wrote suggesting that he might consider reviving the old Clifton baronetcy. Percy wrote saying: 'I think you have forgotten it is Ronnie who is the heir male and not me and surely the cost would be more than a return ticket to the Home Office? I give you free leave and my best thanks for finding out for me. Write to me again.'

Rosslyn exchanged several letters with the Home Office but found the ancient baronetcy was irreparably extinct.

He had written at once to Nellie to condole on the loss of her husband and said how he had prayed for both of them ever since leaving Clifton, and now a sad little note came from his one-time 'sort of mother'.

I have landed in England and go down to Clifton tomorrow but shall not be there long as it will be too sad for me now. My first thought on getting your letter, which I was so glad to receive, was I wish I could share it with Hervey as we should both have been so pleased to heal the unfortunate breach long ago and these few words from you would have done it.

It was a shock to Rosslyn that what had seemed at the time like normal family banter over the pear trees had for seven years lain so heavily between them.

Percy and Evie settled in at Clifton Hall and when the daughter of Mr. Haynes, the agent married, they invited Rosslyn and Rachel to stay for the wedding, with Merlin to be a train-bearer. This invitation Merlin, now into long grey trousers at prep school at Summerfields, Oxford, flatly refused. I was offered instead, curly, blooming and delighted to dress up in pink frills. As we left to catch the train, Rosslyn slid a mahogany letter box hurriedly off the hall table and tucked it under his arm to take as a wedding present.

The return to Clifton would have been even more of a success had I not elected to put my fellow bridesmaid in a water tank in the kitchen garden just before the ceremony.

Merlin was very homesick at Summerfields, and planned his eventual running away as a naval battle, keeping his pockets permanently filled with his needs on the journey. Perhaps it was because his pockets were so heavy that when he swung under his desk their weight pulled the desk on to the top of him. A message came that he was in the San, with a row of stitches above his eye. Rachel was expecting her fifth child so Rosslyn went off to Oxford to comfort him. He stayed as the family subsequently always did when visiting Oxford, with his brother Wilfrid. He and Dorothy and their three little daughters had a beautiful home, Hasely Manor, next to Great Hasely church, whose peal of bells filled the house and garden on Sundays and saints' days. Wilfrid had retired from the navy and farmed Large Black pigs from a mud-caked T model Ford.

Rosslyn next visited Merlin on a speech day. They went down to the river beyond the playing fields to see a duck's nest that Merlin had spotted in a low-lying willow tree. Rosslyn scrambled up the slanting trunk to examine the eggs, lost his footing and fell with a splash into the Cherwell. He waded on to the bank soaked to the skin. But Merlin's real distress was when Rosslyn borrowed a pair of trousers from the headmaster, Mr. Hugh Allington, which, since they had no braces depended entirely on his keeping both hands in his pockets. Rosslyn further embarrassed him by announcing 'the suspense for my son is almost unbearable.'

In the holidays a single-seater biplane made a forced landing near St. Germain's church. Rosslyn took Merlin to investigate it. The young R.F.C. pilot invited Merlin into the cockpit and explained the controls. 'So you can drive one yourself one day,' Rosslyn predicted.

On the Sunday morning that Rosslyn called 'The Birds' Wedding Day', February 15th, 1920, he shepherded Rhalou, Erroll, our nursery maid and myself down the back stairs to clean our teeth in the kitchen because mother was not very well. This extraordinary departure from the normal made more impression on us even than sitting in our dear friends the Keeps' pew before spending the day with them, and being brought home to be shown a new baby. 'But you're still the ex-baby.' Rosslyn hoped to save me from the jealousy he had been warned by the nurse I was sure to feel. Rhalou, as an animal enthusiast, thought the baby a poor specimen. Erroll insisted that it was *his* baby. And I thought I had never seen anything so beautiful or touching in my life. Rosslyn wrote the name LOREMA (to conform with his pattern, meaning, he said 'A bond of love' in a mixture of Greek and Latin) on a piece of paper and pinned it above Rachel's bed as she complained she would never be able to remember it.

The Rev. Lord Byron when asked to be godfather replied: 'As to the honour of standing for Lorema (Lor! what a name!) I should be proud.'

When Lorema was six weeks old our nanny, daughter of the bear-keeper at the Botanical Gardens, broke her leg. Simultaneously Gladly, the bear, hugged off the keeper's arm. Rosslyn announced there would be no more nannies at the vicarage. Rachel proposed to go modern and look after her baby herself. The white lace frocks we had worn were discarded and Lorema was dressed in natural-coloured Shetland jerseys and trousers and was looked upon, when Rosslyn pushed her out in the Botanical Gardens, as a rare exhibit—a 'woolly baby'.

I was taken on parish calls, balanced on the back of his Sunbeam bicycle with one knee on the carrier and one foot—causing increasingly excruciating discomfort—on the step. Rachel would dress me for such an outing in a white fur-trimmed caped coat—a present from the American Buxtons—and a fur-trimmed bonnet to match. Rosslyn preferred a jaunty tam o' shanter—and so did I—so this, after one or two ructions, came to be kept secretly in a drawer in his desk and was smuggled out to be exchanged for the bonnet once we were out in the street.

Rhalou went with him to every possible dog show. Erroll took a long time to recover from appendicitis, so rarely roamed far from home for a while. But Merlin, on his small bicycle, would set out with his father to pedal twenty-four miles to Binton Rectory to visit the much-loved twin uncle and aunt, Lloydie and Gwen. Here Merlin would pick cowslips in the meadow or fish for perch and eels in the pond.

After dark they usually walked, pushing their bicycles, the better to enable Rosslyn to point out the constellations in the sky. Merlin was so fascinated that he determined to be a navigation specialist, like Uncle Wilfrid, and use the stars to guide his ship. From Stratford-on-Avon they took a train to Birmingham.

On these trips Rosslyn suggested other possibilities for a career for Merlin. Banking was much favoured by Rachel's side of the family. Her brother Quintin Gurney was a Director of Barclays Bank, but Rosslyn said a Bruce should either be in the Church or the Fighting Services.

The issue was settled when Merlin, who was more inclined to mathematics than to classical subjects, failed his common entrance to Rugby, but passed creditably into the Royal Naval College, Dartmouth.

In the garden of 4 Manor Road, on summer afternoons we made so much noise, leaping naked in the spray of the garden hose that Rosslyn had to apologise to a next-door neighbour. We pretended that the slowly moving shadow on the lawn was the rising tide at Overstrand, where we bathed during summer holidays spent with our grandmother at Northrepps. 'Don't worry,' said the neighbour. 'I moved my sitting room specially on to this side of the house so that I could watch their antics better.' Later she reported that the part Rosslyn played in his family circle was 'as remarkable and beautiful in its way as the position which he occupied in the parish and beyond it. He brought the interest of his interesting life home and seemed never too tired to play with his children and entertain his friends. He was all strength and splendid kindness and wit and heart and understanding.'

Only when tired from too much dashing about and adulation did he sometimes behave like a spoilt child. Thus he was never referred to in the family as merely 'cross', but always 'cross-and-tired', which was eventully shortened to C and T. For a short time he might be cantankerous and contrary, questioning any serious point, as he had the school rules as a child. Knowing his own limit of control, he was more likely to rise from his chair with his plate, knife and fork during a family meal and retreat to his study with the same dignity that he bore the collection plate to the altar in church. Ever sensitive and squeamish, he also left the table if the conversation turned to operations or even the dentist. Certain words set his teeth on edge, not the least of which was teeth. The combination 'false teeth' was absolutely banned. He discouraged all shortenings, 'phone', 'bike' and nicknames. 'Call each other by the names the angels know you by,' he said. But the angels can hardly have guessed which of us he meant when he used one of his own terms of endearment 'Bumpus', 'Woolly-bump' or 'Cockyolly bird'.

He would pick one of us up for a 'grunty hug' while condemning the word 'chap' for a fellow, 'when everyone knows it's a pig's thigh'.

Though he encouraged us to show off within reason for the entertainment of his friends, if we kept it up too long he would remind us of his mother's warning to him in the same circumstances: 'First time funny. Second time silly. Third time naughty.'

It was hardly surprising that when in a rage, I stamped my foot and said 'I won't' and he forbade me to use the expression again, I stamped the other foot and yelled 'I shan't', and, when that was forbidden, roared, with both feet off the ground 'I refuse'. Once when

I had told a transparently blatant lie, he warned me: 'God could strike you down for that.'

I think he believed it as we stood looking down at the ground as though expecting to see me fizzled out or melted away. But my mother just snatched up my hand impatiently and said: 'Of course He won't. And anyway there was some truth in what you said.'

Among the visitors who came to stay was Rose Fyleman whose children's poetry included 'There are fairies at the bottom of my garden'. She would talk fairies and elves to Rosslyn over my head as other people would talk God and Heaven. Rosita Forbes, another fairly regular guest, would talk sheiks and mirages in the desert. She was an old friend of his who lectured on the remarkable journeys she made into little-known parts of the world, 'always slipping just in time behind a palm tree', Benjie teased her, 'to escape the attention of some would-be oriental follower.'

In 1922 Kathleen was busy falling in love with Sir Edward Hilton Young M.P., barrister, scientist poet and sailor. She complained that 'Bill' was self-conscious and full of contradictions, but she had to admit that he stood on his head with great skill while smoking a pipe, to amuse Peter. They went off to Tunisia and came back engaged. They were married that summer.

Rosslyn's life was perhaps as busy as it had ever been before. Under his leadership, a new branch of the Rotary started off in Birmingham at a gallop, and a new Masonic Lodge. He was on the councils of and attended the concerts and prize-givings of three schools in Birmingham. He formed the Birmingham Fox Terrier Club which had regular meetings after dog shows, usually in pubs around the Bull Ring. It brought together all sorts of people, breeders and fanciers, many who had started with a pair of Rosslyn's puppies. Merlin was introduced as the 'tan-headed pup'. The usual prizes were silver teaspoons with terriers' heads on them.

A cartoon appeared of him in *Our Dogs* as 'the well-known smooth-coated fox terrier breeder, exhibitor and judge'. He was presented with five hundred postcards of the cartoon.

When he preached his first radio sermon from the new Birmingham radio station he could not resist sending a personal message to

Rachel to say he would be home soon and hoped dinner would be ready. It was still the days of 'Can you hear me, Mother?'

Rosslyn had now been at Edgbaston eleven years. His work there could now only increase. The war years had been as great a strain on him as if he had been serving abroad the whole of the four years—in some ways even greater. When he was offered a living in East Sussex he and Rachel went down to see it just before Christmas. They came back glowing with excitement. Herstmonceux reminded Rosslyn of his beloved Carlton, his first remembered home. The two large sunny rectories had much in common and their farm buildings were of the same period too. Not only were the two parish churches early English, but both, by a curious chance, had important medieval memorials in them to the Dacre family.

The Dean of Norwich wrote:

My dear old friend and comrade, it is with the greatest interest and profoundest good wishes that I have heard of your acceptance of a new and most important charge. Its name has always appealed to me as one of the most—perhaps *the* most—romantic and old world designations in all England. I can hardly think of another to match it and to think of you as Rector of Herstmonceux is quite delightful. I hope with all my heart that you and yours will be most happy there. God go with you.

Yours affectionately, J. W. Willink.

This time the farewell parties and presentations were really overwhelming. Among the presents was a new Ford car. Into this were packed all the animals including a goat who gave birth in the back to a pair of kids on the way, with Fox at the helm. Rosslyn stayed behind in the almost empty house for a last week of meetings and services and adulation. I stayed near-by with the family of the surgeon, Jack Jameson-Evans, who had operated on my eye. I came to tea one day and was shocked to find my father's bed unmade and cold rice pudding for tea. But clearly he was surprisingly happy camping here by himself. I made his bed as best I could and laid two plates for the rice pudding. But that, he thought, was quite unnecessary. 'All you need is a spoon each and you just dig in.'

CHAPTER TWENTY

The Goodly Heritage

The rest of the family were delighted by the move to Herstmonceux but I shared the feelings of many of the devoted parishioners, one of whom—Vi Keep—cried when she heard the news. We belonged to Birmingham. Sussex was too far away—and there would be no street lighting.

According to Crockford the gross income was £1,293, much of which was derived from a farm and a hundred and thirty acres of glebe. But Rosslyn had to pay a quarter of this out in pension to the last rector and the upkeep of car or curate also had to be reckoned with. The parish was twenty-seven miles round and there were three churches to serve. All Saints, an early English church standing on the edge of Pevensey Marsh, two miles from the rectory; St. James', a corrugated iron shed, lined with pine wood, known as 'Tin Jimmy.' in the village a mile from the rectory, and a small white wooden chapel at Cowbeech, two miles in the opposite direction. Later a fourth was added when the chapel in Herstmonceux Castle, now the Royal Observatory, was restored and rededicated.

Rosslyn had read the dramatic story of Herstmonceux Castle in Augustus Hare's *Memorial of a Quiet Life*. This beautiful pink brick, moated manor—built by Sir Roger de Fiennes who fought at Agincourt—had been partially demolished by Hare's ancestors in the eighteenth century and the bricks used to erect a grand Palladian style house on the hill above it, known as Herstmonceux Place. Augustus Hare was brought up at Herstmonceux and spent some miserable times with his neurotic uncle at the rectory, drawings of which house and garden appear in his book. The Hares had privately built, and added to, this large country house with its shallow slate roof and rows of tall Georgian windows. In an angle formed by two of the outside walls a spherical conservatory had been built that looked, from the fields, as though a Bubble had floated on to the side of the house. The Bubble made a perfect sunny place for Rosslyn's birds, Rachel's plants and our wooden bricks. Steps led down to it from the elegant drawing room whose french windows opened on to the lawn and a magnificent distant view of the sea and downs. Here the Mothers' Union met monthly, overflowing on special occasions into the large dining room.

When Rosa was out with her young man, Ada brought the food into the dining room; wrapping her right leg round the door in an attempt to close it as she departed with the tray. This never failed to bring Rosslyn to his feet. Not that he remained seated after saying grace, throughout any meal. He would leap up mid-sentence to collect visible evidence of some statement, or to fetch a book from which to read an apt passage. On Monday—Father's Rotary Day— we always had cold beef; Tuesday, mince; Wednesday, boiled lamb; Thursday, slivers of lamb in gravy; Friday, fish; Saturday, rissoles and Sunday, roast beef and Yorkshire pudding (almost indistinguishable from Sunday cake). Rosslyn ate it all with gracious thanks provided his dietetic views had been heeded. Granulated sugar gave you a cold in the head; ducks' eggs gave you infantile paralysis; pork gave you all sorts of unmentionable diseases out of Leviticus. Yet for breakfast he merrily ate bacon and sausages from a silver-plated egg-shaped dish whose cover slid under its tepid belly, which was supposed to be filled with boiling water to keep the food hot. Hardly a morning went by without Rosslyn wishing it could be given away as the next wedding present.

When we toyed with our food we heard about those stoic Victorian nursery days when jam and butter never met on the same slice of bread. We also heard that in his youth cream and the best fruit was kept for adults and now it was set aside for the children so that all his life he lost both ways. Playing with food—making castles and moats with it, brought forth his attention. Food that was too highly decorated counted as someone else having played with it. Cutting up cubes of bread and dividing it into two parts, one for Holy Communion, to be taken to church in a small carved box in his pocket and the other to be soaked in milk and carried off into the study for his tame rats, was all right.

Rosslyn had always favoured a bare, workmanlike study. Here, since there were built-in shutters to cover the windows at night, he was able to abandon curtains altogether. The walls were lined with books and bird-cages. His roll-top desk stood in the middle of the carpetless floor with the Archbishop's prayer desk behind it. His spacious cloakroom across the hall was papered with dog show prize cards and edged with glass battery cases, in which mice and rats lived and ate and bred.

Two steps, several doors and a walk long enough from the dining room to cool the hottest dishes were the kitchens that had been added two rectors before. In Archdeacon Hare's day the kitchens and servants' quarters were under the house in a cellar that could only be kept free of water in winter time with a hand pump. A semi-rotary pump brought the drinking water up from a well, and another brought up the rain water that had run off the roof into an underground tank. Electricity was still a long way off. The rectory was lit by oil lamps and candles which, with its long drive a quarter of a mile from the road or any other building, caused at least one of us younger town-dwellers to pray fervently for safety every night. One bedroom, down a short flight of winding stairs, contained the claw-footed bath into which a trickle of rusty water could be encouraged by some fierce pumping in the back yard.

Rosslyn's bedroom—discreetly known as his dressing room—was as curtainless and bare as his study, with his bed, raised high with mattresses like a plinth, alone in the middle of the room, 'to leave room for the angels to walk all round it'. With crayons he coloured the stiles of the door to stand out like a cross.

His collection of hats gradually filled one wall of his dressing room, his homburg rubbing shoulders with his biretta, the tassel of his St. Edward's rowing cap entwined with the peak of a French bus conductor's cap.

'I shouldn't be the least bit surprised,' he said in the hushed voice used for both piety and impropriety, 'if one day that big leghorn next to my straw-basher laid an egg and a raw bed-hasher hatched out.'

Rachel's room, with a balcony looking towards the sea and downs became a marshalling yard for children and troubled parishioners, with now only an armchair that had belonged to Elizabeth Fry reserved for Rosslyn. Next to it was the small room in which Augustus Hare had suffered as a child, which I occupied with pride.

Even at home Rosslyn found it quite impossible to go into a room without making an entrance. Either he would enter carrying some spectacular animal or bird or a picture or ornament, or he might be wearing an unusual hat or garment or facial expression or he would be making some resounding noise with voice or instrument, although he was always careful not to break his own rule that you should never enter a room already talking. Or worse still enter a room already blowing your nose. This he said was something that should be done in private, preferably in the lavatory. Sneezing seemed to be all right in public, or anyway his own sneezes were of such tremendous volume that it was impossible to keep them private. Every morning after he woke he gave three enormous sneezes that shook the house with their violence and ended on a sustained and triumphant roar.

Then there were his hunting cries when he left the house 'Gone away!' he halloo'd as the great old double front door with its chains rattling, slammed behind him. When he returned it was a more musical cry of 'Ho ho!' His method of quietening us was to raise his voice above ours and call 'Pretty noises'. He never descended the staircase without making use of the platform it gave him. In the evening as he came down changing his collar for dinner as he descended, he would call out a blessing on us all: 'God bless you and make you good, and healthy, and happy'—pause—'and perhaps cleve'r.

In the grounds that surrounded the rectory, Rosslyn moved about, often in a cassock girt with a wide leather strap, rearranging or separating birds or beasts. Outside the front door he would stand and whistle, on two notes, shaking a pan of corn. From the roof would flutter, with their curious falling flight, his flock of black tumbler pigeons.

Head and Charlie, gardener-kennelman and chauffeur-gardenboy did the main feeding and grooming of the animals, assisted in the gardens by Rachel and in the kennels by Rhalou.

There were cowsheds for kennels, and stables for the ponies which

Rosslyn gradually acquired—some borrowed, some bought and some bred. Chestnut paling dog-runs were erected in pairs so that the dogs would exercise each other rushing up and down. On the gate of each dog-run was the name of a former parish Rosslyn had lived in, either as incumbent or child. Soho was a group of thatched cowsheds and pigstys with a boarded-in cow-yard which made a sheltered puppy-run.

The names of the dogs themselves were founded on Rosslyn's own initials. His earlier dogs began with R. Then with F for Francis, those bred at Clifton having one syllable, those bred at Edgbaston two and at Herstmonceux, three. Among his best terriers were Freeze, Foremost, Francis, Flodden, Champion Floorcloth, Flambro, Future, Forethought, Fo'castle, and his finest stud dog, Firstmonceux. The star of the Herstmonceux kennels at that time was the famous Champion Wrose Indelible, a great breeder to whom many a royal and ducal bitch came lumbering up the drive in a dog box aboard the village carrier. To me, 'Champion Non-Rub-Out', as I called him disparagingly, was quite the dullest company I knew.

The glebe and more distant parsonage farm were let to the splendid families of Elphick and Walker which supplied verger, grave-digger, organist and most of the choristers in the church. Rachel supervised the six acres of garden, part of which was enclosed as a kitchen garden in a mellowed old wall. Every fine evening after tea she dug and planted and weeded in her huge herbacious borders.

Meanwhile, in April 1923 the Bishop of Newcastle, Herbert Wild, a former rector of Herstmonceux, had written:

My dear Bruce,

It was delightful to have so prompt and early a letter from you and to hear that you and yours have happily settled into the Rectory with the summer before you. I was sure that the people would give you a warm welcome. They are dear people and will respond to quiet understanding. I think you are wise to let all but the near fields. The cows were a great interest to my father but they were momentarily an expense and I think I should have done as you have done and let the fields. I should certainly like more time to come and sit on your lawn. You will find the village taking a paternal and maternal interest in your young folk.

Merlin, aged five, Rhalou, three, and Erroll, one, at Edgbaston. The doll represented the expected Verily.

Rosslyn with Rhalou, aged twelve, and Champion Wrose Indelible at Herstmonceux beside 'Stokesley', one of the dog-runs called after beloved parishes.

Wedding reception at Herstmonceux Rectory for Rosa Bane from Northrepps, after eighteen years with the Bruces. Rhalou, Lorema, Grace Newnham (Rosa's successor) and Verily sitting on the grass.

Rosslyn, Lorema (bridesmaid), Sub-Lieutenant John Casson, R.N. (best man), with Merlin and Joan at their reception at Lord Hailsham's London home.

I think that Archdeacon Hare planted the garden to look as much like Italy as possible; e.g. Arbutus, Portuguese Laurel, Ilex. The marshes served for the Campagna and the Downs for the Alban Hills.

Yours always, Newcastle

P.S. By the way the right spelling is Herstmonceux or Herstmonceaux. It has nothing to do with Hurst or Hurstpierpoint. It was always spelt with an e until Hare adopted u.

Forthwith Rosslyn began research on the subject and discovered, as he pointed out in a letter to *The Times* that there were sixteen different ways of spelling Herstmonceux and only two were wrong. Gradually he managed to replace the *Hu* spelling with *He*.

'The lot is fallen unto me in a fair ground; yea I have a goodly heritage,' was the text of his first address at Herstmonceux to be reported in the local paper.

I had no knowledge of anyone or anything in Sussex except Bishop Burrows, my instructor twenty-five years ago, to whom I succeeded eleven years ago and who is a Sussex man. My first impressions are profoundly and delightfully happy ones. During these early weeks and months I shall concern myself first with the young people of the parish. Can there ever be a more delightful nursery than that of the children of a congregation? The existence of a little specimen of nearly every child age in our own family is a sesame which opens the magic door. Regard me not as a professional domestic chaplain but as a responsible friend of every family, whose friendship will especially be associated with times of crisis and change, solemn times of illness and glad times of rejoicing.

One of Rosslyn's first steps was to turn the Sunday School into the Ministering Children's League on whose central committee Rosslyn remained in London, with the league's 'parents' Lord and Lady Meath, until he himself became Chairman. Even old Mrs. Alcorn, grandmother and Sunday School teacher to half the village, allowed herself to be enrolled with a metal cross costing a penny. Plans were made early for the first of the annual M.C.L. 'One Day Holidays' on Pevensey Beach. The open charabanc started early in the morning and the seven miles across the marshes were part of the delightful experience. Rosslyn organised a regatta of swimming races, diving and other sports in the sea. Most of the children bathed in vests and underpants or frilly drawers. Mrs. Alcorn, still wearing a Queen Alexandra bonnet, distributed meat pies and strong tea mixed with condensed milk and then tucked up her skirts to paddle. Rosslyn managed to lure a brass band out of the pub to come down and play for dancing. The climax of the outing was the burying in the shingle by the industrious choir, of the rector himself. It was a rather terrifying operation to watch in case, his nose, the only part that was allowed to protrude, got covered up by mistake. 'Why do you let them do it, Sir?' Mrs. Alcorn asked. 'It's the only chance of resting undisturbed. Why don't you lie down beside me?' he suggested, which invitation she remembered with little chuckles till her death bed.

Summer parties were reminiscent of Clifton. Three hundred members of the Dallington Deanery Mothers' Union would assemble for a mass service in the garden, all bringing their own parsons. If the invited speaker failed, as they sometimes did Rosslyn dressed up one of his children as an adult—masking us if necessary—and gave a spoof introduction after which we had to carry on advising on rearing children or dogs. After a gigantic tea the guests would wander about the garden looking at Rosslyn's animals and birds. Sometimes the Wartling silver band would play and if the mothers felt spry enough, they could dance on the lawn. Or Rosslyn would get the Fire Brigade to give a demonstration of putting out a 'house' made of cardboard and paper that we had made for the purpose in the morning. Rosslyn was torn between wanting his Fire Brigade to win, without actually leaving any paper and cardboard to blow about the garden. Rachel, to whom every drop of water on the place was precious, soon took the decision into her own hands and forbade the firemen to draw another bucket of water from the well.

Rosslyn's annual open-air interdenominational Hospital Sunday also became an annual event, with a fancy dress parade and decorated ponies and prams. He and the priests and ministers of the various neighbouring communities preached on a hay wagon outside the Woolpack Inn with one brass and one silver band to lead hymns. When he took the collection to the general store to change it, Mrs. Smith cheerfully said, 'Been robbing the poor box?' and Rosslyn instantly chided her with 'So you recognise your own miserable pittance?'

Rosslyn was soon drawn on to the committee of Princess Alice Hospital and other committees in Eastbourne. He became an Eastbourne Rotarian and a founder member of Hailsham Rotary. He joined a new Masonic Lodge, and was lured into a great many canine matters in the district.

At first there was only a weekly carrier without seats that 'went round by Pevensey' but before long a regular bus service covered the ten miles to Eastbourne in one direction and to Hastings in the other. Rosslyn soon became a well-known source of entertainment on the route.

After Fox returned to Edgbaston, the Ford stood for a month in the coach house. Then the first visitors arrived, Vi and Sylvia Keep, and Rosslyn set off to meet them at the station It was a long time since he had driven and Rachel never had but she remembered water had to go in somewhere. She emptied a jug into the petrol tank, on which the driver sat, and helped to push the Ford into the drive, where it effectively blocked the incoming cars.

Next time Rosslyn went off on a lecture tour, Rachel sought out Jack Newnham at the garage and took six lessons in driving, having packed all of us in the back so that we should all go together in case of an accident. When Rosslyn returned she met him proudly at the station. At first he disapproved strongly of being driven by a woman but presently saw the advantages. From then on each successive car— they were all Fords—seemed to become more and more Rachel's.

For independence, he pedalled off on his Sunbeam. I had now graduated from its step to a small bicycle on which I followed him, sometimes a hundred yards behind if there was a good hill for him to spin down ahead. I came down more cautiously, though once on the way to a christening, not cautiously enough. The christening party had picked me up and bundled me, bleeding, in with the baby before Rosslyn had turned round to come back and look for me.

Rosslyn became a subscriber to the East Sussex Hunt and took Rhalou out on foot. She burst excitedly into a missionary meeting in the drawing room when she got home. The speaker looked up from her Bible and asked earnestly: 'And you, dear, brought up in the sanctity of a rector's home must surely know the Master?'

'Yes I do,' Rhalou beamed with pride. 'And I opened the gate for him into the plough.'

'Dear Doctor, Do you still want a bloodhound?' wrote a dog enthusiast. 'My boy has got into the Royal Sussex Regiment and is off to India. I can therefore get rid of the young bitch by Champion Dark of Brighton.'

Rosslyn bought the young bloodhound and called her Bright of Darkon. One day when he was away, the police called to ask whether she could be used in a search for a young wife who had left a suicide note and disappeared into the woods near Hellingly. Rhalou, aged twelve, volunteered to lead her and left a note on Rosslyn's desk describing the incident.

They got an old pair of combinations to give Bright the idea of what she was looking for, and then off we went expecting at every turn to find Mrs. D. hanging from a tree or floating face down-wards in a puddle. Bright worked like anything sniffing round the trees and going in places no would-be suicide could have managed, but never mind, Bright was obviously on the scent. Then suddenly we found her clothes folded up in the middle of the wood. The only thing was, there wasn't a puddle for miles for her to drown in. I thought she'd probably have died naturally of cold by the time she found one. Bright led us bounding back to the house and there she was quite starkers—I mean naked and dotty. Good old Bright. At least she did her stuff. The police thanked me and said they'd ask me to come again next time.

Every day he walked to the post-box at the end of the drive in a ten-gallon hat, tweed cape, black trousers, a shepherd's crook with, on a lead, Bright, the bloodhound. Usually Molly Reed, who looked after the trug shop when she got back from school, came out to sharpen her wits—which had already won her a County scholarship—

in cheeky arguments with him. The trug baskets were made by her brother Rupert from the willow slivers over which he philosophised as he soaked, bent and nailed them into shape.

Rosslyn always had an enormous mail to deal with and to save both time and postage he had extra large postcards printed with his name and address on to which he could cram a hundred or so words, costing a penny to post (as against a penny-halfpenny for a letter), or, for only five words, a halfpenny. He bought halfpenny stamps by the roll. He called his daily sessions at his desk 'doing his lessons', as though still at school, lightened his tasks by taking 'pot-shots' at his wastepaper-basket with rolled up papers on which there was no space left to write again. Serious writing he reserved for the evenings, after the family had gone to bed. He rarely left the study before 1 a.m.

His weekly contributions to *Our Dogs* were full of quips and often touched on non-doggy subjects, but his serious books, *Fox Terrier Breeding, The Line and Family Method* and his subsequent annual *Fox Terrier Year Book*, were accepted as important contributions to science. Then came *The Popular Fox Terrier*.

The Rev. A. J. Skinner, retired schoolmaster, dog-breeder and strong protagonist of Mendelism, wrote:

A thousand thanks for this delightful volume it has painted a drab day red for me . . . *The Popular Fox Terrier* has suffused it with light and cheer, when I thought fit only for a quiet day, so have read it through. I like it all from cover to cover. You must be very pleased to have left so clear and indicative a footprint on the sands of time; it will shine here when we are all in a wider show ring, please God!

Rosslyn's reply on a postcard was to quote the sixteenth-century Bishop of Bath, Dr. Still:

Body and Limb go cold, go cold,
Both foot and hand go bare;
God send teroures, so bold, so bold,
Heart will harbour no care.

Another terrier-loving parson Rosslyn was fond of referring to was

Parson Jack Russell 'about whom more rubbish was invented than about any other breeder. Anyone,' Rosslyn debunked, 'who owns a fox terrier too bad to show, calls it a Jack Russell as though it were a separate breed.'

> I believe, [he prophesied] that if someone were to choose any apple-headed, crooked-fronted, broad-chested, flat-sided, short-necked, bulgy-eyed a terrier and call it a Parson Jack terrier you would find enough admirers to form a club and make a small fortune in stud fees and pups.

> It is true that the type he strove for has been improved beyond all knowing, but the length of leg, quality of skull and thick hard dense smooth coat were all as much a joy to the old parson's eye as they are to ours today. This model is our model and I could find today a team of modern smooths that would make his dear old eyes twinkle again.

> Jack Russell had many fox terriers from his undergraduate days on, but his best and certainly best known was Juddy, a direct ancestor of countless champions. Though all smooth fox terriers descend from the old sporting parson's strain, only certain ones descend from its direct female succession.

The *Manchester Guardian* said of a lecture Rosslyn gave on Mendelism called 'Birds, Beasts and Clergymen', that 'the lecture, which teemed with interest, revealed a facility of expression and description which held the large audience spellbound for nearly two hours, and that without a reference to a note of any sort.'

In May 1924 Rosslyn received an unlooked-for honour. He was admitted as a Fellow of the Linnean Society in the Society's rooms in Burlington House at an anniversary meeting. What Linnæus had done in classifying the natural system of plant life so did Rosslyn, after forty years of practical experience, in the field of dogs, mice and bird breeding. Rosslyn had proved, through the crossing of different coloured mice, what Mendel had already proved by crossing different coloured sweet peas; through careful choice of sires he proved that the Bruce-Lowe system of breeding racehorses also applied to fox terriers. He was now entitled to add F.L.S. to the D.D. after his name.

In a two-page review of Rosslyn and his work in *The Illustrated*

Sporting and Dramatic News, A. Croxted Smith, under DOGS OF THE DAY. *The padre and his fox terriers*, wrote:

Rev. Dr. Rosslyn Bruce, Rector of Herstmonceux in Sussex, bases his biological beliefs upon Bruce-Lowe's system of figure breeding, and tells us why he does so in 'Fox Terrier Breeding.' He deserves our thanks for the exhaustive study that he has given to the question. Few men would have the time, patience, or diligence to pursue the matter so thoroughly. I suspect that Dr. Bruce had not the time really, but like most busy men, he has managed to do what an idler would shun. Fox terriers must be provocative, for the literature devoted to them is probably more extensive than that of any other breed, unless perhaps it is the Alsatian, which seems to impel men to put their ideas, or expose their lack of them, on paper. In his introduction Dr. Bruce tells us that he has 127 volumes, all of which deal more or less with the smooth variety of fox terriers, the variety that he has adopted.

No one will regret that he has added another, for any theory that is advanced with sincerity and ability should be the means of stimulating thought. What Bruce-Lowe did for the thoroughbred race horse is tolerably familiar to most, I imagine. The task of reducing order into fox terrier breeding was more complicated. And he goes on to explain Rosslyn's system of indicating descent through male and female lines, with examples.

Although Dr. Bruce is best known as a smooth fox terrier man, his tastes are of a catholic nature, he having had Skyes, Cairns, Scottish terriers, Retrievers, Great Danes, St. Bernards, Greyhounds, Borzois, Dalmatians, Bulldogs, Pugs, Spaniels and Bloodhounds, and he has also shown Foxhounds. This is why we have recently seen him judging with confidence all sorts of breeds that we had imagined were more or less strange to him. He also writes learnedly upon terriers every week in *Our Dogs*.

Under POPULAR SMOOTH FOX TERRIERS—265 AT LONDON SHOW, *The Times* said:

The increasing popularity of the smooth fox terrier, a breed of over 100 years old, was again shown yesterday when the S.F.T.A.

held its first championship show in Bloomsbury. A record entry of 265 of these dapper—though somewhat vociferous-little animals was a fitting compliment to the judge, the Rev. Dr. Rosslyn Bruce, Rector of Herstmonceux, who was not only the first President of this association, but is one of the highest authorities on the breed.

When judging he would bend down to examine the dog rather than put it unnaturally up on a bench. By Kennel Club rules he was not allowed to judge at any shows not under the rules. Thus comic dog shows for the children, which he enjoyed as much as anything for the children's sake, had to be given some fancy name other than Dog Show.

The *Daily Graphic* said a reverend genteman asked three hundred pounds for his smooth-haired fox terrier at a show and suggested that he did it with the intention of putting would-be buyers off. Rosslyn replied indignantly that the price was not a 'mere prohibitive figure based on quixotic sentiment' but a reasonable commercial valuation. The terrier had won four first prizes and his sister won six second prizes; the latter was entered not for sale and so he was able to return a cheque for a hundred and fifty pounds which was sent for her. The same month a friend accepted five hundred pounds for a young dog which was no better a specimen of the breed than his. 'The extreme difficulty of breeding a dog of such merits as to stand out from the thousands bred annually, gave the dog a rarity value that the public doesn't realise. There are two or three dogs of this breed for which any practical enthusiast would gladly give five hundred pounds if he had it and it would be a good financial investment.'

Rosslyn sold a smooth fox terrier to King George V and bought one from the Duke of Grafton, who wrote under the strawberry leaves: 'My bitch is a comely little bitch and ought to breed something nice.'

Through Rudyard Kipling's fondness for dogs in what Rosslyn called disparagingly 'a claustrophobic way', Rosslyn was invited to his home, Batemans, a few miles from Herstmonceux. 'Kipling could not agree with his wife, Carrie, any more than I could with either of them.' He found Kipling difficult to talk to on any subject.

Rosslyn advised him against buying a bulldog for a baby

goddaughter. It was ill-tempered and when it bit the baby, Rosslyn had to restrain himself from saying 'Told you so!'

An easier neighbour to talk to, who had also started life as a journalist, was Horatio Bottomley, financier and breeder of a winner of the Cesarewitch. He had just come out of prison for fraudulent conversion, but still had a kind of grandeur about him left over from the three fortunes he had lost.

CHAPTER TWENTY-ONE

Our Father which Art in Herstmonceux

When Rosslyn was in London he visited Kathleen as usual. He got on well with her new husband, Bill, though he was shy. Like Rachel and other Bruce spouses he admired but could not emulate their outgoing, demonstrative ways. 'Tell Rachel,' he said, 'it's *not easy* being married to a Bruce. But it's rewarding.'

In July Kathleen's second son was born in a wild thunderstorm. Kathleen told Rachel she liked it. It made the job more exciting. The baby, wrapped in a Chinese shawl, was christened Wayland in Chelsea Old Church. Among the godparents were two old friends of Rosslyn's, Mrs. Lloyd George and Mrs. Austen Chamberlain. Austen Chamberlain, brother of Neville, now Chancellor of the Exchequer, and his children's governess, Miss Fortescue, came straight from 11 Downing Street to teach us girls at Herstmonceux Rectory. Intriguing as was the political gossip at meal times between Rosslyn and 'Forty', it bored Rachel and Forty's lessons bored us.

Meanwhile the Neville Chamberlains remained friends and Dorothy came to stay at Herstmonceux and handed on her orange velvet Sunday frock to me.

All the silver was brought out from the bottom of the chest and cleaned when Percy and Evie Clifton came to stay. It was still out but less sparkling when Percy's twin, Ronnie, the current Sir Hervey Bruce, turned up without warning with his wife, Margaret, three children, and an Irish nursery maid. The troubles in County Derry had made it imperative to leave Downhill at once. The two younger children had mumps.

Rosslyn helped them to find a furnished house in Eastbourne. They came to his services on Sundays and usually on to lunch with us. When Margaret went over to France to look for a holiday house there, Rosslyn lunched with Ronnie in Eastbourne and suggested bringing the children over as usual on Sunday. The following night, during the height of another thunderstorm a call came from Princess Alice Hospital for Rosslyn to come at once. His cousin had had a serious accident. Before he had time to start out, another call came to say Ronnie had died.

Headlines in the papers next day announced: DEATH IN THUNDERSTORM. DAZZLED BY THE LIGHTNING. BARONET FALLS OVER PARADE RAILINGS. TRAGIC FATE WATCHING STORM.

At the inquest on Sir Hervey Ronald Bruce, 5th Bart., formerly a major in the 14th Irish Rifles, and the Irish Guards, aged fifty-one, a passer-by stated that he was on the top of the parade at Eastbourne watching the lightning. Some of the flashes were so vivid that people cried out.

A waiter at the Queens Hotel said he was sitting on a seat near the pier, and he saw the deceased approach and stand with his hands on the back of the seat on which witness was sitting. Deceased turned to go on to a vacant seat close by, and as he was walking in sideways, the seat tipped up and deceased pitched over the railings on to the lower parade. Witness jumped up to save him, too late.

A policeman stated he was on duty when he heard a thud and shout and found the deceased lying on the pavement with a cut over the temple. He was unconscious and suffered from a lacerated wound on the temple. When admitted to hospital it was found there was a fracture of the skull and laceration of the brain. The verdict was accidental death. The fall was not very great but the deceased was a tall and very heavy man. It was easy to understand how the accident happened in view of the blinding flashes of lightning.

Margaret, his widow, had already started for home and Rosslyn and Rachel had to meet her at the station and break the news. The children came over as planned and played with us while Rosslyn buried their father, his own childhood friend and cousin, in Herstmonceux churchyard. The sixth Sir Hervey was not quite six years old. For the next year he and his sister Beryl came often to

Herstmonceux. Rosslyn would salute Hervey in the middle of a
meal that he did not particularly want to finish with a reassuring:
'We men must stick together!'

The Bruces stayed on at Eastbourne till Margaret remarried.
Rosslyn took the quiet little service, extracting Beryl and me from a
pew just before it began, to walk, somewhat to our surprise, behind
the bride.

Another Bruce establishment was set up ten miles in the opposite
direction, at Battle, after the first of Rosslyn's brothers and sisters
died, within weeks of Ronnie. Lloydie, after his usual quiet day in
the parish at Binton was found by his twin Gwen, apparently asleep
in his chair. Binton was packed up and Hilda came too to teach at
Battle Abbey school, and a favourite niece from Australia, whose
auburn hair inspired Rosslyn's nickname for her of Squirrel. On
Sundays they all came creeping over from Battle in a small car to
church at Herstmonceux and often to lunch at the rectory. Kathleen
returned to Binton to leave in the churchyard a crucifix she had
sculpted, portraying her brother Lloydie's Christ-like face.

After the death of his twin, Percy became even more intolerant of
the incumbent of Clifton than his father had ever been over Rosslyn
cutting down the pear tree.

Rosslyn old boy, [he wrote late one evening]
    Thank you very much for ringing up. Of all the damned cheek,
Bird about takes the cake. He had never even *consulted* me about the
date of the Harvest Festival and not consulted me either about the
preacher and asking *you*, my cousin, to come and preach is a bit
over the odds. Going next month thank heaven and we shall be well
rid of him and his cursed niece who is at the bottom of the whole
trouble. *I see red.* Look here, and don't think I am being beastly to
you, telling you not to come, but for Bird to come and tell me as a
piece of news your cousin is going to preach my harvest thanksgiving service (and stay *where?*) would be a bit thick. It's all very
thinly veiled insolence. Will you and Rachel come here for a
Sunday in November? Bird goes, I believe, the middle of October
and I shall have to find another one but fix your own Sunday
and I will say Dr. Bruce will preach on such and such a date.

We, in the village would love it—If my letter is incoherent, forgive me, but I have never heard such damned insolence in all my life.

From Hellingly station, two miles from Herstmonceux rectory, a small train wound along a single line, stopping at every station on its way to London. Not far from the station, at Carters Corner Place lived Sir Douglas Hogg, Attorney General, with whom Rosslyn travelled often. The Attorney General brought his family to Herstmonceux church and later he became church warden. His schoolboy sons Quintin and Neil came to the rectory to help Rachel dig up the garden. Their half-brother, Edward Marjoribanks, whose brilliance had already brought him success at the bar, came to discuss with Rosslyn the book he was writing.

In May 1925 Lady Hogg died and Quintin replied to Rosslyn's letters to his father, who was 'really too overwhelmed to write himself'; so Quintin was taking over part of his letters.

He's had about 350 so far and his secretary, myself and my half-brother are taking all we possibly can. At the moment it is almost impossible to believe I shall never see her again. I suppose time will allow me to recover but I don't know if my father ever will. She was so well and happy before she collapsed and both he and she thought she was recovering, as indeed she was, from her two years illness. It was as if a cloud had lifted off her, I believe, but I was at Eton and did not know.

He continued with a charming and poetical fantasy concerning the way his mother had died and how he felt she must be able to see them still.

Rosslyn, whose own mother had died while he was away at school, wept unashamedly.

The Hoggs' Elizabethan manor house was within safe—then—bicycling distance from the rectory and we pedalled to and fro exchanging ducks and rabbits. Quintin and Neil joined us for bathing at Pevensey and other family outings.

In the parish church the rectory pew was at right-angles to the

Hoggs so that we could see Quintin's notebook on his knee. His pencil was rarely still during the sermon.

On Remembrance Day 1925, Rosslyn preached a four-minute sermon on the unknown warrior that was to be remembered for half a century. Just as Nottingham people had flocked out to Clifton to hear Rosslyn's sermons, so did Eastbourne people now come out to Herstmonceux. His voice rang dramatically through the church with the question 'Where Are You?' The reply came, as though from elsewhere: 'I am all over the country and throughout the Dominions and I am everywhere except, perhaps, under that great stone in Westminster Abbey, everywhere where human hearts remember and grieve and wonder and love, wherever parents, widows or lovers touch things eternal with a proud remembrance of those great days.'

'Who Are You?' he asked. 'Though known as a warrior unknown, I am well known as an ordinary fellow, a farm hand in Sussex, a factory hand in Lancashire, a gardener, a miner, an artist in Chelsea, a dustman, a doctor, a carrier, a public school boy, a dock labourer, an actor, a shop walker, an unemployed bloke. I am a reflection of Jesus Christ.'

'What is your work now?' 'I am never idle. I live to point the thoughts of all who will think beyond the cares of the moment, to the great past and on to the great future. I live to soften true men and women, to wean them from cynical sneers and assumptions of selfishness. I live to unite all sound-hearted people, I live to inspire to the glory of the grand adventure, a life well worth living that may be led to a death as well worth dying.'

Present at this service was a young novelist and survivor of the war, Norrie Walker, and his widowed mother. Norrie had won the M.C. and lost a leg simultaneously. He too was writing a book, and came almost daily to the rectory to discuss it. Despite his disability he romped with us children, climbed trees and crossed perilous bridges before settling down to talk gardening to Rachel.

One of Rosslyn's first questions to Norrie was, 'Are you a Communist?' Norrie replied that Stalin was a Conservative compared with what he was.

Once when Norrie was sliding with us down the Long Man of Wilmington after a picnic on the downs, an angry farmer threatened him with prosecution for leaving his car on a sheep track. Quintin Hogg leapt to the defence of 'a poor helpless wounded soldier' in a masterly counter-attack thereby prompting Norrie's prophecy: 'That boy will find himself on the Woolsack if he doesn't watch out.'

A colourful friendship developed between Rosslyn and the eccentric owner of Herstmonceux Castle, Colonel Claude Lowther, who had all the charm and flamboyancy of his Lonsdale forebears. He had bought the castle gatehouse and ruin fifteen years before and was slowly restoring it, taking enormous pains to find material of the right period. His dinner parties, in the few medieval rooms he had revived, were legendary. Rosslyn and Rachel were frequently invited. Bishop, his ancient butler, would follow up the invitation with a telephone call begging each lady to wear a colour that would blend with his master's curtains and cushions. During dinner it was not unusual for a scene to break out, half playful and half in tears, with the master hurling abuse and even a pewter plate or two at the departing figure of his butler. There would then be heartrending appeals for forgiveness before Bishop led the ladies upstairs to a bedroom with a screen in it, behind which he had prepared an ornate chamber pot. The lack of plumbing at Herstmonceux Castle remained contemporary with its original building.

Colonel Lowther was much concerned with his impending death and sent for Rosslyn every time he remade his will. He had plenty of descendants but, when in various small ways each had offended, he left the castle for a brief period to Rosslyn. He was generous with land for the graveyard and 'alms for your poor'. On a visiting card attached to a cheque for a hundred pounds he wrote: 'I send you my mite for your dear poor and only wish I could add another nought to it! Claude.' He gave Rosslyn a beautiful statue of a weeping cupid to put in All Saints church. The fact that the new Bishop refused a faculty for its entry made no difference to either. Colonel Lowther started a whimsical rumour, which Rosslyn did nothing to contradict, that supernatural agencies had introduced the statue into the church.

When Rachel's mother died, Rosslyn added a note to her obituary in *The Times* mentioning the delight she took in sending *Punch* to lonely missionaries in the Far East and to vicarages in the slums and outlying country parishes. He spent the small legacy she left him on buying hymnbooks for Herstmonceux church, in each of which he inscribed her name and his.

Her nephew, Noel Buxton, now Minister of Agriculture and Fisheries, continued his demands by note and telegram. Rosslyn did his best to comply. 'Further request for boons. I am interested in farm wages and if you have any farm labourers earning less than twenty-five shillings all told, I do wish you'd show me his home and teach me how on earth he brings up a healthy family.'

'Your writing a great comfort in times of distress. What a blessing to know that somebody wishes the truth to be told about farmers! Why do you never propose to come to lunch with me and cheer me up?'

MAY I COME FOR SATURDAY AFTERNOON AND LEARN ABOUT FARM LABOURERS.

MIGHT I COME TO TEA AND BRING TWO OR THREE INFANTS ON SATURDAY?

He signed himself 'Cogishall of Macedonia'.

'My dear R,' he wrote after one of his visits, 'It was very jolly to see you, and the children were most attractive. You are quite right. The question of slavery is important. I am too much inclined to apologise for it. I would like to hear you and the Bishop. You anyhow.'

After Miss Fortescue left, complaining of the feeling of a rubber band round her head brought on by barking dogs and noisy Bruces, we were taught by an imaginative, embryo musician only a few years older than Rhalou. From Joyce Weston I learnt more than in any other year in my life.

As Rhalou had little use for her books, climbing out of the schoolroom window if hounds went by, Rosslyn decided to send her to a boarding school at which hunting was an almost compulsory subject. This extraordinary bizarre school, housed in Lord Brassey's Victorian palace, Normanhurst, was run by a magnificent cousin of Rachel's and her foxy little husband, who took the girls out hunting as though leading a platoon into battle. Rhalou loved the Edwardian sportsmanship; some of the girls still rode sidesaddle. Rosslyn loved the dances and Rachel the garden parties to which they were both inevitably invited. Daisy Battine reduced her fees drastically for relations and girls with the kind of talent she wanted. Rhalou already knew more about kennel management than some of the hunt servants and so gained her scholarship that way. Meanwhile, Lorema and I were taught for a while by our parents. Rosslyn set me a weekly general knowledge paper and I happily covered reams of paper giving the answers in the form of short stories. Sometimes excerpts of these turned up in his sermons. Rachel's method was to read the classics aloud to me and any gardening books she happened to be consulting while I busily used my hands sewing or making doll's furniture. Lessons were only interrupted for a few days after my appendix was removed on the kitchen table.

The family was now joined every holiday by Ken Rice, whose father was in the Hong Kong and Shanghai Bank. Ken arrived, aged seven, a small, sun-dried, nervous little boy who had been rescued with his mother from the debris of the great Japanese earthquake and then shipwrecked. This was nothing, he said, to his first term at prep school. In the holidays he slept in the girls' room, because of nightmares. He called his parents Mummy and Daddy and ours Mother and Father. Rosslyn pointed out to him that it was the same moon that he could see at school as we could at Herstmonceux and his parents could see in China; 'But they can't see the same clouds,' he sniffed tearfully.

John Betjeman was a master at Heddon Court and remembered being presented by Ken to Rosslyn, 'for whom he had immense affection and pride.' Ken told him afterwards that the rectory was like a second home to him and we were like sisters. John Betjeman wrote:

He was always talking about Herstmonceux when he was at Heddon Court, so much so, indeed, I think that some of the boys loved to tease him about it. He was a lively waif-like figure and Father and Mother were his anchor. I was about twenty at the time but still recall that there was this devotion of this boy to the Rev. Rosslyn Bruce and that it singled him out from the other boys in the school. He had been given a great present of a family background when his parents were in China, and when China could only be reached by a long sea voyage.

Ken went on to Stowe. Erroll joined Merlin at Dartmouth, and I joined Rhalou at Normanhurst. My scholarship was won, Rosslyn said, for my fuzzy hair, which Daisy Battine needed in a pageant she was producing. There was a spate of pageants in the neighbourhood and Rosslyn appeared in many of them. In the Rushlake Green pageant based on Kipling's Sussex novels, he played the Archbishop of Canterbury. In the great pageant of Battle Abbey he played the Lord Warden of the Cinque Ports. Everyone for miles took part, including the no longer young Battle aunts. Normanhurst provided the Normans and their mounts. The pageant master was Gwen Lallie, one of the first to direct a pageant through a microphone which was wired to loudspeakers in the trees. Rosslyn told a story of the final dress rehearsal when one of the grooms, who should have been in Norman dress, appeared in the arena. At the same moment, in a quiet country lane, a commercial traveller in London attire, walking to the nearest pub for lunch was astonished to hear a voice as from heaven boom: 'Take off that bowler hat!'

When Sir Douglas Hogg was created a peer Rosslyn suggested he should call himself Lord Herstmonceux. The reply came from the House of Lords thanking him for his congratulations—'I had a telegram from the village of Herstmonceux making the same suggestion as you do, but I thought that it would not be reasonable to expect Colonel Lowther to agree to such a suggestion. You'll see that I have gone to my own parish town for my title. (Hailsham). See you next week.'

A few months later Lord Hailsham became engaged to a pretty widow with one little daughter, Domine Lawrence. Lord Hailsham, thanking for a wedding present, said: 'I hope before long that you will have Mrs. Lawrence as an additional member of your congregation.'

Quintin had now been elected President of the Oxford Union. Quintin wrote delightedly: 'It is always pleasant to score something in open competition.' Then came the triumph of him getting the First he 'had hardly expected'. And then 'I find it all a little difficult to accustom myself to the belief that I am really an All Souls Fellow. However, I went there yesterday and they seemed to expect me. Yours, Quintin.'

Lord Hailsham brought Lady Baden-Powell, Chief Guide, to church at Herstmonceux on Easter Sunday. Instead of a sermon, Rosslyn made a personal statement on his belief on life after death.

First, because all other earthly things continue scientifically in-destructible. The character of a human being is probably eternal. Secondly, because by the consent of the most effective men and women thinkers of all races in all ages, life has been believed to be eternal. Thirdly, because the inequalities of human happiness demand some readjustment.

He gave three grounds for his belief on the rising of Christ.

First, the empty tomb and no record of the bestowal of the body has been ever claimed. Secondly, the change to Sunday from the seventh day Sabbath has no other explanation. The reason must have been very weighty. Thirdly, the lives of the early Christians, the Apostles, the martyrs and heroic missionaries could not have been based on a delusion.

Those who love most, feel the most deeply the paramount necessity of love beyond the grave.

Lady Baden-Powell wrote thanking him.

The same year Lord Hailsham brought Mr. Winston Churchill, then Chancellor of the Exchequer, to Herstmonceux church. Rosslyn's sermon was based on the new peace pact.

Rosslyn usually invited distinguished visitors to the church to read the lesson. A French diplomat read beautifully in, apparently, his mother tongue, but even our current mademoiselle was unable to translate it. Afterwards Rosslyn asked him to point out what he had read instead of the appointed lesson, beginning: 'Can the Ethiopian change his skin or the leopard his spots.'

'But that is what I read,' he objected in English. Afterwards

Rosslyn gave an imitation of this passage with an exaggerated French pronunciation, ending in 'or zee Lee-o-parrrd eesbo!'

When Colonel Lowther died, his funeral was one of the most theatrical services Rosslyn had ever taken. Music that he had loved to hear Dame Clara Butt sing, was played as a voluntary. The church was filled with expensive flowers from London shops and exquisitely dressed mourners, wearing the black that was forbidden at Colonel Lowther's dinner parties. Rachel could not help expecting Claude Lowther, who had believed so fervently in the castle ghost, to appear as he always had done with such ceremony after dinner, to wander among his guests.

The castle was offered for sale at a hundred thousand pounds, but bidding stopped at thirty-five thousand. It was bought by Mrs. Lawson, a widow whose only contribution to its restoration was to allow the ivy to grow more thickly over it.

As soon as Rhalou left school, Rosslyn took her on a tour of the United States and Canada in which he combined preaching sermons with judging at dog shows and attending a Rotary Convention at Minneapolis. Spry in his half-high hat, light summer suiting, black bib and clerical collar, he smiled charmingly out of the many photographs that appeared of him in the press. Rhalou, in low-cut, double-breasted costume with a skirt above her knees and a cloche hat pulled down over her eyebrows, looked, as she was, extremely pretty and nearly grown up.

The following summer Rhalou combined a part-time London season as a debutante with receiving canine members at the Dog's Bath Club, in Beauchamp Place.

Rachel swept aside parish duties and went off to her dress-maker to prepare to present Rhalou at Court. Queuing in the Mall in a borrowed Daimler before entering Buckingham Palace, Rhalou was spotted by a press photographer who had last photographed her showing one of Rosslyn's dogs at Crufts. 'Surely you've got one of your father's famous fox terriers tucked under your train? — he insisted and her photograph appeared in the front page of the *Daily Mirror* under 'Doggy Deb'. Rosslyn accompanied her and Rachel to the next Buckingham Palace garden party. On the way they met Rosslyn's favourite 'Doggy Duchess', Kathleen Duchess of

Newcastle, a frequent co-judge with him at dog shows. His sister Kathleen was there and took them back to see her new home, Leinster Corner, 100 Bayswater Road. It was here that Rosslyn had first met James Barrie, its former tenant.

While they were there two Geoffreys appeared, both of whom Rosslyn had known well as small boys, as sons of old friends. Geoffrey Dearmer, B.B.C. Children's Hour producer, his first guest at Clifton, and Geoffrey Shakespeare, Labour M.P. for Norwich, who shortly afterwards became Parliamentary Secretary to Kathleen's husband, Bill Hilton-Young, when he was made Minister of Health in the coalition government.

By the time he was sixty, Rosslyn's old friends had mostly reached the tops of their professions or received public honours. John Simon, now investigating the R101 airship disaster, had long been a knight. Bill Hilton-Young had just been knighted. Rosslyn met Nigel Playfair, now a well-known actor and impresario, in what he called 'the dark period between the honours list and the accolade' and asked if he were truly a knight yet. 'I think so,' Nigel said, 'at least in the sight of God.' F. E. Smith who had become Lord Chancellor at forty-six, was now the Earl of Birkenhead and Viscount Furneaux.

Noel Buxton had just been created a baron, using his own name with a hyphen 'Lord Noel-Buxton' to distinguish him from his first cousin the Earl Buxton.

Neville Chamberlain was heading towards Premiership. 'Dear Bruce,' he wrote from 37, Eaton Square after a family bereavement: 'It was very good of you to write and in face of a host of difficulties it is helpful to know that one is in the thoughts of one's friends. Yours sincerely, Neville Chamberlain.'

Rosslyn's old Oxford Union rival, Hilaire Belloc, had written a prodigious number of books. Rosslyn had written ten. Neither had received any official literary award.

Rosslyn probably had more letters in *The Times* on a wider range of subjects than any other contributor of his day. It was his letter that closed the extended correspondence on how long it took readers to do *The Times* crossword puzzle. 'I always do it at breakfast,' he wrote, 'while my egg boils.'

He had been installed Past Grand Chaplain of the Grand Lodge of

England by Lord Cornwallis supported by six hundred Masons and was 'honoured by command of the Duke of Connaught, the dignity of Past Grand Standard Bearer of England in the Grand Chapter of Royal Arch.' There was hardly a cathedral in England Rosslyn had not preached in, but his preferment in the Church had stopped at Herstmonceux.

'If Rosslyn had stayed at Edgbaston,' Bishop Burrows said, 'he would almost certainly have been into gaiters within a year or so.' And his Archdeacon said: 'Throwing up the active Midlands and burying himself in the south coast lost him the opportunities of preferment.'

But Rosslyn did not consider himself buried. And there was no doubt that in one field—as a fox terrier breeder and judge—he had reached the top.

Throughout the dog literature of the day he was referred to as 'The greatest living fox terrier expert and one of the six most famous fanciers of our time', 'one of the best-known all-round judges'. As 'The Factor', he edited '*Fox Terrier Facts*', a weekly column in *Our Dogs*.

He also wrote a regular weekly nature column in the *Evening Standard*, which produced a huge and lively correspondence.

The *Scottish Field* said:

A successful man, beloved as a clergyman, Dr. Rosslyn Bruce's name has a special significance for dog lovers. He has for long been recognised as one of the greatest living authorities on the smooth fox terriers. A distinguished breeder and judge, he has written learned scientific works on the breeding of smooth fox terriers and has been for many years a regular contributor to the canine press of this country. An American authority says he has sought to adapt the old Bruce-Lowe system of breeding horses to the breeding of smooth fox terriers and has with great labour worked out fox terrier pedigrees and sorted the dogs into Lines, and bitches into Families for the application of this method.

As an all-round local sportsman, curtain-raiser at public entertainments and after-dinner speaker, Rosslyn was in constant demand.

Whether it was the East Sussex milkmaid's game of stoolball, or cricket, football or billiards, he was keen to be there. He attended all local point-to-points, and always went on the firemen's outing to Goodwood races. He proposed the Immortal Memory on Burns nights, and chaired a variety of annual dinners. He still followed the East Sussex Hunt on foot, and reported its activities in the local paper under the pseudonym of 'Old Dog Fox' from the point of view of the fox with such endings as 'altogether it was a very satisfactory day for hounds, horses, riders, footmen, cyclists and motorists. Archibald and I provided enough sport for the greediest. All honour to the East Sussex. I feel proud to have lived and run in their country and when my time comes, well, I wouldn't ever want to be a spongey-gummed toothless old fox, not for toffee.' Later Rosslyn was presented with an East Sussex Hunt button, a rare distinction for a non-riding subscriber. Probably even more gratifying were the letters that poured in daily.

'My dear Rosslyn,' Losco Bradley wrote from Sherwood Rise. 'You are really a marvel at the fox terrier job. You are the one of the world certs. As soon as I begin to catch salmon I will send you a beauty. We ran for two and a half hours yesterday and had a ten mile point.'

'Dear Doctor, You excelled yourself this week. Topping stuff and absolutely right about the size faddists.'

'Dear Doc, Your speech was a pippin. We enjoyed it hugely.'

Rosslyn was playfully known in the dog world as the Bishop of Brighton. The local press took it up and said 'Perhaps coming events are casting their shadows before them. We are sure the gaiters would become him.'

When asked if there was any truth in the rumour, Rosslyn said he could never wear gaiters. His hunting accident had left one leg longer than the other—or else the press had. Anyway he was too busy cross-ing bantams with pheasants to produce phantams.

Some suggested that Rosslyn would have adored to be a Bishop but his lack of self-restraint, particularly at diocesan conferences, shocked the higher ecclesiastics into withholding their recommendations He could not help suggesting, for instance, at a discussion on the Fundamentalists and the Sacramentalists, that the former speaker 'was neither fundamental nor sacramental, but just plain mental.'

Even at parish meetings he could not resist tossing off such remarks as, after the very deaf organist had been considered too old to play at weddings: 'He plays with as much feeling as ever. You can almost hear the babies crying in the vestry.'

When approached by a rural dean, beaming and rubbing his hands with 'I have heard so much about you.' Rosslyn replied brusquely: 'Yes, but can you prove it?'

And then there were his words of comfort to the bishop's wife moaning about her many bereavements: 'Yes, yes, I know how you feel. Golgotha and Gethsemane all rolled into one.'

And then his inability to resist his twin interests in pretty girls and the vagaries of the English language in a story he told after a rurideaconal meeting.

One of my parishioners in Birmingham who made a lot of money came to me in great trouble with a letter from his daughter. 'My only daughter!' he cried. 'And I have given her the best of everything, sending her to the finest schools and now look.' I read the letter with its shattering contents and tried to comfort the poor fellow that at least his daughter loved him enough to tell him herself that she was no longer a virgin. 'Yes, but my dear padre,' he went on uncomforted. 'All that money spent and she still spells vergin with an E.'

CHAPTER TWENTY-TWO

Seventh Heaven

There were seven ponies in the glade and a white donkey in the paddock. Ken and Lorema and I floated home-made rafts on the pond and fell in. We built crows' nests in the trees reached by rope ladders. Merlin and Erroll shot rabbits and the occasional pheasant in the glebe assisted by Quintin Hogg, hysterical with laughter over the antics of his own uncontrollable dog, with us girls beating through the undergrowth. Rosslyn stood on the croquet lawn with his old hammergun—Rachel pruned the vine in the Bubble—Rhalou could be seen in the distance surrounded by a pack of twenty or more dogs of different breeds, with Erroll striding past her on his way down to the marshes to photograph peewits.

Merlin joined a flying club, gained his pilot's ticket, and set his sisters to work to remove the mole hills from the park so that he could land near the house.

Colonel Lindbergh, Atlantic flyer, came over from his Sussex home near by, to buy a dog. He asked Rosslyn to lunch and advised Merlin against attempting to land on his homemade runway. So the clover field half a mile away continued to be used.

Rosslyn, a goat, a pekinese and eventually each one of us in turn—and finally Rachel—were taken up for Merlin to demonstrate the sensation of looping the loop in a small open Moth. One day he turned up with a dual-control learner plane and, once up, Rosslyn found himself taking over. He first flew by airliner to The Hague to take part in an international sporting conference. From then on he flew whenever there was a choice of air, land or sea. For a while, in these early days of aerial transport, he was known as the Flying Parson.

Kathleen wrote from Leinster Corner:

My dear,

Here is a ridiculous old coat which, being of unwearable-out material, has outlived its fur lining. Both my men-kind are too short for it. If it is too shabby for your august person, you might like to give it to one of your parishioners. Hope all is well with you. All well here.

Ever K. Love to R.

This was Scott's fur-lined British warm, taken from a Museum case. Merlin wore it at sea for some years. Peter used his father's sword to poke out wasps' nests. Before Merlin went abroad for long spells he would begin a game of chess with Rosslyn that they continued to play by post. Postcards sped across Siberia to and from Japanese waters with such messages as: 'Have noted your move 13, and Kt to QB3. If you move KR pawn, I will take your castle, if not I shall have to think again. Let me know your move 14, and if poss. forecast 15.'

When Merlin returned the game was completed on the regular chessboard in the study.

Then Erroll's cruises to Far East countries began. Both boys saw Ken Rice's parents in Hong Kong and later Ceylon. Rosslyn had sent me to the Royal College of Music on the advice of his old friend and organist, Doc H, who struggled to inject the basic principles of harmony and counterpoint into my wandering mind.

His Oxford Union friend, Dr. Percy Buck, had little more success in diverting my attention towards musical history. Dr. Malcolm Sargent, with whom Rosslyn had made friends over cage-birds, however, occasionally managed to hold my attention as I scraped away on my violin in the third orchestra, and later sang in his choir.

Sometimes Kathleen would ring up my student's lodgings at about 6 p.m. and say 'Wash your hair, cancel your next engagement, put on your best evening frock and come and help me to give a party.'

Malcolm Sargent appeared at one of these, hot from conducting at the Albert Hall. 'Do play us something,' Kathleen pressed him and he sat down at the piano and played the latest jazz hits to which we danced.

At Herstmonceux rectory dance music was confined to sheet music, which Merlin bought at Woolworth's, sixpence a copy, for me to play on the piano, and to three records which Ken had swapped at school with a clockwork gramophone, for his outgrown bicycle. Then, after the first few repetitive renderings, Ken was only allowed to play in the field beyond Merlin's landing place.

By now love had entered the rectory by all doors. Ada, in the kitchen, had at last consented to marry the—now—head gardener at Clifton Hall after a nearly twenty-year courtship by post and was busily sewing her beige satin wedding dress. They were married at Northrepps. Rosa had been married at Herstmonceux with Lorema as bridesmaid, and the reception at the rectory.

Merlin brought home a different collection of girls every time he came on leave. Rhalou brought sophisticated deb's delights from London and sporting squires' sons she had met out hunting. I brought an occasional flautist from the R.C.M. or a shy bassoonist. But once Erroll had returned from abroad with the whole of his Dartmouth 'term' of fifty acting sub-lieutenants at our disposal, I got into my stride, had my pigtails cut off and bought some red lipstick.

Rosslyn warned us all that we must not lead others to believe we loved them more than we really did, and we girls must never allow young men to propose unless we intended to say yes. The result of heeding this warning was that I found myself engaged to four naval officers at once, and Merlin became seriously engaged to Joan Hitchcock. Rosslyn married them in his old church of St. Anne's, Soho, with Sub-Lieutenant John Casson, R.N., son of Sybil Thorndike, as best man. Truda, one of Rosslyn's first loves at Oxford forty years before, steeled herself to appear at the wedding but was too overcome by the sight of him to join the reception at the Hailsham's London house, 17 Bryanston Square.

In April that year we were all at the East Sussex point-to-point at Hellingly when Rosslyn was called away urgently to the Hailshams' country house near by. Lord Hailsham's stepson, Edward Majoribanks, barrister, writer and M.P. for Eastbourne—young, brilliant and beautiful—had been found dead beside his gun.

At the inquest the coroner asked the family to suppress the evidence which showed that Edward had shot himself. This, neither his devoted stepfather nor half-brother would do. Both said: 'the truth is the truth.'

As a result the Bishop of Chichester refused to allow Edward to be buried in consecrated ground. There followed three unhappy days trying to comfort the family and trying to persuade Bishop Bell, holidaying on Lake Windermere, to change his mind. At last Rosslyn contacted him, but the telephone line was bad and Rosslyn's own reception faded out altogether when the bishop not only expressly forbade him to bury Edward in the churchyard but also ordered cuts in the funeral service. The bishop gave up and sent a telegram.

MOST DEEPLY GRIEVED FOR LORD HAILSHAM AND ALL MOURNERS AT SUCH HEART-BREAKING TRAGEDY AND FEEL KEENLY FOR YOU. CONFIRMING CONVERSATION PLEASE BEGIN WITH PSALM 39 OMIT HEARD A VOICE FROM HEAVEN SUBSTITUTING PRAYERS. BISHOP.

'I heard a voice from heaven,' Rosslyn said casting it aside. 'But I couldn't hear a voice from Windermere.'

He buried Edward in a part of the churchyard that could be seen from Carters Corner Place, and though Bishop Bell admitted afterwards that Rosslyn was right, Lord Hailsham never forgave the bishop for the part he played.

Quintin wrote a free translation from a poem by Catullus, whom Edward loved above all Latin poets, and whom had been similarly placed.

> Over sea and land come I,
> Brother dear, to say good-bye;
> To hear the ancient words I dread
> Muttered softly o'er the dead:
> 'Ash to ash and dust to dust'.
> Though you hear not, speak I must
> And tell your silent body how
> In bitter grief I mourn you now.
> Custom's servant, not her slave
> Stand I weeping at the grave
> Take this wreath as tolls the bell;
> Brother dear, a long farewell.

Quintin's wreath, which Edward would have understood, carried the original Latin of the last line: *Frater ave atque vale.*

A small aircraft flew over the church and dipped in salute. It was said to be the Prince of Wales.

Frederick Vanderberg, K.C., in whose chambers Edward had been a pupil, wrote that the funeral 'at the picturesque little church at Herstmonceux opposite the castle which he and I had often visited together—it was his favourite walk—was the saddest sight I ever witnessed. No one who was there can ever forget it.'

The Hon. Mrs. Rupert Gwynn, a cousin of Edward's, wrote thanking Rosslyn for 'your stout heart and grand attitude. We all thought it a lovely service. F. Vandenberg took a great fancy to you. Edward always said he was one of the most brilliant young persons at the Bar. Elizabeth would so like it if you can lunch here.'

Her two young daughters, Elizabeth, now Elizabeth David, and Priscilla, now Mrs. Longland, had felt the tragedy very deeply and their mother knew, she said, that Rosslyn could help and cheer them.

Among the Members of Parliament at Edward's funeral was Sir Paul Latham, M.P. for Scarborough. He wandered along Edward's favourite walk with Rosslyn and so came upon the enchanting rosy battlements of the castle on the edge of the marshes. Rosslyn told this willowy, golden-haired young man that the owner was leaving. Paul decided instantly that he would live there. Within days he had made an offer for the castle, just as it stood. Even the owner's clothes and library books were still in it. Work began at once to rebuild the castle according to old prints of the original. It had once been enormous and so it would be again, at a cost of a quarter of a million pounds. The moat was to be filled with water again and not only would there be forty bedrooms but also full modern plumbing. Sir Paul asked for Rosslyn's suggestions and, with them, restored the castle chapel to be used not only as a domestic chapel, but regularly by the parish. At the head of the swimming pool among ancient yew hedges, stood a statue of a blindfolded boy sculpted by Kathleen over the legend 'The Kingdom of Heaven is within'.

Rosslyn was among the clergy officiating at the wedding of Sir Paul Latham to Lady Patricia Moore at St. Margaret's, Westminster.

Rachel, Rhalou and Kathleen were among the guests at this fabulous wedding. Later Paul, as a churchwarden at Herstmonceux, insisted that his strange guests staying in the castle should attend church on Sundays. Several of Rosslyn's old stage friends came, including Nigel Playfair and his son Giles, who found the food and tobacco at the castle too overpowering for him and so spent much of one day at the rectory, only returning with Rosslyn and Rachel for a dinner party.

Later Nigel brought his Shakespearean Company to play in an Eastbourne garden where a real nightingale drowned the voices of his actors.

Inside the castle the chapel was consecrated in time for the christening of Paul and Patricia Latham's baby son, Richard. At the first parish service in the chapel, Rosslyn asked for a collecting plate and Paul emptied the sugar basin on the breakfast table and brought the basin to the chapel.

Barbara Hutton, in the days when nothing in Woolworth's, from which her fortune derived, was over sixpence, asked to borrow that sum for the collection. I offered my half-crown pocket money, for my own sixpence was to be my donation. But she insisted on taking the sixpence and I was left with the half-crown to put in the plate. However, when I explained the predicament in the vestry, Rosslyn gave me two blessed shillings change.

After three years in China seas Erroll was home doing courses at the Royal Naval College, Greenwich. Merlin was abroad again and his baby son, Euslin, came to live at the rectory with his mother. Lorema was at our aunt Kathleen's holy school, St. Michael's, Bognor. Rhalou got engaged to Kirkby Peace, a veterinary student, whom she met out hunting; and I had reduced my naval entanglements to one. For one glorious summer we were both 'unmarried daughters living at home'. Rhalou helped with the dogs. I helped in the parish. I, who ran a Brownie Pack and taught twenty-seven Mixed Infants in the Sunday School, rather fancied myself as a lay pillar of the Church of England. However, just to watch reactions, I said to my father one day as we pushed our bicycles up the hill to church: 'I've been rather thinking lately of becoming a Roman Catholic.'

He turned round and, looking down at me over his shoulder, observed crushingly:

'I should be only too happy to see *any* signs of *any* religion in *any* of my daughters.'

Now I was presented at Buckingham Palace and, with Erroll and his 'term' at Greenwich Royal Naval College, enjoyed the London dances and nautical fun that he and his special friends, John Kennard, Dick Beckwith, Laurence Kettle and later Alec Hunting laid on. Even more memorable were their visits nearly every week-end to the rectory, when Rosslyn proved that he could still play tennis and cricket.

When we rolled up the carpet in the evenings to dance, he was always first on the floor. But his greatest delight was to have us all round him playing paper and pencil games. A favourite version of Consequences was called 'Noël Coward' in which, between us, we wrote reams of pert dialogue, with a maximum of three words to the line. The games were continued with the making of a forty-two-foot-long stair carpet. Rachel spread the canvas over our knees and provided each person with strands of wool and a rugging hook, to be exchanged at intervals for the pencil and paper. Surviving from a party game, written on Dick Beckwith's knees, tucked under the rug, are lines alluding to the first Lord Hailsham's elevation to the Woolsack.

> Lord High Chancellor
> Presiding up in Westminster
> Frowning through the fringes of his
> Full bottomed wig
> With a hand on the pulses of
> Kings and Cabinets
> Scarlet and magnificent
> Really very big
> Old country gentlemen
> Brooding down in Herstmonceux
> Swirling through the wrinkles of a face full of fun
> With his hair hanging over his
> Butterfly old collar
> Walking round in public
> With his buttons undone.

Rosslyn, standing on the doorstep blowing his bugle, saw a party of twelve of us off in three old crock cars. Erroll was taking us on the Norfolk Broads in three unwieldly sailing wherries to practise, he said, for future transatlantic crossings. We returned after a fortnight to find a procession in the rectory drive, of a fleet of imposing limousines from which were expelled, at intervals, Indian guards who lay in the grass awaiting events. It was Rosslyn's old friend the Maharajah of Pittapuram and his ladies, in bead-curtained vehicles who had come to admire the dogs. When the Maharajah's Champion, Diana Danesgate, for which he paid five hundred guineas and which stayed for a while at the rectory, won the Fox Terrier Club challenge cup he celebrated his success with a lunch at the Savoy for twenty-six, which Rosslyn, Rachel and Rhalou attended. Later the Maharajah paid a thousand guineas to Dr. Miller for Champion Boreham Belsize, whom Rosslyn introduced to him. The doctor retired on the proceeds.

At the height of the summer of 1934 Rosslyn and Rhalou went off to Richmond Dog Show with the car loaded with would-be champions. Near Epsom they stopped to take them out of the car to give them a run. Rosslyn was putting them back when another car ran into the back of the Ford and once again Rosslyn was carried off with his right leg broken. For five months he lay in Epsom Hospital with Rachel staying in a near-by hotel much of the time. Meanwhile Rhalou and I struggled to keep the parish going and to look after the stream of 'guinea pigs' (substitute clergymen) who came for the weekends to take the services.

At Epsom inquiries were so extensive that Rosslyn had five hundred copies of a card printed with 'Thank you very much indeed for your kind and cheering message; it has been a painful and trying time, but the worst, one may hope, is over now, and your kindness has helped greatly. Forgive this print, I cannot write much yet.' In the midst of his misery came the news of Nigel Playfair's sudden death from a heart attack.

When Rosslyn returned to Herstmonceux, his regular nurse for broken legs, the same Chloe who had also attended my birth, came to care for him. Though older and stouter she was still good-looking and gay and came willingly out dancing with all of us when we made our way to 'The Monkey Puzzle Road House' or 'Druscilla's'.

Colonel Claude Lowther's weeping cupid, said to have flown from Herstmonceux Castle into the church against the Bishop's orders.

The sailors' return, Herstmonceux, 1934. Merlin, Rhalou, K. Peace, Verily, Erroll, Lorema. *Front row*: Joan (holding Euslin, the first grandchild), Rosslyn and Rachel.

Of the many varieties Rosslyn bred, showed, judged and wrote about, his two favourite breeds were Skye terriers and smooth fox terriers. He is holding here Fearlessness and Formosa.

While he was recovering Rosslyn wrote some new verse and revised poems he had written before. The main literary product of this fracture was a kind of whimsical repeat of the *Oxford Verses* he had edited forty years before. It was called *Sussex Sacred Songs, selected by Rosslyn Bruce*. Selector's notes pointed out the qualities of each poem and excused defects: 'This colloquial little fragment, with its quaintly ambitious title, rings strong and true: again if not technically sacred in phrasing, the essence is spiritual.' Each, secretly written by himself, was signed with an anagram of his name. The book was illustrated with portraits of some of the poets drawn by a young artist who cunningly incorporated some feature of the common source, even though the relevant poet might appear as a nun or a naval officer.

When Rosslyn recovered from his accident he published *Sussex Sacred Songs* himself, and its three editions were sold through local shops or direct from his study. Few guessed the identity of the 'nineteen poets'.

A case was brought against the drunken driver who had caused Rosslyn's accident and £871 was paid in court at the Sussex Assizes for solicitors and other expenses. If Rosslyn had not been seen dancing six months after the accident at the Hunt Ball, considerably more would have come his way.

Rhalou was to be married on the joint anniversary of Rosslyn's hunting accident and her parents' wedding, October 21st, 1935. The restoration of Herstmonceux Castle was now complete and Sir Paul Latham's wedding present to her was a reception for five hundred friends and relations. So many were the wedding presents that, when laid out, they filled the whole of the long gallery. As before, efforts were made to secure a bishop, and eventually three took part. Bishop Burrows wrote that he had hoped to enjoy the wedding from a pew.

I still hope you may allow me to be unrobed and you will let one of the clergy, who is better known to your daughter, have the privilege you offer me. Please do. I would really rather be unseen and your daughter will have a happier and less official wedding. Don't think me ungracious, unsympathetic and unkind. Let her wedding be homely and unprelatical. I'll give her my prayers and my blessings in silence.

Benjie Bruce wrote from a hospital in Zurich.

Divine doctor and earthly cousin, your letter asking me to help to marry your daughter reached me through the family solicitor. I have no idea how long it has been wandering, meanwhile I normally reside in Budapest where I am a noise. The reason I'm here is because I was caught bending in the train on the way from Budapest to Geneva and had to get out here and be operated on for kidney trouble. We have been here eight weeks but it is now time to return to the fortunes of our little Rhalou. I see that she marries one Peace.

It's a year or two since in the billiard room at Downhill you expounded to a wondering me your reasons for wishing to dodge devils; to wit, you wanted to wash dirty babies.

You must apologise to the bride for me. Any possibilities of sending a wedding present are reduced here to a roll of elastoplast or a tube of argosol, useful but unsuitable offerings for romantic occasions.

Yours as of old, Benjie.

There were eight bridesmaids and Rosslyn wrote a hymn for the occasion and gave the bride away. The party at Herstmonceux Castle was magnificent, and afterwards the bride and bridegroom trundled off to their new home in a horsebox filled with two ponies, five dogs and a number of smaller items of livestock.

The next party at Herstmonceux Castle was a dance for six hundred of the village and their friends. Rosslyn conducted the dancing and games; Rachel and Patricia dispensed pies and cake and Paul and I knocked the tops off the bottles for want, in this sumptuous millionaire establishment, of a bottle opener.

The parish birth rate rose by fifteen within a week the following year.

One day Kathleen blew in for tea at the rectory on her way from Eastbourne to London. When Rosslyn saw from *The Times* Court Circular, next day, that she had not bothered to mention that she had been lunching with the King and Queen at Compton Place, Eastbourne, he wrote accusing her of 'not letting us share your feather'.

She wrote back on a postcard: 'You both might have thought I came to boast and not because I loved you.'

Rosslyn said, on reading it, that Rachel was one of the few people whose opinion of her, Kathleen cared about.

Bill was raised to the peerage in 1936 and took the name of Kennet of The Dene. In Rosslyn's list of family and close friends he prayed for, he pencilled against Bill's name 'Lord Kennet'. 'In case the Almighty hadn't heard about it?' Merlin asked. Rosslyn teased Kathleen on having changed her name from Miss Bruce to Mrs Scott, and then to Lady Scott, then Lady Hilton-Young, and now Lady Kennet with:

> When an artist has once made a name,
> He is properly proud of his fame;
> But when one can contrive
> To have not one, but five,
> She is clearly quite good at the game.

That year after judging two breeds of terriers at Crufts where he had won his first championship forty-three years before, Mr. Cruft presented Rosslyn with a souvenir medal in recognition of his long association with the show. During all the busy activity he had tea alone with Mr. and Mrs. Cruft, who admitted that their favourite animal was a cat.

Quintin Hogg's little half-sister, Domine, wrote to Rosslyn:

As Mummy is coming down to Carters Corner I send this by her. My cousin is doing lessons with me. Is your advice forthcoming? We have made a little image of the inside of a chapel with an altar. It is exactly like a real one in the main details. I realise we could not, I suppose, have it blessed. But can we say our prayers in it? Do write and tell me what you think. It's only an idea. My love.

From Domine.

Rosslyn explained away Domine's fears and blessed the little chapel with love and approval.

Herstmonceux Place, standing on the hill above the castle, was now lent by Sir Paul Latham to General Nation, whose wife had been the widow of Rosslyn's Oxford friend Paul Rubens, musical comedy composer. Olive Nation immediately formed an amateur dramatic society and regularly produced ambitious plays. She asked me to write a thriller for her but my first attempt, 'Rosie's in the Garden', in which a man melted down his wife in sulphuric acid and watered the roses with her, was she said, too lurid. With Quintin's help it was adapted for Domine's latest project, a puppet theatre for which Rosslyn and I then wrote a ghost play starring the voice of Stella, Lady Reading, who was staying at Carters Corner Place.

I wrote two more plays for Olive Nation, neither of which she produced. One, however, with a hunting theme, was put on in London at St. Martin's Theatre as a curtain-raiser and Rosslyn came to its first night, and provided the appropriate hunting noises.

The Nations' lunch parties to which we were invited had a strong theatrical and literary flavour greatly to Rosslyn's taste. Here he met the Harold Nicolsons, and Virginia Woolf.

In the months before the Second World War Rosslyn married Erroll to Daphne Bradley in Dorset. Not long before war broke out came a letter from John Simon, who was soon to become Viscount Simon, on the typed envelope of which he had inked in, after Rosslyn's name, 'Member for Dogs and Cats!'

'It really is great fun being appointed to the Woolsack if it produces echoes from old friends like you. Dear old F. E. would not have failed to point out that Wadham had produced three Lord Chancellors within a century and thereby has deseated all other Oxford colleges as certainly as did the rugger team we played in in 1895! I'm delighted to hear from you.' And later: 'At dinner at 11 Downing Street the other night (Wish you had been there) were twelve contemporaries including C. B. Fry, Lord Roche, E. C. Bentley, *Trent's last case*, Bishop Blagdon, F. W. Hurst. Belloc could not come.'

As soon as war was declared, evacuee children began to arrive at Herstmonceux rectory but were soon moved on to a less vulnerable part of the coast. The rectory then became a haven for local nervous wives with young children, after their husbands were called up. Some of the people from the hamlets nearby came to spend the night in the cellar, as much for the company as for the reinforcement that Rosslyn had made.

Dogs and smaller animals were reduced to a minimum. Rachel joined the W.V.S. and not only 'dug for victory' but packed up and sent off weekly a hamper of fresh vegetables to each of us, with two or three eggs from Rosslyn's remaining hens carefully packed in the middle.

Both the boys, being regular naval officers, went to sea at once. Merlin was in the Fleet Air Arm and Erroll in submarines. Lady Hailsham had persuaded me to become a F.A.N.Y. after the Munich crisis so I too was called up at once. By sheer chance the London Company I belonged to was sent to Herstmonceux Place for the first few months of the war. The Nations stayed in a corner of it till they could find a smaller house. All our young friends went off and even our not so young friends. Norrie Walker and Paul Latham both of whom had lost legs, served on gun sites on the East Coast. Lorema was waiting to go into the M.T.C. in Chelsea.

One night about 9.45 Rosslyn heard several loud reports and hurried to the front door to look out He and Lorema found the whole countryside aflame with brilliant fires of various sizes. This was the night when thirty-five incendiary bombs fell on the rectory lawn, four more on the garden and one on the old coach house where the Ford had been put away with a full petrol tank.

My first reaction was to the terrifically impressive and definitely beautiful sight, [Rosslyn said] till Lorema shouted 'The kennels are blazing.' The old cow byres and stables and granary with the food bins and ferret hutches were all alight. Leading from the granary was the wooden staircase to the loft above the coach house with windows at each end. Up here there were three terriers and four puppies. I was apalled to see flames and thick smoke pouring out of the windows. A pillar of denser flame and smoke was rising from a hole in the floor. Lorema rushed to the telephone for the Fire Brigade wasting a minute, for the telephone wire was down; then for the stirrup pump which, by merciful providence, had arrived after two months delay, only a few days before.

Rachel reluctantly brought buckets of her precious water and the three of them set to work with the pump.

Rosslyn mounted the steps and opened the loft door and then sank on his knees and wriggled in on his stomach to avoid the heaviest of the smoke. He reached the flaming spot just above the car's petrol tank, and started to spray it, as taught in A.R.P. demonstrations. Below Rachel and Lorema tried to push the car out when it failed, as usual, to start. He tried to yell to them to wait till he could come and help but the smoke choked him. It was with some relief that he heard it start and shoot out backwards. Still he could not reach the puppies and then he saw smouldering above his head a fourteen-inch magnesium bomb, spluttering in a piece of wire netting. This had to be put out before he could reach the puppies in the farthest corner, in two boxes. By some miracle they were still alive when he hauled them out, buttoned them into his coat and tipped up the box so that the terriers could leap out by themselves. Hardly had they all got downstairs, with the dogs scampering after him and out into the stable yard, when the smouldering loft floor collapsed into the coach house where the car had just been.

Just beyond the village two parishioners were killed trying to drive some farm horses off the road with torches which were seen by enemy aircraft and machine-gunned.

At one point during the Battle of Britain, anti-aircraft guns were ranged in a line across the marshes only a mile away. Then came the invasion scare and Rosslyn was put in charge of the Home Guard 'hot line' radio transmitter which was hidden in a box at the bottom of the garden. Rachel, as leader of the local W.V.S., was warned that should the enemy arrive it would be her duty to meet them with C. D. Snatt, the butcher. Rosslyn would not of course accept this. A confused American had addressed a letter to him lately as Mayor of Herstmonceux, and as such he expected to be allowed to meet the enemy.

At the time of Dunkirk, Rosslyn and Rachel went down to Pevensey Bay, Rachel with the W.V.S., to give out cups of tea and sandwiches to the troops landing on the open beach, and Rosslyn to jolly along the fit and give comfort to the wounded and dying. Among those who landed on the beach were three of his ex-choirboys including one of his tenant farmer's sons, who had rowed themselves across in a small fishing boat to land on the beach where they had annually buried

Rosslyn at the Sunday School outing. One had lost a thumb and a fourth had been shot and drowned while hauling one of the others into the boat.

I was next stationed in Nottingham and spent my hours and nights of leave at Clifton. Percy's son Peter Clifton was there after being wounded at Dunkirk, and Ronnie's daughter Beryl who was waiting to go into the W.R.N.S. During the brief lull before the inevitable storm of the Battle of Britain Donald Anderson and I decided over the telephone to get married while we were still alive to do so. Although we were married in London, I was virtually, like my father, married *from* Clifton. Like Rosslyn before me I was despatched from Nottingham station by the lady of the manor—Evie Clifton—who, in my case, bought me a quick trousseau on the way.

I was the only one of Rosslyn's five children he did not marry. He had hoped I would marry a younger, more robust man, of his choice. In the ensuing disagreement Donald accused him of applying Mendelism to the breeding of his own grandchildren.

We were married, by an ironical chance, by another doctor of divinity in a church not half a mile from Rosslyn's beloved St. Anne's, Soho, within weeks of its total destruction by high explosives on the night of September 24th–25th, 1940.

But Bruces are quick forgivers. Herstmonceux was in the fifteen-mile coastal limit and we had to have special passes to go home. But go home we did, fairly often.

The following year, between air raids in London, Rosslyn christened two of his grandchildren and married Lorema to Alan Goolden, who was in the R.N.V.R. and later became a doctor.

During the flying-bomb period the extreme danger area narrowed down to a three-mile-wide belt, in which fighters induced the 'doodle bugs' to crash. One crashed on the stream in the rectory park and formed a new pond.

Though the Second World War was less eventful for Rosslyn than the first, he was continually active, not only with his own duties in replacing younger men, but keeping up the morale of others.

'Now you are coming on Hailsham District Council again,' wrote Sir Roland Gwynn, 'it will be a *real* pleasure to have you and I'm *sure* we shall all be the better for your incomparable knowledge and help and good wit. What a joy to think we shall enjoy that!' and when Rosslyn thanked him he replied:

'Your letter was so witty it made me laugh out loud and I re-read it when I am feeling depressed and laugh again. How wonderful to have that brilliant cleverness that you have! Sometimes I feel you are so sadly wasted down here. What a classic you'd have been in the House of Lords!'

Then there were prayers and visits to be made to the families of those who were fighting or prisoners of war. Quintin Hogg had been wounded in the Middle East. Three of our most frequent visitors among Erroll's naval friends were killed. Laurence Kettle went early on in submarines; Dick Beckwith was missing from Singapore and Alec Hunting went down in H.M.S. *Repulse*. Rachel's nephew, Hugh Gurney of Northrepps, was killed in action parachuting into enemy-occupied country. When Paul Latham was in hospital, after a nearly fatal accident, Rosslyn visited him and wrote to him frequently. Herstmonceux Castle was now the headquarters of The Hearts of Oak Insurance Company, but as troubles piled up it was clear Paul would never be able to return there.

'You have proved yourself a good friend—and I am very very grateful,' he wrote, and later:

'I never expect to live in the big house again, but I do hope that, after the war, I shall be able to live at Church Farm or some other house and learn to love the country more than even I do now. I am looking forward to the day when I see you again—for I shall always love Herstmonceux.'

When he came back a widower, with his son Richard, it was to live at Herstmonceux Place near by.

Rosslyn's eldest brother, Douglas, had come out of church, looked up to point to an enemy aircraft and died instantly of a heart attack. Four of his sisters had died of heart attacks and Rosslyn expected to do the same. Once his allotted span had passed, he had tucked individual notes of condolence to each of us into a drawer fifteen years before he died. He called these bonus years his 'Seventh Heaven' and assured us that he was ready to go at any moment when called— and yet, and yet, though no doubt ready, he still found life very precious.

CHAPTER TWENTY-THREE

Green Mouse, Rose Tinted

Soon after the war ended Rosslyn invited a squad of German prisoners of war to attend a Church service. Their chaplain was a discharged German prisoner who read the first lesson and Lord Hailsham, formerly Minister of War, read the second lesson.

One of the most heartening things for Herstmonceux was the settling in the village of the Davis-Gilberts with their horses and eventually five children. Gilbert became churchwarden and succeeded Lord Burghley, ex-Olympic runner, as master of the East Sussex Hunt. Through all the troubles of the parish and field, the Davis-Gilberts supported Rosslyn, teasing him affectionately, 'like family'.

'We might get a bit more out of the bishop,' Gilbert said cheerfully, 'if only dear Dr. Brucey could contain himself from addressing him as Bishmepop.'

In their tactful hands Rosslyn's hospital Sunday became a bonfire night with what Rosslyn called a 'girt' bonfire. When Herstmonceux Castle replaced Greenwich as the Royal Observatory, the Astronomer Royal marched with the villagers and lit the bonfire with a flaming torch.

'When,' Rosslyn asked the Astronomer Royal, Sir Harold Spenser Jones, 'can you get us to the moon?'

'We could go now,' was the reply. 'We've got it all worked out. It's just a matter of paying for it.'

Rosslyn's own pet scientific experiment was drawing to a conclusion. Since he was expelled from one school for keeping white mice in his pencil box, and another for rats in his boot hole, he had been breeding and inter-breeding the different basic colours on the lines of Mendel's sweetpeas, and had produced every colour of the rainbow—

except green. True the blue models were only as blue as a kerry blue terrier, the red only as red as a red setter, the lavender only as lavender as lavender waistcoats—but the champagne and strawberry roans were more aptly named. The apricot vole, which appeared at Rotary dinner, was said to be distinctly striking.

Now he bred a green mouse, as green as, if not greener than, a green monkey. To one whose glasses were always rose-tinted, who saw good—which is what he wanted to see—in all men, the mouse seemed as green as a field of sprouting corn in June. He was interviewed by the *Eastbourne Herald*, which wrote:

After breeding 50 generations Dr. Rosslyn Bruce has succeeded in producing the first Green Mouse. This mouse was grass green and its first offspring was bottle green. Now he has the first family from the bottle green mouse. Their chief tendency is back to grass green, but two of the family are white—the first sign of the original Japanese white strain for many generations of this family.

'It is obvious to me that I have to get more yellow and blue into my strain to improve the green,' said the rector, 'so I shall have to introduce further crosses. I am still hopeful of producing something approaching perfection in green mice. Some of my latest young mice may be better than I think. It is early yet to be quite sure of their colour.'

The national press took it up immediately, and even the American press. ENGLISH RECTOR GETS GREEN MOUSE AFTER 50 TRIES was a headline in the *Chicago Tribune*.

And of course it was frivously suggested that the grass had been hayed and the bottle filled with whisky.

Rosslyn could take mockery but not gross inaccuracy and he wrote to Alan Kemp of the *Daily Sketch* in those terms, who replied:

Dear Sir,

I am much obliged for your letter which greatly entertained me. The reason for my vague but I hope inoffensive reference to yourself was one which you as a journalist will appreciate, the law of libel. You never know nowadays where any personal reference, however innocent and good humoured, will land you. With a sympathetic jury I am not sure that you couldn't claim say £500 from me but whether you could actually extract it is another matter! Anyhow, as I am sure you realised, my little jest was meant in nothing but a congratulatory and friendly spirit. No journalist, who has to try to be funny every week could be expected to resist the temptation of a Green Mouse.

At Battle, Rosslyn's sister Gwen had had heart trouble for some time and Kathleen had kept her supplied with the champagne to sip, as their mother had done seventy years before, between spoonfuls of broth. When Rosslyn heard in 1947 that Kathleen had leukaemia, he wept openly. He asked me to go and see her in hospital; she looked bright and pretty. I told her I was expecting a baby and she insisted: 'It must be a boy this time. Every woman should bear a son at least once.' Peter came in, very distressed; but she was not. She knew she was dying and had long before asked Bill to put on her gravestone:

'Kathleen. No happier woman ever lived.'

On Noel Buxton, trouble upon trouble was heaped. He went almost blind, his son was killed and his daughter died tragically, but his faith was profound. Smilingly he tapped his way along with his white stick, telling of the joy of his other children and of his hopes for his great causes.

In his last decade after the war Rosslyn saw the end of so many of his contemporaries, many of whom he buried himself.

At one funeral of an old parishioner, Rosslyn was seen to sink down on one knee at the graveside, apparently overcome with grief till a perceptive mourner noticed him scoop a grasssnake up into the sleeve of his surplice and, as he rose, almost imperceptibly transfer it to the pocket of his cassock.

Lord Hailsham, who was a year younger than Rosslyn, died six years before him. His funeral was as simple as any village service could be with 'Music' as Rosslyn called Margery Elphick, playing the organ as she had done since she was a schoolgirl, and the members of the village with whom Lord Hailsham had been used to worshipping, all taking part. The eminent statesmen, judges and other great men who attended were touched by the affection which his country friends felt for him. Rosslyn paid tribute 'to one of the most eminent men of our times, whose secret of his immense influence was his intense devotion to his great ideals.' There was no faltering in an address that was full of Rosslyn's old fire.

Two sergeants and two troopers of the Inns of Court Regiment carried Lord Hailsham's coffin to the grave next to that of his stepson, Edward Marjoribanks. The 'Last Post' and 'Reveille' were sounded by a trumpeter of the Royal Horse Guards. This was followed by a memorial service in St. Paul's Cathedral where Rosslyn and his family were seated beside Lord Hailsham's own family, all of whom were deafened by the row little James Hogg made with the plaster cast on his recently broken leg.

Quintin, the second Lord Hailsham, now read the lessons in church and brought his own young family. When Frances was two, having been told she was not to talk in church, she pointed a finger at Rosslyn as he began to preach. 'You naughty man. You mustn't talk in church.' 'Don't be disturbed by the voices of little children,' Rosslyn replied in the same spirit. 'I can talk louder than them.'

Rosslyn, who had already brought out a guide to Herstmonceux church, was now writing a guide to the castle. He asked Paul Latham for a list of royal visitors to it. Paul wrote back telling him that Queen Mary had come in April 1937 and in 1934 and again in 1935 with King George V, the Duke of York, later George VI, and his Duchess; Princess Alice and the Earl of Athlone came in August 1933.

Prince and Princess Christian of Hesse and Queen Marie of Rumania had also been there. Rosslyn was there in 1938 when the Duke and Duchess of Devonshire brought Princess Elizabeth and Princess Margaret who were staying with them.

Before the guide was finished Paul became very ill again and died within weeks of planning, with Rosslyn, a new school on land he had given for it. He too was buried in Herstmonceux churchyard with the same simple, loving service in which Rosslyn could inspire hope, however sad he felt himself.

In 1950 Merlin was in Korean waters for a while in charge of air-craft activities in H.M.S. *Triumph*. He was mentioned in despatches and later awarded the O.B.E.

Erroll, also a Lieutenant-Commander, was skipper of the thirty-foot yacht *Samuel Pepys* which had been entered by the Royal Naval Sailing Association in the transatlantic race of nearly three thousand miles from Bermuda to Plymouth. She had a crew of three. The race began on July 2nd, after taking part in the famous race from Rhode Island in the United States to Bermuda.

Rosslyn led his congregation in prayer for a calm passage for Erroll and sang Hymn 370. Erroll, in mid-Atlantic, led his crew in prayer for a gale to help them win. 'The Almighty,' Merlin explained after-wards, 'resolved the inconsistency by obliging the man on the spot.'

On July 24th Rosslyn received a telegram from the *Daily Express*:

SAMUEL PEPYS OFF LIZARD LAST NIGHT.

Then came another:

ARRIVED PLYMOUTH MIDNIGHT SUNDAY AFTER EXCITING RACE FROM BERMUDA PROBABLY SECOND. ERROLL.

In fact he was first. This was the first of three crossings he made as skipper in this race.

Another family triumph was Hervey's; the sixth Bruce baronet's horse won the Cesarewitch, 'my second friend to do so', Rosslyn claimed. Downhill, Hervey's great white elephant in Derry, was far too large and unwieldy for him to inhabit and reluctantly he had it demolished, all but the beautiful Mussenden Temple that the Earl-Bishop had built on the very edge of the cliffs, which he handed over to the National Trust.

In 1951 Cecil Roberts was surprised to receive, among the letters about his new book *A Terrace in the Sun*, one from Rosslyn Bruce and later wrote:

He was then eighty and I thought he had long forgotten a small boy to whom he had shown his animals at Clifton. After some complimentary words on my Nottingham novel he reproached me for a liberty I had taken. I had described a squire driving to church in his carriage with a liveried, cockaded footman on the box seat. 'What on earth do you mean by giving Sir Hervey gout, in order to have him drive to church so pompously—nonsense! The hall was only five hundred yards from the church and he walked through his private gate into the churchyard.'

Rosslyn congratulated Cecil Roberts on his career with: 'It doesn't surprise me. You were a most inquisitive, intelligent boy.'

The writing was firm, [Cecil Roberts wrote]. For over eighty years he had brightened the world with his rich personality whether taming pets, running a campaign for better conditions for stage children, for poor young widows with babies, acting as chaplain to the troops in France, going on missions with Noel Buxton to the Balkans and America, organising a Maypole dance on the village green at Clifton or lecturing on Dante.

He was still producing the *Fox Terrier Year Book*, writing weekly for *Fox Terrier Facts* and, as President of the Smooth Fox Terrier Association, writing and speaking on their behalf. He was Chairman of the Eastbourne Canine Society and persuaded the Duke of Devonshire, with whom he corresponded and occasionally met over terriers, to become its patron.

Travelling was becoming increasingly difficult. Rosslyn was invited to preach at the Harvest Festival at Dinting, his first parish as a curate. Regretfully he had to refuse. 'But I hope to come to Dinting at some time in the future. Dinting and Paradise are the only two places in which I should prefer to spend September the 28th. If it were practicable I should choose the former. After all it is only forty-two years ago that I was one of you, and what is that compared with eternity?'

Rosslyn continued to keep and show a few smooth fox terriers and a Skye. He also still had birds in his study and, if anything, more mice than ever. There was a revival of the green mouse interest but now Rosslyn took no chances of being teased by the press. He teased them. One serious young reporter wrote in detail how the great doctor scientist had made the amazing discovery that it was possible to cross a mouse with a bat. He had even been shown, in a glass tank, the expectant mother which was about to give birth to at least one *bouse*. Other papers 'carried the tail' as the *Manchester Guardian* put it. The *Daily Mail* telephoned Quintin at his chambers and reported that Lord Hailsham had replied, 'Dr. Bruce is a considerable biologist like Dr. Mendel. But he is also notable for his sense of humour.' Quintin rang Rachel who told him, 'Those young men don't know the facts of life. Anyone could see it was a male mouse.'

The Times had a fourth leader on it. 'All Peter Scott's geese are swans. All Bruce's mice are bouses,' quipped *Our Dogs*. Rachel answered the telephone when the *Daily Mirror* telephoned and told them shortly to go away. 'And don't put anything in your paper about it,' she told them. 'It only encourages him and then he does it again.'

Rosslyn's sailor brother, Wilfrid, had a stroke which left him smiling and active as ever except in one respect. He would talk with the same old interest and enthusiasm but in words that belonged to no known language. He would burst out laughing and start again, but still make no sense. Finally he would shrug his broad shoulders, still good-humoured, and try to explain with his hands. Writing down his perfectly lucid thoughts and needs was no better. After writing his address and to whom he addressed the letter, utterly meaningless words appeared from his pen:

'Dear Rosslyn,
 Tlma hwsidy u wwur savrls mnwt. Dnror . . .'

After a short illness he died.

But there were christenings and weddings as well as funerals. There were dog shows and after-dinner speeches and sermons. Sometimes he was not quite sure which he was doing. But if the baptism service merged into a funeral or a dog show speech, his followers only loved him all the more for it His eyesight remained perfect and he could hear as well as anyone. He was lame, but so he had been for more than half his life. Now arthritis merely made it worse. In old age he kept the dignity of an innocent child that had gone with him all his life. Though he grew thinner and his silvery hair less, his periwinkle blue eyes still twinkled and his voice remained as strong, eloquent and musical as ever. Only his memory intermittently let him down.

It never worried him if in church he momentarily forgot his lines, for his inventive powers always came to the rescue. His additions were always in perfect keeping with the text of the Common Prayer. Sometimes it was hard to tell at first that they were not part of it.

'I baptise this child Alexandra,' he said of my youngest, as he signed the cross on her baby forehead. 'The twenty-fifth of my descendants,' he rolled out as though he were reading Genesis, 'and I hope it will be the last.'

This christening, in June, was described in a poem by John Hersey, painter and proxy-godparent. 'The day was a fine one, sunny in Sussex and the old gentleman, once at school with Belloc, said several times it was the first fine day this winter. Then cocks an eye to see if you are awake.' At the lunch at the Woolpack inn, 'at the top of the table, sunk low in his chair, sits the oldest of kings, king of the christening melodious king. He sings to us all, we stiffly sit, expecting a glance. He's bold; and in a perky, cheerful rhythm he sings of Alexandra and of Hercules, his trick being to change the last line to suit his whim.' John Hersey describes 'standing by the Sussex-pale graves and wind-buzzed grass' and 'the church with the wideawake view'.

The church was clean, clean and historical, as though the flood had just subsided. Before the curtain rose, before the curtain call, he, frocking himself in loose white linen near two dead knights stretched stiff as pitchforks, set aside from amateurs, lead the choir answers, standing near the font, his role assured. We were asked to do, asked to be, to keep her innocent. Yes, we murmur, yes, we will.

At tea, back at the rectory, he expanded on his twenty-five descendants, and then, with a naughty grin, added to the boast, 'And I've bred forty-five different kinds of dogs, nineteen shades of mice and eleven of my friends have been Prime Ministers, and one was once President of the United States.'

Rosslyn wrote to Rhalou:

Most precious and lovable of all daughters! Fifty thousand million thanks for your lovely birthday present. Of all my four thousand volumes it is *the* one I read most and enjoy the most. I wonder if the author is still alive! Saturday will be my eighty-third and almost certainly my last birthday, as I grow *much* older every day, but still your loving father. Come again soon please.

She had sent him a little paper-covered book on *Breeding Birds in Captivity*.

In fact he lived to see his eighty-fifth and in those two years, because I lived near enough for frequent visits, he let me help with dressing and an occasional hair-cut with his nail scissors. Sometimes I would come over for a night or two to relieve Rachel. Once, after a short illness, he had appeared to be almost in a coma for a day and night. Rachel was resting after her vigil. At two o'clock in the morning he sat up and said he'd never felt better in his life. 'Let's have some milky kind of tea or teay kind of milk,' he suggested, and we had a riotious tea party till dawn. We told each other funny stories and agreed that at last we were able to see eye to eye.

Sometimes he was ill enough to be sent to hospital. But not for long. Either he caught the nurses by hooking them by their ankles with his walking stick to his side to give them a kiss, in much the same spirit in which, at the age of six, he had lifted up the mistresses' petticoats to see if they had legs. Or he secretly dressed and limped out to the nearest bus stop and took himself home.

He had always enjoyed hitch-hiking but as he got older his addiction grew. He would limp the quarter of a mile to the end of the lane and stand in the road waiting for a car to slow down. Once the driver asked him where he wanted to go. 'Where are you going?' Rosslyn asked.

'Well, actually to Nottingham.'

'How absolutely whopping!' Rosslyn exclaimed. 'That's exactly where I want to go', and he got in, prepared to go the two hundred and fifty miles. People said they enjoyed his company so much they were happy to go out of their way to drive him around for a little and then take him back home again.

When Rosslyn climbed up into the pulpit of the Norman church, where he had ministered for over three decades, the years seemed to fall from him. At Evensong the light from the candles, that were still lit on long spiked sticks throughout the church, shone on his face, emphasising the simplicity and innocence that was part of his whole spirit.

'Verily I say unto you,' his voice was still clear and ringing, 'whosoever shall not receive the Kingdom of God as a little child, he shall not enter therein.'

Cecil Roberts was right. All his life Rosslyn had retained something of the small boy—often the small mischievous boy. Now he often returned to his childhood as though he had never left it.

His rabbits were once again called by such names as Evelyn, Beatrice and Chloe, names that were recalled from his fleet of girl friends in the old days and rarely to be found any more among his confirmation candidates. Rosslyn often wrote now for fun in his old schoolboy hand, using the same old nursery expressions, to his sister, Hilda. Her mind was as brilliant as ever and she still taught pupils. He wrote using her baby nickname and she had the wit to reply in the same vein.

The bishop had many times hinted it was time to retire.

'Retire?' Rosslyn retorted innocently, as though it were an entirely new idea. 'I retired thirty-three years ago when I came here.'

Now, at last, Rachel persuaded him to give in at New Year 1956. They would build on to a bungalow beside our house and so still remain in touch with his beloved Herstmonceux.

Rosslyn wrote to Hilda about it:

Dedee Presus,

What a gorjus long letter all about you; Hurrah! *Here* there is nothing like that. We are leaving this house (and the Rectorship!) at CHRISTMAS time to live 8 miles away, in a *much* smaller house (there are 24 rooms in *this* house) here we have 3 families of helpers! (i.e. guest helpers!) here there are 4 acres of garden ($\frac{1}{4}$ acre is the ideal). I am still rather limpy lame in my right thigh, but can get about, with a 'Prefect' motor which I gave to Rachel as a birthday present, it cost £440, but she drives me wherever I want to go, further than I like to walk. She is very fit and makes a capital 'Wurse' (wife nurse). We had a row yesterday because she took the second perch out of my dove's cage—in my 'Bed-study'.

When we go, (about Xmas time) our new house (8 miles away) has no room for my 950 books; so a dealer is going to buy all the ones I cannot carry into the garden and back. I have no horse, but 2 (one black and one white) belong to my tenant, and live and feed in our 'glebargen': they are both virgin mares. Our only surviving sister Zoe once hurt poor old Douglas' feelings by calling *me* her 'favourite brother' at which I gurgled inwardly, but poor dear old Douglas was hurt, and said 'But Zoe, You have known *me* longer, and he only received the reply 'That's just why,'!!! I always keep his photograph visibly in my room, to recall his quiet charm, and forcefulness.

My poor new pen (a recent present) had a disease (politely called 'lack of control,' or a dire rire, 'Stop Bruce before you get worse') All my devoted love

Your only surviving bro. Rosslyn

On Christmas Day, his thirty-third Christmas at Herstmonceux, Rosslyn took the services, with the usual help from Rachel and the Davis-Gilberts, backed by the Elphicks and Walkers, Nance Oldham and Sister Ray.

Quintin brought a bottle of champagne. 'I knew he was dying,' he wrote many years afterwards, 'and wanted him to have a happy Christmas. We drank it all together and he gave me his blessing and his copy of Farrar's *Lives of the Early Fathers*, in which he scrawled an inscription. I still have it.' Two weeks later, a few days before his retirement began, he was taken to the hospital in Eastbourne with —like his mother—kidney trouble.

Erroll and I were both having our first books published. Rosslyn had published fifteen and we expected him to be delighted that the habit was to continue into another generation. But he was not particularly pleased till I took him an advance copy in his last two or three days' illness in hospital.

He turned it over and them said, 'Pooh, I could write a better book than that.'

I offered him a tame mouse, borrowed from one of my children and he was much more pleased. He put it on the white counterpane of his bed and said, 'Look at the light through its beautiful little ears. Isn't that like the gates of heaven?'

Erroll was in command of H.M.S. *Ricasoli*, in Malta. Next day Merlin used the Admiralty signal service to send a priority message to C.O. *Ricasoli*:

INFORMATION RECEIVED FROM COMMANDER M. BRUCE BROTHER OF COMMANDER ERROLL BRUCE, R.N., THAT THEIR FATHER DIED THIS MORNING 19TH JANUARY, 1956.

Index

Aberdeen, 240
Ada, 212, 213, 228, 230, 231, 253, 283
Addleshaw, Stanley (Alan Stanley), 88, 94
Afflick, Mrs., 23, 28, 30
Africa, South, 200, 201
Alcorn, Mrs., 257–8
Alexandra, Queen, 128
Allie, 27, 36, 60, 86
Allington, Hugh, 247
Amelia, Queen of Greece, 12
America, United States of, 177–80, 185, 219, 229, 234–8, 301
Ampthill, 2nd Lord, 72
Amundsen, 201, 203–4, 207, 219
Anderson, Alexandra, 304
Anderson, Donald, 295
Annie, 247
Astor, Viscountess, 236
Athens, 12, 55, 82
Athlone, Earl and Countess of, 300
Australia, 85, 200, 209, 268

Bach's Christmas Oratorio, 127
Baden-Powell, Lady, 275
Baines, Bishop, 198
Baird, Dorothea, 79
Balcarres, Lord, 78, 91
Balfour, A. J., 133
Bane, Rosa (Mrs. Colbran), 230, 253, 283

Barnard, Lady, 20
Barrie, Sir James, 123–4, 193, 277
Barton-in-Fablis, 24–25, 28–33, 101
Bath Club, 126, 131, 142
Battine, Mrs, Daisy, 272–4
Battle, 268, 274, 299
Beardsley, Aubrey, 87, 99, 171
Beauchamp, 7th Earl, 78, 84
Beckwith, Dick, 287–8, 296
Beerbohm, Sir Max, 66, 67
Beeston, Notts., 202
Belgrade, 154
Belloc, Hilaire, 77–78, 82, 84, 90–92, 229, 277, 292, 304
Benson, Sir Frank, 121
Bentiened, Henry, 149
Bentinck, Henry, 198
Bentley, E. C., 292
Berlin, 161
Bermuda Race, 295
Betjeman, Sir John, 273
Binton, Warwick, 146–7, 164, 170, 183, 200, 201, 225, 229, 268
Binyon, Lawrence, 94
Birmingham, 85, 211–77, 280
Birmingham Repertory Theatre, 219, 231–2
Bishopthorpe, 19, 23, 36, 37, 50, 71, 226
Blackburn, Judge, 24
Blackwood, Basil, Lord, 80

Blyth, Rev., 187
Boot, Dorothy (Mrs. Wilfrid Bruce), 225, 246
Boot, Sir Jesse (1st Lord Trent), 147–8, 206, 225
Boot, John (2nd Lord Trent) 147, 225
Boot, Lady (Lady Trent), 147, 206
Born, Baron von, 89
Bosporus, 153
Boston, 231
Bottomley, Horatio, 265
Boucicault, Nina, 152
Bournemouth, 40
Boys' Brigade, 59, 60
Bradley, Daphne (Mrs. Erroll Bruce), 292
Bradley, Losco, 279
Brassey, 1st Earl, 272
Bristol, 1st Earl, 21
Bristol, 4th Earl, Bishop of Derry, 21, 54, 74, 307
Brittain, Sir Harry (Pilgrim Emeritus), 79, 95, 96, 97, 133
Browning, Robert, 45, 50, 51
Bruce, H. J., 'Benjie', 53–54, 100, 116, 121, 141, 142, 145, 161, 162, 183, 189, 198, 200, 208–10, 240, 245, 290
Bruce, Beryl, 267–8, 288, 295
Bruce, Rev. Douglas 25, 27, 29, 40–46, 51–52, 61, 76, 86–87, 101, 113, 146, 147, 151, 234, 240–1, 296, 307
Bruce, Elma, (Mrs. Keating), 23–24, 29, 46, 51, 75–76, 240, 241
Bruce, Erroll, 226, 247, 282–3, 286–8, 292–3, 296, 301, 307–8
Bruce, Euslin, 286
Bruce, Gervase, 145, 197, 208, 228
Bruce, Gwen, 27, 29, 36, 47, 51, 86, 147, 164, 187, 201, 229, 248, 268, 274, 299
Bruce, Rev. Sir H. Hervey, 1st Bart., 20

Bruce, Sir H. Hervey, 3rd Bart., 18, 21, 46, 52–54, 68, 86, 97, 99, 100, 110–11, 120, 125, 128, 140, 145, 146, 165, 210
Bruce, Colonel Sir Hervey J. L., 4th Bart., 21, 99, 100, 142, 145, 168, 208–210, 211, 214–15, 245–6, 302
Bruce, Sir Hervey R., 5th Bart., 'Ronnie', 53, 97, 100, 130, 189, 245, 266–7
Bruce, Sir Hervey, 6th Bart, 266–8, 301
Bruce, Hilda, 'Presh', 38, 46, 63, 75, 86, 109, 113, 182, 268, 274, 306
Bruce, Irene, 29, 86
Bruce, Admiral Sir James and Lady, 131, 184
Bruce, Janie, 'Podge', 38, 46, 56, 86, 109, 162, 164
Bruce, Kathleen (Mrs. Falcon Scott, Lady Scott, Lady Hilton-Young, Lady Kennet), 38, 46, 50, 76, 87, 89, 97, 99, 112–13, 115–16, 122, 125, 125–32, 134, 138–42, 144, 153–4, 161–3, 171–3, 177, 184–9, 191, 195, 197, 200, 204, 207, 219, 220–1, 224–5, 230, 233, 242, 250, 266, 277, 281–2, 285–6, 290–1, 299
Bruce, Canon Lloyd, 16–25, 27, 30–32, 36, 38–41, 46, 50–55, 185–6
Bruce, Rev. 'Lloydie', 27, 40, 42, 44–46, 52, 86, 101, 147, 151, 170, 193, 200–1, 229, 248, 268
Bruce, Lorema (Mrs. Alan Goolden), 247, 273, 281, 283, 286, 293–5
Bruce, Merlin, 196, 198, 204, 206–7, 225, 241, 246–8, 250, 281–3, 286, 291, 293, 301, 308
Bruce, Nikita, 240
Bruce, Percy (Colonel Clifton), 53, 97, 114, 145, 197, 220–1, 245–6, 266, 268, 295
Bruce, Peter (Lieut-Col. P. T. Clifton), 295

Bruce, Rhalou (Mrs. Kirkby Peace), 202, 204, 206–7, 242, 247–8, 255, 260, 272–3, 281, 286, 288–90, 305

Bruce, Robert, 147, 234, 241

Bruce, Rev. Doctor Rosslyn, 28–29, 30–308

Bruce, Sheila, (Clifton, Lady Crawshaw), 145, 197, 208

Bruce, Verily, (Mrs. Donald Anderson, Mrs. Paul Paget), 226, 228, 237, 241, 244, 246–9, 250–2, 255, 259, 282–3, 286–8, 290, 295, 301, 305, 307–8

Bruce, Captain Wilfrid, 46, 56–57, 86, 109, 183, 185–6, 191, 193, 200–4, 219, 221–2, 225, 246, 248, 303

Bruce, Zoe, (Mrs. Newham), 24, 29, 50–51, 86, 307

Bruce, Colonel, 15

Bruce-Lowe system, 262–3, 278

Bryce, Ambassador, 162

Buck, Sir Percy (Mus. Doc.), 80, 282

Buckingham Palace, 28, 276, 287

Buckingham Palace Rd., 174, 185, 204, 233

Burghley, Lord (Marquis of Exeter), 297

Burne-Jones, Sir E., 64

Burrows, Rev. W. A., (Bishop of Truro), 103, 211, 229, 257, 278, 289

Bussage, Glos., 39

Buxton, Lady Catherine, 166

Buxton, Charles, M.P., 166

Buxton, Harold (Bishop of Gibraltar), 181

Buxton, Mabel (Mrs Crowdy), 141–2, 164, 181

Buxton, Noel (Lord Noel-Buxton), 55, 99, 125, 133, 138, 152–5, 157, 161–2, 165–8, 176, 181, 207, 226, 228, 234–7, 277, 302

Buxton, Sir T. Fowell and Lady Victoria, 55, 181, 220

Buxtons of Boston, 172, 192, 235, 248

Byron, 6th Lord, 24, 160

Byron, 8th Lord and Lady, 24, 29, 32, 189

Byron, Rev., 9th Lord, 154, 198, 243, 247

Cadbury, Christopher, 243–4

Cameronian Rifles, 234

Campbell, Captain Harry, 186–7

Canada, 118, 130, 276

Cardiff, 225

Cardwell, Rev. J. H., 'The Saint', 116–18, 153–4

Carlile, Prebendary, 136, 210–11

Carlton-in-Lindrick, 33, 35–37, 41, 46, 48, 53, 107, 147, 198, 251

Carnot, President, 85

Carroll, Lewis (Rev. Charles Dodgson), 88, 131

Carters Corner Place, 269, 284, 291

Carter, Mrs., 190

Casson, John, 283

Ceylon, 282

Chalmers, Port, N.Z., 201

Chamberlain, Austen, M.P., 266

Chamberlain, Dorothy, 243, 266

Chamberlain, Frank, 243

Chamberlain, Sir Neville, M.P., 243, 266

Charles I, King, 81, 150, 151

Charlesworth, Derbyshire, 109, 113

Chatsworth, Derbyshire, 114

Chelsea Old Church, 266

Chesham, 4th Lord, 164

Chester, Betty, 231, 233

Chichester, Bishop of (Dr. George Bell), 271–2, 284, 306

Chicago Tribune, 298

China, 273, 274, 282, 286

Cholmondeley, Lord George, 198

Christchurch, N.Z., 225

Church Army, 210–11

Churchill, F. A., 48
Churchill, Sir Winston, M.P., 193, 275
Clemens, Elfrida, 152
Clifton Book, The, 151
Clifton, Notts., 24, 99, 100, 144, 149–52, 175–7, 183–4, 189, 194–5, 197–9, 202, 204, 205, 207, 208, 209, 210, 212, 240, 245–6, 258, 283, 295, 301–2
Clifton, Sir Gervase, 99–100, 150–1
Clifton, Sir Juckes, 100
Clifton, Marianne (Lady Bruce), 18, 22, 24
Clifton, Sir Robert, M.P., 18, 100
Colarossi's Studios, 128
Collier, Rev. E. C., 106–7, 113–14
Compton Place, 290
Connaught, Duke of, 278
Constantinople, 158–9
Cornwallis, 1st Lord, 278
Coster Gazette, 135
Coughlan, Dr., 163
Coward, Sir Noël, 231–2, 287
Cowbeech, Sussex, 252
Cozens-Hardy, W. H. (2nd Baron Cozens-Hardy), 65
Crane, Walter, 127
Crimean War, 14, 15
Cromer, Norfolk, 190
Croxted Smith, A., 263
Cruft, Mr. and Mrs., of Cruft's Dog Show, 291
Curzon, 1st Marquis, 242

Dacre family, 33, 251
Daily Express, 307
Daily Graphic, 264
Daily Mail, 134, 135, 142, 303
Daily Mirror, 186, 276, 303
Daily News, 216
Daily Sketch, 298
Daily Telegraph, 131, 164

Daniel, Dr., 62, 74, 220
Daniel, Mrs Emily, 62, 73, 88
Daniel Press, 95
Daniel, Rachel, 73, 81, 88–89, 95–96
Daniel, Ruth, 'Thrisby', 73, 81, 88–89, 96, 134
Dante, 70, 136–7, 199, 231, 302
Danube, 155
Dartmouth, Royal Naval College, 248, 274, 283
Davis-Gilbert, Major Gilbert, 297, 307
Davis-Gilbert, Mrs. Sybil, 297, 307
de Bunsen, Mr. and Mrs. Lothair, 155
de Fiennes, 252
de Quincey Society, 80
Dearmer, Geoffrey, 144, 219, 233, 277
Dearmer, Mrs. Mabel, 144, 219
Dearmer, Rev. Percy, 79, 144
Delabere, Rev. Bagot, 52, 67
Delabere, Johnnie, 62, 67, 80
Denmark, Crown Prince of, 65
Devonshire, 10th Duke and Duchess of, 300, 302
Dewey, Admiral, 253
Dieppe, France, 152
Dinting, North Derbyshire, 106–18, 302
Discovery, 171
Donoughmore, Lord, 126
Douglas, Lord Alfred, 79, 80
Downhill, Co. Derry, 20–21, 53–55, 76, 97, 110, 115, 130–1, 145, 210–11, 266, 290, 301
Drinkwater, John, 121
Du Maurier, Angela, 209
Du Maurier, George, 45, 79
Dublin, 110
Dunbar, Scotland, 56, 86, 147
Duncan, Isadora, 129, 132–4, 195, 208, 225
Dunedin, N.Z., 201
Dunkirk, 294–5

East Sussex Hunt, 260, 279
Eastbourne, 251, 259, 266–8, 270, 290, 302
Eastbourne Herald, 298
Edgbaston, Birmingham, 211–19, 227–32, 233, 239, 241–5, 247–51, 278
Edgbaston Botanical Gardens, 217, 248
Edgbaston High School for Girls, 217, 243
Edinburgh, 30, 40, 50–56, 58–61, 75–76
Edward VII, 15, 65, 130, 160, 186–7, 198
Elizabeth I, 100
Elizabeth, Princess (Queen Elizabeth II), 300
Elphick family, 256, 307
Epsom, Surrey, 288
Erroll, 20th Earl of, 31
Euston, Earl of, 115, 116
Evans, Lieut. R.N., 200
Evans, Seaman E., 223
Evening Standard, 278

F.A.N.Y., 293
Ffolkes, Rev., 140
Filey, Yorks., 19, 20
Flynn, Mr., 237
Football Post, 166
Forbes, 21st Lord, 31
Forbes, Jane (Mrs. James Skene, of Rubislaw), 12, 14, 16, 55
Forbes, Sir William, 5th Bart., 12
Forbes, Sir William, 6th Bart., 12
Fortescue, Miss, 266, 272
Fox, Fred, 143, 213, 228, 230, 251, 259
Fox terriers, 38, 129, 278
Fox Terrier Association, Smooth, 263, 302
Fox Terrier Breeding, 261
Fox Terrier Facts, 278, 302
Fox Terrier Year Book, 302

Freemasonry, 80, 229, 250, 277–8
Frewen Hall, Oxford, 15–20
Frontiersmen, Legion of, 227
Fry, C. B., 79, 292
Fyleman, Rose, 250

Garner, J. Parker, 218–19
Garrick Club, 27
Gaul, Alfred, 217
Geneva, 76, 290
George V, 205, 224, 264, 290, 300
Gillet, Gabriel (Rev.), 87, 94, 97, 99, 194
Gladstone, W. E., M.P., 15, 26, 45, 65, 107, 160, 235
Glebe, The, Clifton, 143, 184
Globe, The, 135
Glossop, Derbyshire, 106, 111
God and The Allies, 238
Goolden, Alan, Dr., 295
Gotham, Notts., 168, 169
Granger, Frank, 195
Greenwich, 286–7, 297
Gritten, Howard, 84
Gurney, A. G. H., 80, 194
Gurney, Christopher, 182–3, 192, 224, 228, 229
Gurney, Mrs. Dorothy, 229
Gurney, Gerard, 190
Gurney, Gladys, 'Turveydrop' (Hon. Mrs. Rome-Wynn), 167, 173, 177, 179, 187, 195, 205, 206
Gurney, Hudson, 21
Gurney, Hugh, 296
Gurney, Mrs. (of Keswick), 191
Gurney, Quintin, 173, 192–3, 228, 248
Gurney, Rachel (Mrs. Rosslyn Bruce), 167–98, 206–8, 212–13, 216, 219, 221–2, 227, 234, 243, 248, 248–9, 250–1, 255, 259, 266, 270–1, 273, 276, 281, 286, 287, 288, 291, 293, 294, 303, 305–6

Gurney, Mrs. Richard, 166–7, 172, 175, 179, 189, 190–2, 196, 271
Gurney, Richenda, 166–7
Gwynn, Elizabeth (Mrs. David), 285
Gwynn, Priscilla (Mrs. Longland), 285
Gwynn, Sir Roland, 295, 296
Gwynn, Hon. Mrs. Rupert, 285

Hailsham, Sussex, 295, 296
Haines, Mr., 13, 210, 246
Hale, Wilts., 23
Hamilton, General, 237
Hampton Court, 72, 126–7, 150, 185–6
Hare, Augustus, 17, 167, 252, 255, 257
Harrington, Earl of, 163–4
Harris, Cecil, 213, 217
Harris, Sir William, 'Doc H', 217, 228, 230, 243–4, 282
Harrison, Andrew J., 218–19
Harvard University, U.S.A., 238
Harvey, Sir Martin, 195–7
Hayfield, Derbyshire, 113
Head, Harold, 255
Heddon Court School, 273, 283
Hellingly, Sussex, 269, 283
Hersey, John, 304
Herstmonceux, Sussex, 251–7, 266, 268, 270, 271–5, 281–98, 299–307
Hesse, Prince and Princess of, 300
Heythrop hunt, 62
Hilton-Young, Wayland (2nd Lord Kennet), 266
Hilton-Young, Sir William, 'Bill' (1st Lord Kennet), 250, 266, 277, 291, 299
Hitchcock, Joan (Mrs. Merlin Bruce), 283, 286
Hogg, Sir Douglas (1st Lord Hailsham), 269–70, 274–5, 283, 287, 291, 297, 299, 300
Hogg, Frances, 300
Hogg, James, 300

Hogg, Lady, 269
Hogg, Neil, 269
Hogg, Quintin (2nd Lord Hailsham), 269–71, 274–5, 281, 283–5, 291–2, 296, 300, 303, 307
Home Guard, 293
Horsfall, Truda, 73, 283
House, Colonel, 234, 236–8
Hull, Bishop of (Dr. R. F. L. Blunt), 60, 101, 124, 182
Hong Kong and Shanghai Bank, 273
Hulton, Chloe, 109, 164, 166, 228, 288
Hunt, Holman, 89
Hunting, Alec, 287–8, 296
Hurst, F. W., 292
Hutchinson, Arthur, 152
Hutton, Barbara, 286
Huxley family, 67
Huxley, T. H., 63

Ickworth, Suffolk, 21, 54
Ingram, Dr. Winnington (Bishop of London), 98, 140
Inns of Court Regt., 300
Ireland, 109, 266–7
Irish Guards, 267
Irving, Harry, 79
Irving, Henry (Sir), 45, 72, 79
Isis, 65, 75, 76, 78, 83–84, 89, 90, 93, 96, 104
Italy, 192, 194, 230

Jackson, Sir Barry, 195
Jackson, Margaret (Lady Bruce), 267
Jellicoe, F. G. G., 42
Judd, Mr., 38

Kaiser Wilhelm II, 207, 235
Karsavina, Tamara (Mrs. 'Benjie' Bruce), 240, 245
Keating, Canon J.F.S., D.D., 75
Keating, George, 240

Keating, John, 240
Keating, Maurice, 240
Keepe family, 247
Keep, Vi (Mrs. Carrington), 252, 259
Keiland, Antarctica, 203
Kemp, Alan, 298
Kennard, John, 287, 288
Kennel Club, 89
Kensington Square, London, 105, 112
Kerle-Smith family, 140, 177, 183
Kerry, Earl, 80
Keswick, Cumberland, 153
Keswick, Norfolk, 191, 192
Kettle, Laurence, 287–8, 296
King, Croker, 104
Kipling, Mrs. Carrie, 264
Kipling, Rudyard, 264, 274
Knutsford, 1st Viscount, 219

Lallie, Gwen, 274
Lancashire, 104–5, 108
Lang, Andrew, 73
Lapidi, Princess Zoe, 11
Lascelles, Sir Francis, 161
Latham, Sir Paul, 2nd Bart,, M.P., 285–6, 289, 290, 293, 296, 300
Latham, Richard (Sir, 3rd Bart,), 286, 291, 296
Lauder, Sir Harry, 175
Law, Hugh, 'Hugo', 55, 67, 80, 89, 97, 105, 110, 112, 114, 125, 128, 134, 171, 194
Law, Hugh Francis d'Assisi (Colonel), 105, 110, 112, 240
Lawrence, Domine, 274, 291
Lawrence, Mildred (Viscountess Hailsham), 274, 293
Laycock, Joe, 198
Le Brun, Madame Vigée, 54
Leeds, 98, 101, 103–4
Leinster Corner, 124, 277, 281–2
Leith, 'Evie' (Mrs. Percy Clifton), 197, 246, 266

Letters from Turkey, 161
Levillon, Lily (Mrs. Harold Lion), 183
Liddon, Dr. H. P., 108
Lincoln's Inn, London, 127, 131
Lindbergh, Colonel, 281
Line and Family Method, 261
Linnean Society, 262
Lion, Leon M., 183
Liszt, 12
Liversidge, Howard, 77, 83–84
Liverpool, 108
Lloyd George, M.P. (1st Earl), 226, 266
Lloyd George, Dame Margaret, 226
Lockhart, R. Bruce, 56
Lodge, Sir Oliver, 220, 229, 236, 243
Löhr, Marie, 122–3, 209
Lord, Margaret (Mrs. Douglas Bruce), 86, 147
Lowther, Colonel Claude, 271, 274, 276
Lusitania, 238
Lyttleton, N.Z., 201, 204, 209, 222

Macdonnell, P. J., 92, 93, 94
Macedonia, 138–9, 141, 153–5, 161, 165, 168
Mackenzie, Sir Compton, 56, 58
MacNaughton, Jean, 155
Mafeking, 130
Mallett, Sir Louis, 133
Malta, 11
Manchester, 106, 108, 131
Manchester Guardian, 94, 262, 303
Manor Road, Edgbaston, 231, 240, 243, 249
Manvers, 3rd Earl and Countess, 61
Mappin, Lady, 48
Mappin, Sir Luke, 45
Margaret, Princess, 300
Marjoribanks, Edward, M.P., 269, 283, 284, 285, 300
Markham, Admiral Sir Charles, 224
Martyn, May (Lady Playfair), 152

Mary, Queen, 29, 300
Maude, Cyril, 209
Max-Muller, Professor, 16
Meath, 12th Earl and Countess of, 257
Melbourne, 201
Mendelism, 262, 295, 303
Mendelssohn family, 241
Meredith, George, 67
Merton College, Oxford, 66
Miller, Dr., 288
Milner, Lady Georgiana, 29, 30
Ministering Children's League, 146, 257–8
Minneapolis, 276
Monkton-Milner, Amy (Lady Fitzgerald) 31, 36
Moore, Lady Patricia (Lady Patricia Latham), 285–6, 290
Morganthau, Herr, 235
Morning Post, 84, 127
Morrah, H. A., 78, 84, 91, 94
Morris, William, 64
Mothers' Union, 104, 233, 242, 252, 258
Motor Transport Company, 293
Mudd, Mr., 183, 195, 205
Murray, Mary, 150

Napoleon, Prince, of Greece, 82
Nation, General Jack, 291, 293
Nation, Mrs. Olive, 291–3
National Trust, 301
Nauheim, Germany, 206
New York, 172, 234–8
New Zealand, 201, 203–5, 219, 224
Newcastle, Bishop of (Dr. Herbert Wild), 256
Newcastle, Kathleen, Duchess of, 276–7
Newham, Rev. Cecil, 50–51, 86
Newham, 'Squirrel', 268
Newnham, Jack, 259
Nicolson, Sir Harold, M.P., and Lady, 292

Nightingale, Florence, 15
Nijinsky, 240
Norland Nurses, 87
Normanhurst, Sussex, 272, 274
North Pole, 201
Northrepps, Norfolk, 166–7, 172, 176–7, 179–80, 186–7, 190, 192, 194–5, 206, 227, 230–1, 283
Nottingham, 100, 143–5, 147–8, 163–4, 175–6, 194–5, 199, 200–1, 206–7, 210, 295, 302

Oates, Capt., 223
Observer, 216
Octopus, 84, 90
Okeover, Ruth (Mrs. Ronnie Bruce), 130, 238
Olympus, Mount, 11
Our Dogs, 250, 261, 263, 278, 303
Overstrand, Norfolk, 180, 216, 227, 248
Oxford, 14–15, 20, 28, 50, 54, 58–59, 61–67, 70, 72, 81–82, 84–85, 87–89, 94–95, 97, 104–6, 138, 142, 170, 173–5, 178, 225, 274–5, 283, 292
Oxford, Bishop of, 112
Oxford House, Bethnal Green, 98–99
Oxford Review, 65, 94
Oxford Union Society, 64–66, 70, 74, 79, 83–84, 87, 89, 274, 282
Oxford University Dramatic Society, 79
Oxford Verses, 92

Paget, Aletheia (Mrs. Percy Bruce), 114, 145
Paget, Sir Ernest, 1st Bart., and Lady, 115–16
Paget, Francis (Bishop of Oxford), 43, 151
Paget, Hylda (Mrs. Tilney), 115–16
Palmerston, Lord, 16
Pankhurst, Dr. and Mrs., 132

Paris, 12, 28, 37, 40, 128–31, 138–9, 192, 194

Parker, Mrs. (Mrs. Lloyd Bruce), 44–46, 50–52, 61, 76

Pater, Dr. Walter, 70–71, 80

Patmore, Coventry, 67

Patriarch, Greek Ecumenical, 160

Patrick Campbell, Stella, 209

Patten, Dr., 104

Peace, Kirkby, 286, 290

Peary, R. E., 201

Pelham family, 174

Pelham, Rev. Sidney, 187, 193

Pelham-Burn Lucy (Lady Noel-Buxton), 208, 226

Peter Pan, 124, 135, 193

Petrograd, 240

Pevensey, Sussex, 252, 258, 269, 294

Phillimore, J. S., 91, 93

Phillimore, R. C., 78, 91

Picasso, Pablo, 129

Pilgrim Dinners, 133

Pitsligo of Monymusk, 12

Pittapuram, Maharajah of, 288

Plant, Percy, 218

Playfair, Audrey, 88

Playfair, Nigel (Sir), 66, 88, 94–95, 121, 125–32, 152, 232, 277, 286, 288

Ponsonby, Rev., 187

Ponting, 225

Popular Fox Terrier, The, 261

Portland, 6th Duke of, 195

Portsmouth, 225

Prestbury, vicar of, 67

Punch, 216, 271

Pusey, Dr., 67–69

Pytchley hunt, 164

Quartermain, Charles, 208–9

Queen Magazine, 95, 196

Queen's College, Oxford, 14–15, 33

Raglan, 1st Lord, 14

Ramsden family, 35, 37, 41

Ramsden, 'Robby', 35

Raphael, 93

Rattle, 72

Read, Donald, 134

Reading, Stella, Marchioness of, 292

Reed, Molly, 260, 261

Reed, Rupert, 261

Referee, 122

Reynalds, Edwin F., 213

Rhineland, Germany, 206

Ricardo, 'Nellie' (Lady Bruce), 100–140, 150, 168, 177, 182, 189, 195, 207, 210, 245, 246

Rice, Ken, 273–4, 281–3

Richelieu, Cardinal, 150

Richmond Dog Show, 288

Richmond, 7th Duke of, 100

Rizo-Rangabee, Cleon, 57, 161

Rizo-Rangabee, Prince Jacovaki, 11, 18

Rizo-Rangabee, Princess Rhalou (Mrs. James Skene), 11–14, 16, 20, 27–28

Roberts, Cecil, 124, 199, 301–2, 306

Robin Hood's Bay, Yorks., 103

Roche, A. A. (Lord Roche), 78, 292

Rodin, A., 129, 145, 187

Rodin, Madame, 187

Roosevelt, Theodore, President, 235, 236, 238

Roosevelt, Mrs., 235

Rossetti, Dante Gabriel 64, 67

Rosslyn, Countess of, 30

Rosslyn, 4th Earl of, 30, 94

Rotary Club, 218, 250, 253, 255

Roughton, Norfolk, 187

Royal College of Music, 282–3

Royal Geographical Society, 224

Royal Horse Artillery, 198, 199, 227, 233

Royal Horse Guards, 300

Royal Observatory, 252

R.S.P.C.A., 133

Royal Zoological Society, 224

Rubens, Paul, 79, 88
Rufford hunt, 163
Rumania, Queen Marie of, 300
Runton Old Hall, Norfolk, 167
Ruskin, John, 67
Russell, Parson Jack, 38, 262

St Anne's, Soho, 122, 125, 127, 230, 131, 142–3, 283, 295
St. Augustine's, Edgbaston, 229, 239, 244, 277
St. Edward's School, Oxford, 40–41, 50, 54, 56, 62, 80, 106
St. Germain's, Edgbaston, 213–14, 229, 244, 247
St. James', Herstmonceux, 252
St. Mawes, Sir Ernest, 116
St. Michael's School, Bognor, 76, 286
St. Paul's Cathedral, 217, 300
Saints, All, Herstmonceux, 251–2, 269–70, 271–2, 275–6
Salisbury Plain, 198–9
Samuel Pepys, 301
Sargent, Sir Malcolm, 282
Scalby, Yorks, 31, 72
Scarborough, Yorks., 60, 86–87, 101, 103, 109, 162, 228, 285
Scotsman, 135
Scott, Captain Falcon, R. N., 171–3, 177, 184, 186–7, 200, 206–7, 219, 220–5, 227, 282
Scott, Mrs., 221
Scott, Peter, 195, 197, 200, 201, 204, 219, 220, 224, 225, 233, 242, 250, 282, 299, 303
Scott, Sir Walter, 11, 12, 78
Scottish Field, 278
Scriabin, 224
Seaton, J. B. (Rev.), 103, 108
Seely, Sir Charles, 2nd Bart, 148
Shackleton, (Sir Ernest), 204
Shakespeare, Sir Geoffrey, 277
Shaw, G. Bernard, 162, 242

Sheffield, 72, 76, 95, 97, 265
Simeon, Algernon Barrington, 41–43, 48, 50, 61
Simmondley, Derbyshire, 113
Simon, John (1st Viscount Simon), 78, 91, 104, 225
Sitwell, Sir George, 101
Skene, Carrie (Mrs Rizo-Rangabee), 28
Skene, Felicia, 'Fifi', 12, 15, 17–18, 20, 28, 33–34, 40–42, 54–55, 58–59, 61–68, 70–71, 75, 80–81, 83–87, 106, 115, 119
Skene, Rev. George, 12, 15, 17–20, 52, 81
Skene, James (Junior), 11, 12, 13, 34
Skene, James, of Rubislaw, 11, 12, 20
Skene, Janie (Mrs. Lloyd Bruce), 12–38, 40, 65, 81, 115, 133, 162, 249
Skene, William, 13, 27–28, 51–52, 56–59, 75–76, 109
Skene, Zoe (Mrs. William Thomson), 12–33, 37–41, 50, 53, 65, 67, 72, 76, 112, 126–7, 185–6, 197, 211, 219, 226
Slade School, London, 113, 121, 130
Smith, Mrs. Eddy, 259
Smith, F. E. (Earl of Birkenhead and Viscount Furneaux), 78, 84, 91, 277, 292
Smooth Fox Terrier Association, 263, 302
Snatt, C. D., 294
Sofia, 158
Soho, 117–21, 125, 140, 142–3, 154, 169, 283
Soho Square, London, 131, 134–5
South Pole, 200–1, 203, 207, 225, 227
Southwell, Bishop of, 106, 112, 113
Southwell Cathedral, 112
Spencer-Jones, Sir Harold, 297
Speyer, Sir Edgar, 205, 227
Spooner, Dr. W. A., 72–73
Sporting and Dramatic News, 263

Stein, Gertrude, 129
Still, Bishop, 261
Stokesley, Yorks., 32–33, 50–52, 107
Stowe School, Bucks., 274
Strafford Club, 81, 151
Stratford de Redcliffe, Lord, 15, 57
Stride, Mr., 78
Stuart, Williamina (Lady Forbes), 12
Stud, W. K., 74
Suckling, Sir John, 150–1
Suirdale, Viscount (6th Earl of Donoughmore), 80, 88, 89, 91, 126
Sunday Pictorial, 216
Sussex Sacred Songs, 289
Swan and Edgar, 119
Swinburne, A., 67
Sydney, N.S.W. Australia, 201

'Taffy' (Mrs. Trowsdale), 167, 173–4, 178, 187
Teniel, 45, 88
Tennyson, Lord, 67
Terra Nova, 200, 201, 219, 221, 225
Terry, Beatrice, 209
Terry, Dame Ellen, 45
Theotokas, Dr., 159
Thessalonika, 158
Thompson, Lady, 138, 140, 141
Thomson, Basil, 36, 72
Thomson, Ethel, 37, 49
Thomson, Dr. William, Archbishop of York, 14–17, 24, 28, 32–33, 36, 40–41, 44–45, 49, 50–53, 59, 64–65, 68, 71
Thorndike, Sybil (Mrs. Casson), 283
Thrumpton, Notts., 24, 114, 254
Times, The, 90, 94, 127, 131, 239, 257, 263, 271, 277, 290, 303
Titheradge, Madge (Mrs. Charle Quartermain), 122, 125, 208, 231
Titheradge, Mrs., 209
Toklas, Alice B., 131
Toller, Rosalie, 209

Tonga, Queen Salote, of, 72
Tredwell, Jessica, 180, 229, 248, 253
Tree, Sir Beerbohm, 79, 196
Tresseder, Dr. Stanley, 164
Trilby, 79
Trollope, Anthony, 45

Upshire, Essex, 153

Van Triplitz, Admiral, 225
Vanderberg, Frederick, 285
Victoria, Queen, 65, 72, 82–83, 125–6

Walker family, 256, 307
Walker, Norrie, 270, 293
Wartling, 258
Warwickshire Territorials, 227
Washington D.C., 237–8
Washington Times, 237
Wayne, Louis, 208
Webb, Sydney and Beatrice, 132
Wellington, 1st Duke of, 65
Wellington, N.Z., 222, 224
Westmeath, 11th Earl of, 80
Westminster Gazette, 136
Weston, Joyce, 272
Whitechapel, 105
Wigan, 104
Wightman, Lady, 23
Wilberforce, Bishop, 16
Wilde, Oscar, 45, 79, 80
Willink, J. W. (Dean of Norwich), 251
Willoughby, Lady Anne, 150–1
Willoughby, Sir Henry, 150–1
Wilson, Woodrow, President, 234–5, 237–8
Wilson, Mrs., 221–2
Wimereux, France, 233
Windermere, 153, 284
Windsor, 82, 119
Wodehouse, Mrs., 168–9, 181
Women's Voluntary Service, 293–4
Woodward, Henry, 183

Woolf, Virginia, 292
Worcester College, Oxford, 61–63, 66, 73–76, 80, 85, 88–89, 95–96, 104, 152, 174–5, 220
Worcester College Debating Society, 66
Workington, Cumberland, 153
Wright, Archie, 198

York, 33, 41, 72
York, Duke and Duchess of (King George VI and the Queen Mother), 97, 300
Young People's Service, 243, 244
Young Pretender, 12

Zoological Evidences of Man's Place in Nature, 63
Zoological Society of London, 224
Zurich, 290

Firstmonceux, 256
Fearlessness, *illus.*
Formosa, *illus.*
Hilda, 63
Juddy, 38
Lennie, Lord Lennox, 82
Picasso's fox terrier, 129
Rona I, Champion, 58, 75, 82–84
Rona II, 83, 84
Roosevelt's dog, 236
Sandringham Peg, 205
Scamp, 49, 71–72
Tatters, 58, 63, 115
Una, 38, 44, 49
Wrose Indelible, Champion, and *illus.*, 256
Worcester Jim, 79

Horses
Aerial, *illus.*
Audrey, 143, 168
Bryant and May, 192

Others
Amateur Zoo, 101–3
Dorothy, iguana, 63
Elephant, at Oxford, 66
Gladly, bear, 218
Green mice, 297–8, 299, 304
Purity, dove, 124 and *illus.*

Animals

Dogs
Boreham Belsize, Champion, 288
Bright of Darkon, 260
Cheviot, 49
Dark of Brighton, Champion, 260
Diana Danesgate, Champion, 288
Dixy, 197
Force, 205